Self-Perspectives

Across
the
Life Span

SUNY Series, Studying the Self
Richard P. Lipka and Thomas M. Brinthaupt, Editors

Self-Perspectives
Across
the
Life Span

Edited by
Richard P. Lipka
and
Thomas M. Brinthaupt

STATE UNIVERSITY OF NEW YORK PRESS

1992

Published by
State University of New York Press, Albany

For information, address State University of New York
Press, State University Plaza, Albany, N.Y., 12246

Production by E. Moore

Marketing by Fran Keneston

Library of Congress Cataloging-in-Publication Data

Self-perspectives across the life span / [edited by] Richard P. Lipka
    and Thomas M. Brinthaupt.
        p.   cm.
    Includes bibliographical references and index.
    Contents: Self-complexity and self-esteem in middle childhood /
Karen M. Anderson — The tasks of self-development in middle
childhood and early adolescence / Stephen R. Shirk and Andrew G.
Renouf — Self in school / Richard P. Lipka, David P. Hurford —
Self-concept stability and change during adolescence / David H. Demo
and Ritch Savin-Williams — Variations in self-esteem in daily life
/ Anne J. Wells — The best and worst of it / Daniel Ogilvie and
Margaret D. Clark — Trait distinctiveness and age specificty in the
self-concept / John Mueller . . . [et al.]
    ISBN 0–7914–1003–X (acid-free). — ISBN 0–7914–1004–8 (pbk. : acid
-free)
    1. Self.   2. Developmental psychology.   I. Lipka, Richard P.
II. Brinthaupt, Thomas M., 1958–   .
BF697.S438   1992
155—dc20   91–16383
                                                                 CIP

        10 9 8 7 6 5 4 3 2 1

Contents

RICHARD P. LIPKA
THOMAS M. BRINTHAUPT

Introduction

The purpose of this volume is to arrive at a broad understanding of the study of the self across the life span. For the researcher interested in studying the development of the self across the life span, there are many issues that must be addressed. One must first identify the most important characteristics and dimensions of the self. Then, attempts can be made to answer when and how the self is acquired, as well as what characterizes and affects its development.

For the past two decades, psychologists and other social scientists have devoted a great deal of attention to the cognitive, affective, and behavioral implications of the self. They have employed a large number of interesting and innovative methodological approaches and have studied the development of the self across all periods of the life span.

As these contributions to a companion volume, *The Self: Definitional and Methodological Issues* (Brinthaupt & Lipka, 1992), illustrate, any effort to study the self is affected by the answers which one gives to the questions of *what* to study and *how* to study it. Researchers differ widely in how they believe the self should be defined and measured. These differences also become very important when the question of *whom* to study is raised.

As previous theory and research have shown, the self can be defined in many different ways. Thus, when one studies the self across the life span, an important initial question concerns exactly *what* is to be studied. Several different answers to this question are offered in this volume.

For example, some contributors focus on the structural properties of the self (Ogilvie & Clark in chapter 6). Others emphasize some of the processing aspects of the self (Shirk &Renouf in chapter 2). Still others consider both the structural and processing aspects of the self (Anderson in chapter 1, and Mueller et al. in chapter 7). In addition, some contributors (Demo & Savin-Williams in chapter 4; Lipka et al. in chapter 3; and Wells in chapter 5) devote their attention to self-esteem and self-evaluation, whereas others (Anderson in chapter 1, and Ogilvie & Clark in chapter 6) consider both the descriptive and evaluative aspects of the self.

One's definition of *what* to study both influences and is influenced by *how* it can or should be studied. Thus, even if researchers agree in principle about what they are studying, there are often disagreements about the best way in which to study it. For example, some structurally oriented contributors (Anderson in chapter 1) rely on open-ended interviews and self-descriptive tasks. Others rely on memory and reaction-time procedures (Mueller et al. in chapter 7). Some contributors who are interested in self-esteem rely on standardized questionnaires (Demo & Savin-Williams in chapter 4; Lipka et al. in chapter 3; and Shirk & Renouf in chapter 2). Others prefer interviews or a combination of questionnaire and interview (Anderson in chapter 1), and still others use techniques that do not even require a testing site or the presence of the investigator (Wells in chapter 5).

Beyond that which is discussed in this volume, most research on the development of the self has been concerned with the self in infancy, childhood, and adolescence (Honess & Yardley 1987). It is during these years when most of the action regarding the development of the self is assumed to be occurring. For example, research with infants attempts to establish the onset of visual self-recognition and knowledge of self and others (Harter 1983; Lewis & Brooks-Gunn 1979; Ryce-Menuhin 1988).

One of the commonly observed findings in developmental research into the self is that, from childhood to adolescence, the person's understanding of self changes from an emphasis on concrete, external, and overt dimensions (such as behavior and physical attributes) to an emphasis on more internal, psychological, and covert dimensions (such as traits and attitudes) (Bannister & Agnew 1977; Livesley & Bromley 1973; Montemayor & Eisen 1977; Rosenberg 1979). Developmental differences in the self have also been associated with different cognitive abilities and structural processes (Damon & Hart 1986; Harter 1983).

How do the selves of those who are five, ten, twenty, forty, and eighty years of age differ from each other? What are the theoretical and developmental implications of the use of quite different methodologies with different age groups?

In an effort to address these questions, we have included selections in this volume that focus not only on the early stages of the life span, but also on adulthood and old age as well. Recent research from a variety of theoretical and methodological perspectives is presented. There are three sections to the volume, including early and middle childhood, late childhood and adolescence, and adulthood and old age.

How can we study the selves of very young children? In the first part of her chapter 1, Anderson reviews the conceptual and methodological issues in studying the self in early childhood. She notes that there are differences between the two developmental periods of the preverbal infant and the verbal preschooler when studied separately. The major conceptual issues here concern the developing awareness of the self as an agent and object as well as the impact on the self of the emergence of verbal and other cognitive abilities. Her presentation of the unique methodological challenges to studying the self in early childhood is especially interesting.

One important question about the self in childhood concerns the relationship between cognitive complexity and self-evaluation. As the structure of the self increases in complexity, what effect does this have on the child's self-esteem? In the major part of her chapter, Anderson proposes that the intensity of feelings attached to specific components of the self are affected by the complexity and integration of the self. She tests this proposition by examining the differential effects of receiving a school report card on the self-esteem of third- and sixth-grade students.

During the transition from childhood to early adolescence, there are a great many changes in the person (Blyth & Traeger 1983). In addition to new role requirements, the child develops more sophisticated reasoning and cognitive abilities and begins to show the bodily transformations that characterize puberty (Simmons & Blyth 1987). What effects do these changes have on the self of the early adolescent?

In their chapter 2, Shirk and Renouf describe the effects of these changes in terms of a series of pivotal socioemotional tasks that affect the self. Central to these tasks are concerns about mastery and identity formation. Shirk and Renouf describe how, during this period, accurate self-evaluations, feelings of competence and self-worth, conservation of self, and the maintenance of positive self-esteem have important implications for both development and mental health.

In addition to more sophisticated cognitive abilities and pivotal socioemotional tasks, researchers have also been interested in the impact of contextual and situational factors (Gecas 1982; Markus & Kunda 1986; McGuire 1984). Chapter 3, by Lipka and his colleagues, falls into this latter tradition. In particular, they are interested in the effects of school transition on the self-esteem of early adolescents. Much debate has arisen over the extent to which changes in school structure (in addition to or as opposed to age changes) have positive or negative effects on self-esteem. Lipka and his colleagues examine this question by comparing not only students with different school-organization experiences but also students of different ages within the same grade.

There has been a great deal of controversy over whether adolescence is a period of storm and stress for the self. In their review and integration of the research surrounding this controversy, Demo and Savin-Williams argue in chapter 4 that, except in early adolescence, the self during this period is characterized by growth, stability, and increasing self-acceptance. Despite this conclusion, they note that there are several unresolved conceptual and methodological issues concerning the self in adolescence. They suggest several areas of research in which increased attention can help to resolve the controversies that still remain.

As we move from studying the self in childhood and adolescence to studying the self in adulthood and old age, a whole set of new and quite different issues emerges. The idea that the self continues to develop throughout life has led to much recent interest in studying the self in later life (Breytspraak 1984; Whitbourne 1986). Most of this research emphasizes the effects of life events and transitions on the self. For example, researchers have considered the effects of occupational changes, changing family responsibilities, the death of one's spouse or parents, retirement, and a variety of other crises, dilemmas, and role changes on the self (Meyer 1986; Rossan 1987; Wells & Stryker 1988).

Is it accurate to speak of the self as developing all across the life span? One might argue, for example, that, if development is defined as the acquisition of new perceptual, memory, and reasoning abilities, then after adolescence the self does not develop any further.

The adult self is not really getting any "bigger or better"—or is it? How does it change during adulthood, other than by adding new experiences and events and by utilizing new interpretations of past experiences and events? As one ages, does the self reverse its development? Are aspects of the self that were previously held now lost? Does self become obsolete in old age (Esposito 1987)? These are the types of issues that emerge when we study the adult self.

In her chapter 5, Wells presents a conceptualization and methodology for studying the fluctuations in self-esteem across the life span and in different contexts and settings. She reports a study designed to investigate the variations in self-esteem of a group of working mothers as they went about their daily lives. Among her more important findings is that self-esteem varies as a function of specific activities as well as specific persons with whom the mothers were interacting. An important aspect of her research is that it is based on an innovative and relatively recent methodological approach to studying the self in naturalistic settings called the *Experience Sampling Method.*

To the extent that young adulthood is a time of looking forward to the future and that older adulthood is a time of looking back toward the past, what are the resulting implications for the self? Ogilvie and Clark address this question in their chapter 6 on age and sex differences in individuals' perceptions of ideal and undesired selves. They review previous research on real-ideal self-discrepancies as well as their own research showing that the real-undesired self-discrepancy is more strongly related to life-satisfaction than the latter, especially among females. In considering age differences, it seems that young adults believe that their best selves are yet to come in the future, whereas older adults believe that their best selves were realized in the past. This suggests that the self plays a differential role in the motivations and evaluations of young and older adults.

Finally, Mueller and his colleagues compare, in chapter 7, the information-processing aspects of the self among young and elderly adults. They are especially interested in how memory is affected by the self, and they describe a program of interesting studies designed to identify why the self is not as effective of a memory aid for elderly subjects as it is for young adults. Among the possible reasons for this difference which they investigate are that the elderly are less self-conscious than are young adults, and that there are differences between young and elderly adults in the structure and content of their selves. The work of Mueller and his colleagues is an important extension of experimental cognitive methodology to studying the self across the life span.

In summary, this volume explores the study of the self in childhood and old age, as well as during most points in between.

Although some aspects of the life span—such as postcollege, pre-geriatric adulthood—are given only minimal attention, we have tried to cover as many of the distinct stages of the life span as space permits. In addition, because we have attempted to present a mixture of methodological, theoretical, and developmental concerns, some of these chapters are primarily reviews and some are primarily research reports. We think that this variety presents a useful balance for a volume of this kind.

Finally, there are some common themes in this volume that should be noted in advance. Primary among these are the issues of gender and its relation to the self, and stereotypes about the self at different stages of the life span. In terms of gender, several of the contributors report interesting differences between the selves of males and females across many domains. In addition, several contributors address common conceptions (and misconceptions) about the self, such as adolescence as a time of storm and stress and old age as a time of memory deficits. We shall return to these issues in chapter 8 as a final summary.

REFERENCES

Bannister, D., and Agnew, J. 1977. The child's construing of self. In *Nebraska symposium on motivation 1976*, edited by J. Cole. Lincoln: University of Nebraska Press. 99–125.

Blyth, D. A., and Traeger, C. M. 1983. The self-concept and self-esteem of early adolescents. *Journal of Early Adolescence* 3:105–120.

Breytspraak, L. M. 1984. *The development of the self in later life.* Boston: Little, Brown.

Damon, W., and Hart, D. 1986. Stability and change in children's self-understanding. *Social Cognition* 4:102–118.

Esposito, J. L. 1987. *The obsolete self: Philosophical dimensions on aging.* Berkeley: University of California Press.

Gecas, V. 1982. The self-concept. *Annual Review of Sociology* 8:1–33.

Harter, S. 1983. Developmental perspectives on the self-system. In *Handbook of child psychology*, Vol. 4, edited by P. H. Mussen. New York: Wiley. 275–385.

Honess, T., and Yardley, K., eds. 1987. *Self and identity: Perspectives across the life span.* London: Routledge and Kegan Paul.

Lewis, M., and Brooks-Gunn, J. 1979. *Social cognition and the acquisition of self.* New York: Plenum Press.

Livesley, W. J., and Bromley, D. B. 1973. *Person perception in childhood and adolescence.* London: Wiley.

Markus, H., and Kunda Z. 1986. Stability and malleability of the self-concept. *Journal of Personality and Social Psychology* 51:858–866.

McGuire, W. J. 1984. Search for the self: Going beyond self-esteem and the reactive self. In *Personality and the prediction of behavior,* edited by R. A. Zucker, J. Aronoff, and A. I. Rabin. New York: Academic Press. 73–120.

Meyer, J. W. 1986. The self and the life course: Institutionalization and its effects. In *Human development and the life course: Multidisciplinary perspectives,* edited by A. B. Sorensen, F. E. Weinert, and L. R. Sherrod. Hillsdale, N.J.: Lawrence Erlbaum Associates.

Montemayor, R., and Eisen, M. 1977. The development of self-conceptions from childhood to adolescence. *Developmental Psychology* 13:314–319.

Rosenberg, M. 1979. *Conceiving the self.* New York: Basic Books.

Rossan, S. 1987. Identity and its development in adulthood. In *Self and identity: Perspectives across the lifespan,* edited by T. Honess and K. M. Yardley. London: Routledge and Kegan Paul. 304–319.

Ryce-Menuhin, J. 1988. *The self in early childhood.* London: Free Association Books.

Simmons, R. G., and Blyth, D. A. 1987. *Moving into adolescence: The impact of pubertal change and school context.* New York: Aldine De Gruyter.

Wells, L. E., and Stryker, S. 1988. Stability and change in self over the life course. In *Life-span development and behavior,* Vol. 8, edited by P. B. Baltes, D. L. Featherman, and R. M. Lerner. Hillsdale, N.J.: Lawrence Erlbaum Associates. 191–229.

Whitbourne, S. K. 1986. *The me I know: A study of adult identity.* New York: Springer-Verlag.

PART I: EARLY AND MIDDLE CHILDHOOD

KAREN M. ANDERSON

1

Self-complexity and Self-esteem in Middle Childhood

INTRODUCTION

Psychologists have long been interested in the role played by the self in both social and psychological processes. In 1890, William James, for example, devoted a lengthy chapter to the self in his book, *The Principles of Psychology*. This interest in the self has continued to the present day, and has produced a good many theories as well as a great deal of research regarding the self.

However, there has not always been agreement on how to best conceptualize the self. One central debate focuses on whether to treat the self as a process or as a structure. Gergen, for example, argued in 1982 that, because the self can change dramatically from situation to situation in response to external cues, it is best viewed as a process. Other psychologists have also taken a more process-oriented perspective on the self (Carver 1979; Hull & Levy 1979; Wicklund 1975).

Most psychologists, however, treat the self as some sort of cognitive structure that is relatively stable across time (Gordon 1968). For example, Epstein argued that the self is "a subsystem of internally consistent, hierarchically organized concepts contained within a broader conceptual system" (1973, 407). Similarly, Markus also took a structural view of the self in her research on self-schemas (Markus 1977; Markus & Sentis 1982).

If it is true that the self is best viewed as a type of cognitive structure, then it follows that this structure could affect the processing of information in a variety of ways (Bargh 1982; Rogers, Kuiper & Kirker 1977). Additionally, treating the self as a cognitive structure might also imply that there are affective consequences associated with this type of structure (Linville 1985, 1987).

This chapter will deal more specifically with issues focusing on the complexity of this self-structure, the potential relationship of self-complexity to affective reactions regarding the self, and, in particular, to the stability of self-esteem across time. Data from a study looking more specifically at individual differences in self-complexity and the relationship of self-complexity to self-esteem in children will be presented with a review of the relevant literature.

The Development of the Self-concept

Infancy. The earliest studies of the development of the self-concept during infancy focused on the infant's self-recognition abilities. This research has borrowed techniques from the classic research on mirror-image stimulation in animals (Gallup 1968). Typically, between the ages of eighteen and twenty-four months, an infant who is placed in front of a mirror with rouge on his or her nose will respond to the reflection as though he or she understands that it is his or her own image. Evidence for this visual self-understanding comes from the infant's behavioral responses to the infant in the mirror (Bertenthal & Fischer 1978; Lewis 1979).

Prior to the development of self-recognition, which does not occur until the middle of the second year, psychologists have typically focused on the infant's emerging understanding of response-outcome contingencies as an early precursor to the self-concept during the first year of life. More specifically, by the end of the first year, the infant understands the relation between two events (as in "kicking my legs will make the mobile above my crib move"). This understanding allows the infant to anticipate the outcomes of their actions as well as the emotions associated with those outcomes ("making the mobile move will make me happy"). The discovery of contingent stimulation as a reinforcer to organize the infant's discovery of contingency may be the earliest emergence of the sense of agency, which is an aspect of the self.

This understanding of response-outcome contingencies also plays a critical role in the development of caregiver-infant attachment. Initially, the infant does not differentiate between the self and the primary caregiver (Mahler 1972). The infant's awareness of his or her own existence as separate from that of the primary caregiver is an essential precursor for the development of understanding of response-outcome contingencies. It may also be possible that both the awareness of separateness and the awareness of contingency stimulation are products of an increasing ability to move on one's own.

Other researchers studying attachment (Ainsworth et al. 1978) have pointed out the importance of a secure attachment to the primary caregiver in the early emergence of the self. These researchers again emphasize the critical role of the contingent responsiveness on the part of the caregiver in the development of attachment (Shaffer & Emerson 1964). This contingent responsiveness includes both caretaker sensitivity (as in "Does the caretaker correctly interpret the infant's signals?") and cooperation ("Does the caretaker respond to the infant's signals?").

During the second year of life, particularly between the ages of eighteen and twenty-four months, there is a well-documented shift in the infant's mental representational abilities, as exemplified by the acquisition of object permanence (Piaget 1951). Besides the emergence of visual self-recognition during this time, a number of other important abilities that are additionally relevant to the self-concept emerge at this time. For example, in 1981, Kagan discussed five signs of self-awareness: appreciation of standards, distress to modeling, mastery smiles, directives to adults, and self-descriptive utterances. Similarly, others have focused on the child's ability to mentally represent "the relation between two relations" (Higgins 1989, 413), implying a more sophisticated understanding of the relationship between the child and his or her primary caretaker. Additionally, psychoanalytic writers from the object-relations perspective have coined the term *transitional object* to refer to the toddler's use of some self-chosen object as a tangible symbol of his or her experience of the mother-self relationship.

By the end of the second year, the young child's increasingly sophisticated cognitive abilities allow for an understanding of the self as an object (visual self-recognition and linguistic pronoun representation) and the self in relation to others (caregiver attachment and related response outcome contingencies), as well as the self as doer or agent.

Early Childhood. Research into the self-concepts of preschoolers has dealt with two major areas, the emergence of the early categorical self and on the development of self-control. For example,

Keller, Ford, and Meacham (1978) asked three-, four-, and five-year-olds to describe themselves via a verbal open-ended self-description task. This type of task will be discussed in more detail in this chapter's following section.

They found that preschoolers typically describe themselves in very concrete ways and in terms of general categories such as gender, race, and age, and in terms of preferred activities and possessions. It should be noted, however, that one unresolved issue regarding the use of such open-ended self-descriptive tasks is the issue of the preschooler's potential verbal limitations (Clark 1983).

During the preschool years, the self-concept also acquires a strong affective component, conceptualized in the literature as feelings of self-esteem. While there are a variety of unanswered questions regarding the theoretical conceptualization of the construct of self-esteem, this will be discussed further in a later section of this chapter.

Again, because of the potential limitations of the preschooler's verbal capabilities, the assessment of self-esteem could be considered as problematic. Generally, however, the typical preschooler has an undifferentiated set of positive feelings about his or her self that is quite resistant to negative feedback (Harter 1983). Again, as will be discussed later in this chapter, these positive feelings about the self do not become more differentiated (and more realistic) until much later in middle childhood.

Finally, there has been a focus on the development of self-control during the early childhood period. Much of this research has relied upon a delay-of-gratification or resistance-to-temptation paradigm. These studies show that, as would be expected, younger children do more poorly on these tasks than do older children. However, later research (Mischel & Patterson 1978) has shown that, if given specific instructions on how to resist temptation, younger children can perform much better on these tasks.

A fair amount of research has also investigated the construct of locus of control during early childhood. As conceptualized in the adult personality literature, locus of control is a generalized tendency to perceive personally relevant events as being either internally or externally caused. Some researchers (Mischel, Zeiss & Zeiss 1974) have suggested that there is a developmental shift from egocentric internality during the preschool years to decentered externality and then to decentered internality. Other researchers, however, have not found support for this developmental process (Hegland & Galejs 1983). Thus, the issue of whether locus of control is a stable personality characteristic or whether it is instead a characteristic that is developmentally influenced remains unresolved. It should also be noted that, as with many other early childhood personality constructs (such as self-esteem), numerous questions have been raised regarding the measurement of this construct and, again, concerns about the verbal limitations of children at this age and the implications of these limitations for measurement.

As was true during infancy, these changes in the development of the self-concept also appear to be linked to more general cognitive developmental changes. For example, Eder, Gerlach, and Perlmutter in 1987 asked both preschoolers aged 3½ and 5½ years old and adults general as well as specific questions about both behaviors and traits. They found that the proportion of specific responses increased with age, suggesting that changes in the retrieval of information about the self from memory is similar to the retrieval of other types of information. Thus, Eder and colleagues concluded that their findings are similar to other more specific research into developmental changes in other types of memory. This relationship between developmental changes in the self-concept and more general cognitive developmental changes are also seen during middle childhood, which will be discussed in the next section.

Middle Childhood.   The period of middle childhood would seem to be a particularly important period for developmental changes in the self. For example, during this period there are advances in general cognitive skills that might also affect the child's ability to conceptualize the self. Additionally, the child's range of social experiences also greatly increases during this period. During the course of middle childhood, then, we might expect to see a variety of changes in the child's self-concept.

Most psychologists studying developmental differences in the self during this period have focused on changes in children's written or oral open-ended self-descriptions (Guardo & Bohan 1971; Livesley & Bromley 1973; Montemayor & Eisen 1977; Rosenberg 1979. See also Brinthaupt & Erwin 1992). This reflects an idiographic approach to the self, in which a unique set of self-descriptive statements are generated by each child, with very few constraints being imposed by the researcher. The major advantage to this approach is that each child produces a set of rich, descriptive data that is, by nature, unique to that child. The primary disadvantage, on the other hand, is that it is often difficult to compare these data across children.

In the typical open-ended interview, the child is asked by the interviewer, in a one-to-one situation, to simply describe himself or herself. These self-descriptive statements are then recorded by the interviewer for later coding. The classic finding from studies of this type is that, as children grow older, their self-descriptions shift from being very concrete to being more abstract (Montemayor & Eisen 1977; Rosenberg 1979).

Damon and Hart presented a model in 1982 that both supported and extended the idea that, with development, the self-concept becomes less concrete and more abstract. Their model looked at the self at four different developmental levels, from infancy through late adolescence. During infancy, for example, the physical self predominates. During middle and late childhood, the active self predominates. During early adolescence, the social self predominates, and during late adolescence, a concern with one's personal philosophy and belief system predominates. More recent research by Damon and Hart lends support to their model (Damon & Hart 1986; Hart & Damon 1986) and to the more general contention that a shift from thinking about the self in more concrete terms to thinking about the self more abstractly occurs during the middle childhood years.

A second, very different way to assess developmental changes in the self-concept would be to use a questionnaire or similar type of instrument (Long, Henderson & Ziller 1967; Mullener & Laird 1971). This reflects a more nomothetic approach, in which certain features of the self-concept are assumed to be relevant to all children. The major advantage to this approach is that a standardized set of responses is generated, allowing for statistical comparisons across children. One major disadvantage, on the other hand, is that children may be making judgments about features of the self-concept that are not equally important to each child.

A second problem associated with this approach is that, because these measures are often designed specifically for a particular study, the reliability and validity of such measures are often quite poor. For example, Long, Henderson, and Ziller constructed a set of nonverbal measures in 1967, which they called the *Children's Self-Social Constructs Test*, to study age-related changes in five different aspects of the self. Support for their hypotheses was quite mixed, perhaps reflecting problems with their measures.

Mullener and Laird (1971), on the other hand, used a self-designed questionnaire that did lend support for their hypothesis that the self would become more differentiated across a range of content areas with age. They found that, with age, subjects did tend to give increasingly more variable ratings across content areas when evaluating themselves, suggesting that "with age, there was a change from relatively global to relatively differentiated self-evaluations" (Mullener & Laird 1971, 235). Additionally, they found that those subjects who did not vary much in their self-evaluations across content areas tended to have higher scores overall, suggesting that simpler and less differentiated self-conceptions were somehow associated with more positive evaluations of the self.

Taken together, the results from such studies indicate that, as children become older, their thinking about the self becomes less concrete and more abstract. This conclusion is also supported by the literature on developmental changes in person perception (Barenboim 1977; Livesley & Bromley 1973; Peevers & Secord 1973). With age, children's descriptions of other people also become less concrete and more abstract. However, there are still gaps in what is known about the development of the self-concept beyond this now well-documented shift. For example, some researchers (Livesley & Bromley 1973) have implied that not only do children's self-descriptions become more abstract with age, but their organization of this self-descriptive information becomes more complex as well. Thus, not only is the content of the self-concept becoming more abstract, but the structure of the self-concept is becoming more complex as well (Harter 1983; Rosenberg 1986).

Structural Models of the Self-concept

Perhaps the most influential structural model of the self-concept is the hierarchical model suggested by Shavelson and his colleagues in 1976. Because this model will be discussed in detail elsewhere in this series of volumes (Marsh, Byrne & Shavelson 1992), only those studies relevant to the present chapter will be discussed.

Marsh extended Shavelson's original hierarchical model by creating an instrument called the *Self-Description Questionnaire* (SDQ), designed to specifically measure the seven lower-level nodes of Shavelson's original model (Marsh et al. 1983). In a 1984 study, Marsh and other colleagues factor analyzed the SDQ responses of children in grades two through five (Marsh, Barnes, Cairns & Tidman 1984). The same basic seven-node factor structure was found at all grades, but these factors did appear to become both more distinct and more clearly identified in the older grades. This indicates possible changes in the hierarchical structure of the self-concept with development.

Similarly, Marsh and Hocevar (1985) analyzed SDQ responses using structural equation modeling techniques. In testing the various possible models of the self-concept, Marsh and Hocevar found the strongest support for a hierarchical model with one nonacademic factor and two academic factors. However, this model was not equally supported at every grade level. The three factors were more strongly correlated at the lower grades, and were more distinct at the older grades. These results, like those obtained by Marsh and colleagues in 1984, again imply that there may be developmental changes in the structure of the self-concept. More specifically, these findings suggest that the hierarchical structure of the self-concept becomes more distinct with age. However, beyond this conclusion, it is unclear as to what other types of changes in the structure of the self-concept might be occurring because, to date, these issues have not been further investigated.

Jolley also viewed the self as being hierarchically structured in her study of changes in the self-concept across the life span (Jolley 1982; Jolley & Mitchell 1984). Borrowing from Zajonc's paper on cognitive structure presented in 1960, Jolley used a modified Q-sort measure to assess self-structure. The individual first generates a series of self-descriptive statements. These statements are then sorted into groups by the individual, based upon his or her judgments about which statements involve related aspects of the self. From this sorting task, at least four structural dimensions of the self can be assessed: differentiation, complexity, organization, and unity (Zajonc 1960).

Differentiation is the number of different self-attributes which an individual possesses. Complexity refers to the degree to which these attributes are organized, from one single group to a hierarchical organization of groups. Unity reflects the degree to which these attributes are dependent upon or interrelated to each other. Finally, organization (or centrality) measures the extent to which certain attributes are highly central to the self and, thus, dominate the self-structure as a whole.

Jolley looked at changes in the structure of the self-concept in children, adolescents, young adults, and older adults. Her data showed a general trend of increasing differentiation of the self-structure with age. This trend was strongest with complexity scores, and weakest with unity scores.

There is, then, some evidence that children's self-knowledge is structured, most likely in a hierarchical fashion. However, the research reviewed raises a number of important and, as yet, untreated issues.

First, it is unclear as to exactly how the self-structure changes over time. The most plausible hypothesis would be that, with age, the structure of the self becomes both more complex, as suggested by Jolley in 1982, and more stable, as suggested by Marsh and colleagues in 1984 (Marsh et al. 1992).

A second issue in looking at the self-structure in children is the question of whether a child's self-structure might have the same types of cognitive and affective consequences as those of an adult. There is at least some evidence that this might be the case.

Affective Consequences and the Self

As discussed earlier, the evidence indicates that the self as a cognitive structure has a variety of consequences for the processing of information. This seems to be the case for children as well as for adults (Halpin et al. 1984; Hammen & Zupan 1984). Yet, the self could also have important affective consequences as well. That is, the existence of cognitive structures corresponding to the self could also influence an individual's affective responses to self-relevant information. For example, psychologists studying attributional processes have long noted the presence of egocentric and self-serving biases (Bradley 1978; Ross & Sicoly 1979).

More recent research has linked self-structures to affective reactions in other ways. Linville (1985) measured the complexity of knowledge about the self in college-aged students. She hypothesized that students who were high in self-complexity would have more moderate affective reactions to self-relevant information.

An individual who is high in self-complexity is more likely to have a wide range of roles in his or her repertoire. Thus, when negative feedback affects one of these self-roles, he or she has a wide range of alternate roles to fall back on. In contrast, an individual who is low in self-complexity does not have this wide range of alternate roles available and, thus, should experience greater swings in affect.

Linville measured self-complexity using a card-sorting task in which subjects sorted twenty-five different roles into groups according to which roles they thought were self-descriptive and which roles they felt belonged together. From this task, a self-complexity score was created, based upon how many roles were chosen as self-descriptive and how these roles were sorted or organized. Students with high self-complexity scores had both a greater number of self-relevant roles and a greater degree of independence among those roles.

Affect in this study was measured by a scale that the subjects filled out daily for a two-week period. As predicted, Linville found that college students who were lower in self-complexity did indeed experience greater swings in affect, following a success or failure experience. These students also experienced greater variability in their moods over time.

More recently, Linville (1987) also found that subjects higher in self-complexity are less prone to both feelings of depression and physical illness. These results, then, reveal an intriguing link between self-complexity and affective reactions to self-relevant information.

However, Linville's research has, to date, involved only college-aged students. Little is known as to whether the same types of affective reactions occur in children as well. However, it is likely that the self could also have affective as well as cognitive consequences for the child as he or she grows older.

Affect toward the self as assessed in children is typically measured in terms of feelings of self-esteem. Traditional measures of self-esteem tend to be unidimensional—that is, self-esteem is treated as a set of global positive or negative feelings about the self in general (Coopersmith 1959; Piers & Harris 1964).

More recent conceptualizations of self-esteem view this construct as, instead, being a multidimensional set of feelings. Thus, a child can have positive or negative feelings about the self in a variety of different domains. Harter first attempted in 1982 to measure self-esteem in this way by using her Perceived Competence Scale for Children, which measured self-esteem in four specific domains—cognitive, social, physical, and global self-worth. This instrument was revised (Harter 1985) to measure feelings of competence in six separate domains. According to this theoretical perspective, measuring self-esteem in a variety of domains should lead to a more accurate measure of feelings about the self.

In reviewing those studies investigating self-esteem in children, levels of self-esteem seem to be highest (perhaps unrealistically so) in young children, and then decline until adolescence. For example, Piers and Harris (1964) gave their "The Way I Feel about

Myself" inventory to children in grades three, six, and ten. Self-esteem scores were significantly higher in both the third and tenth grades than in the sixth grade. This is a typical result. Self-esteem appears to be high in young children, but then decreases until later in adolescence, when self-esteem scores again rise (Marsh et al. 1992; Rosenberg 1986.

Evidence from a number of other studies indicates that although young children consistently overrate their abilities on a variety of different tasks, their self-assessments do become more realistic with age (Benenson & Dweck 1986; Harter 1982; Ruble et al. 1980; Stipek 1981, 1984). For example, Harter (1982) gave her Perceived Competence Scale to several samples of second to seventh graders. These self-esteem scores were then compared with both teacher ratings of ability and standardized achievement test scores. Correlations among these three measures increased systematically from the second grade until seventh grade. This suggests that it is the younger child's unrealistically high estimate of his or her own abilities that accounts for the low correlations between self-esteem scores and more objective assessments of ability. With age, however, self-ratings become more realistic and thus are more highly correlated with objective measures of academic ability.

What is not clear from these studies is how these age-related changes in self-esteem might be related to the complexity of the child's developing self-structure. Although this issue has never been directly investigated in children, Linville's research investigating the relationship between self-complexity and affective responses in 1985 and 1987 demonstrated just such a link in college-aged subjects. Similarly, Mullener and Laird (1971) noted that, in their data, those subjects having higher evaluation scores also showed less variance across content areas.

Research in the area of self-image disparities also supports this idea. In an early study in 1967, Katz & Zigler found that the disparity between ratings of one's real self-image and one's ideal self-image increased with age. More specifically, not only did ideal self-image scores become higher with age, but real self-image scores declined. It appears that for younger children, there is little disparity between one's real and ideal selves.

The evidence thus suggests that there is a relationship between global self-esteem and self-complexity in children. As the child grows older, self-esteem declines to a more moderate level and more closely reflects his or her actual abilities. What is not clear from these studies is how these changes might be related to self-complexity. We know that self-complexity influences affect toward the self in adults, but it is not known how self-complexity might influence affect toward the self in children, particularly with regards to both global and domain-specific self-esteem.

One promising arena in which to study this relationship is the classroom. Children spend a great deal of time at school, and much research points to the important role played by the school environment in socialization (Minuchen & Shapiro 1983). Focusing upon the school environment has the added advantage of tapping a large part of a child's world in a relatively consistent manner across children. For example, all children take exams, receive report cards, and so on as part of the commonplace routines of school.

One particularly important aspect of the school setting is the formal academic feedback which the children receive in the form of their report cards. Report-card time would seem to be an especially important event for children. Both parents and teachers feel that getting good grades is important, and the grades a child does receive can have a variety of consequences ranging from parental reward or punishment to peer acceptance or rejection—and more.

Because report cards are so important to students, it is likely that the grades which a child receives will have an effect upon his or her self-esteem. In fact, studies have found a relationship between academic achievement and self-esteem (Kifer 1975; Ames 1978). Good grades should lead to increased self-esteem, while poor grades should lead to decreased self-esteem.

However, the same set of report card grades could affect two children in quite different ways, depending upon their levels of self-complexity. More specifically, the impact of these grades might be dependent upon the structure of that child's self-concept, and the complexity of that structure. The following section of this chapter will discuss aspects of cognitive structures in general, and offer hypotheses as to how self-structures might be related to self-esteem.

The Relationship between Self-structure and Self-esteem

Psychologists studying individual differences in cognitive structures have generally focused upon two different structural characteristics. The first—differentiation—is defined as the number of different attributes or roles that make up the self-concept. Scott called the notion of differentiation "basic to any concept of cognitive structure" (Scott 1963, 277). One individual might have many different dimensions that define the self, while another might have only a few dimensions by which he or she evaluates the self (see figure 1.1). In 1960, Zajonc also treated differentiation as an important component of cognitive complexity and, in fact, demonstrated in his study that high differentiation is significantly related to high levels of cognitive complexity overall.

In the present study, differentiation was operationalized as the total number of different categories used by the child in an open-ended self-description task. A child could use anywhere from one to six different self-descriptive categories—scholastic competence, athletic competence, behavioral conduct, social acceptance, global self-worth, and physical appearance—in describing himself or herself. These six categories were chosen in order to correspond to the six subscales of the Harter Self-Perception Profile, which served as the self-esteem measure in the present study.

Using higher numbers of different categories implied higher differentiation. It was expected that children high in differentiation would be less affected by their report cards, because these children have many different self-roles and thus should be less affected than are children with fewer self-roles. This is because a child with a highly differentiated self-structure has many different nodes corresponding to the self in memory. When information about one's report-card grades is being processed, only that node representing the scholastic self should be activated. Because only one aspect or node of the self-concept is being activated, the impact of the grades upon self-esteem should be low.

In contrast, a child low in differentiation has fewer nodes corresponding to the self in memory. Thus, when information regarding one's report card grades is processed, the activation of the scholastic-self node means that a greater proportion of the self-structure is being activated. This, in turn, should lead to a greater impact upon that child's self-esteem.

A second characteristic of cognitive structures is the degree of integration present in the structure. Measures of integration attempt to consider "systematic interrelation(s) among cognitive elements" (Scott 1974, 563). In other words, how the various elements of the self-structure are linked together is another important component of cognitive complexity.

In his 1974 study, Scott studied four different integrative styles—affective balance, affective-evaluative consistency, centralization, and image comparability—among college students in six separate domains of acquaintances, family, self, groups, nations, and

Figure 1.1
High versus Low Differentiation

High Differentiation

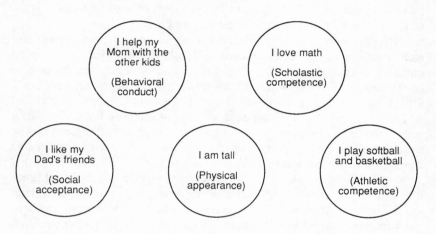

Low Differentiation

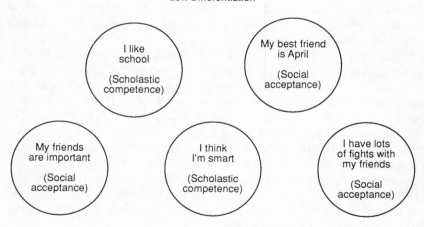

school. The first two integrative styles were characterized as being simpler and less powerful, while the last two styles were considered by Scott to be more cognitively sophisticated. He found that subjects tend to use the same integrative style across the six domains in a consistent manner. Additionally, within any one of these domains, integrative style was significantly related to structural complexity. Students who used a simpler integrative style also had simpler cognitive structures, while subjects who used more sophisticated integrative styles had more complex cognitive structures.

In the present study, integration was conceptualized in a slightly different way. The degree to which the self was integrated around the scholastic self served as the measure of cognitive integration. This variable—scholastic centrality—measures the degree to which a child's self-concept is organized around the scholastic self (see Figure 1.2).

It was expected that children high in scholastic centrality should be more affected by the report card than were children low in scholastic centrality. This is because, when the self is integrated around the scholastic self, and information about the report card is received, the scholastic self node is again activated. This, in turn, activates the surrounding nodes. Because many aspects of the self are being affected by this information, this should have a greater impact on that child's self-esteem. In contrast, a child whose self-structure is not integrated around the scholastic self should show less change in self-esteem. This is because when report card information is processed, only the node corresponding to the scholastic self is activated.

It was hypothesized in the present study that these two measures of self-complexity—differentiation and integration—should mediate a child's affective reactions to an important event. More specifically, changes in self-esteem due to the report card grades received should be mediated by the child's level of self-complexity.

The following four hypotheses were investigated in the present study.

1. The more academic self-descriptive items generated by a child, the greater the impact of the report card on that child's scholastic self-esteem.
2. Children who generate self-descriptive items from a wide range of self-descriptive categories (or high differentiation) will be less affected by the report card than are children who generate items from a more limited range of categories.
3. Children who view their scholastic self-descriptive statements as being highly central to their self-concepts (as in high scholastic centrality) will be more affected by the report card than are children who do not view the scholastic self as being central.

Figure 1.2
High versus Low Integration in Scholastic Centrality

High Integration

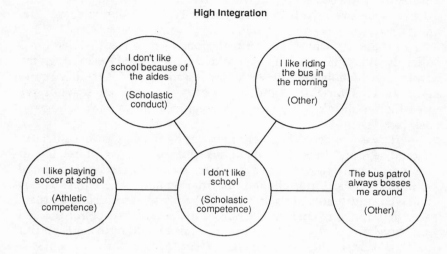

Low Integration

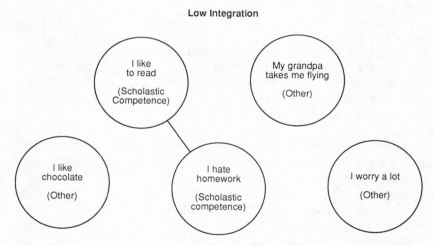

4. With development, children will show greater self-complexity, as evidenced by an increase in the number of different categories used to describe the self (or differentiation), and in the degree to which these categories are hierarchically organized. Integration

or scholastic centrality is not expected to increase with development. Thus, the differential effects of the report card on the two different age groups is unclear.

METHOD

Subjects

Subjects in this study were forty children in the sixth grade (twenty-one boys and nineteen girls), and forty-six children in the third grade (twenty-three boys and twenty-three girls). The mean ages for the sixth and third grades were 11.79 and 8.92 years, respectively. All children attended school in a local public school system, and parental permission was obtained for all participants.

The subjects were randomly divided into two groups. The first group—the target group—consisted of fifty-eight children (twenty-eight sixth-graders and thirty third-graders, with equal numbers of boys and girls at each grade). This target group completed both the self-esteem measure and the self-complexity measures at session 1, and then again completed the self-esteem measure at session 2. The second group—the control group—consisted of twenty-eight subjects (twelve sixth-graders and sixteen third-graders). This group completed only the self-esteem measure at session 2 and again at session 3. Because there was no intervening event between sessions 2 and 3, the control group was designed to serve as a comparison group for the target subjects.

Materials

Self-complexity Measures. The self-complexity measures in this study were all derived from the target children's responses to a series of tasks involving a set of 3×5-inch index cards, each of which contained a short self-descriptive phrase. These self-descriptive phrases were generated by each child so that every child had a unique set of items.

The measurement of the structural aspects of the self-concept, or self-complexity, is a difficult methodological issue. This is particularly true when working with a sample of children, given their more limited verbal abilities. In the present study, self-complexity was measured using a series of tasks that, I hoped, would show individual differences in how children organize self-relevant information. Further issues regarding the measurement of these structural aspects of the self-concept will be discussed again later in this chapter.

Self-Esteem Measures.   Self-esteem was measured in the present study using Harter's (1985) Self-Perception Profile for Children. This instrument consists of thirty-six questions, and is designed to measure six separate components of self-esteem— scholastic competence, athletic competence, global self-worth, physical appearance, behavioral conduct, and social acceptance. Each question follows a forced-choice format, and is scored according to a four-point scale, with four indicating high self-esteem and one indicating low self-esteem.

One theoretical and methodological issue regarding the assessment of self-esteem is the question of whether self-esteem is a global, unidimensional construct or whether it is a more differentiated and multifaceted construct. While each perspective has its supporters, it appears today that the view that self-esteem is a multidimensional construct is more popular (Marsh, Byrne & Shavelson 1992).

Additionally, because instruments such as the Self-Perception Profile measure children's perceptions of their abilities in a variety of areas, they provide a richer as well as a more differentiated picture of self-esteem than do the more traditional unidimensional instruments. For the purposes of the present study, a more multidimensional measure was deemed to be more appropriate, particularly given the focus upon scholastic performance.

Academic Performance Measures.   Academic performance was assessed from the grades which each child received on his or her actual report card. Again, parental permission was obtained in order to look at the school's copies of the report cards. These data were converted to numerical form for data analysis purposes and for use in hypothesis testing.

While report card day did have the advantages in the present study of *(a)* being a naturally occurring event, and *(b)* being an event that the children presumably perceive as important, there were disadvantages to this approach as well. For example, the children may have already had a good idea of what to expect in terms of grades; after all, they most likely received academic performance feedback within the classroom on a regular basis. Despite potential problems, however, it is more ethically acceptable to rely upon a naturally occurring event than to use a more traditional experimental technique to look at changes in self-esteem, such as giving the children false feedback in a laboratory situation.

Procedure

Session 1. As stated earlier, only children assigned to the target group were seen at this time. Each child was interviewed privately in a testing room at her or his school, approximately two weeks prior to the report card date.

The experimenter introduced herself and explained to the child that she was interested in "how children of different ages think and feel about themselves." Once the child appeared to feel at ease, the open-ended self-description task was explained: "Okay, what I would like you to do is to just tell me about yourself. I just want you to tell me all of the things that you think are important about yourself, and what I'm going to do is write the things that you tell me onto these cards."

As the child described herself or himself, the statements were written onto a set of index cards. The child was allowed to generate as many self-descriptive statements as he or she wanted, but was encouraged to generate a minimum of eight items. The number of statements generated ranged from a minimum of eight and a maximum of thirty-one, with a mean of seventeen statements for all children.

A second trained observer also recorded the child's statements in order to establish a reliability check.

Each child generated statements until either the child stated that he or she was ready to stop, or until approximately fifteen minutes had passed. Afterward, the child was shown a five-point rating scale (1 = not at all well; 5 = very very well) and was asked to decide, "How good a job do you think you did of describing yourself to me?" This question was asked to ensure that the children did, in fact, feel that they did an adequate job of describing themselves to the experimenter.

Next, the experimenter placed all of the cards out on the table in front of the child. This was done randomly, except for those cards which the experimenter felt to be relevant to the scholastic self. Again, the trained observer made judgments as to which items were scholastic statements, in order to determine reliability.

These scholastic items were put first in the array, in the upper-left corner of the table. The child was then asked to consider the first such scholastic card: "Okay, now I want you to think about this card for a minute, and I want you to pretend that this card isn't true about you any more. If this card wasn't true any more, would this card change?" This question was asked while the experimenter pointed to each subsequent card in the array.

The same procedure was followed for each one of the scholastic self-descriptive cards. The data from these questions were used to compute the child's scholastic centrality score, a variable designed to measure the extent to which the scholastic self was a central and unifying component of the child's self-concept. The children appeared to have no trouble with this task, and great care was taken to make sure that the child understood the task before beginning.

The experimenter then explained the next task, which was the hierarchical sorting task: "Okay, now what I would like you to do is to put together into groups all of the cards that you think go together." Once the child had completed this initial sort, the child was asked to consider each group of cards separately, one at a time.

For each group, the child was asked whether "this group could be made into other, smaller groups." If the child responded "no," then the next group of cards was considered. If the child responded "yes," then he or she was asked to show the experimenter how these new groups could be made. This process of breaking down the original groups into other, smaller groups continued until either the child said that no smaller groups could be made, or until there were only two cards left in a group.

All card sorts were recorded by the experimenter. Data from this task were used to compute three self-complexity variables: number of levels, number of groups, and hierarchical complexity. All of these variables were designed to measure the complexity of the child's hierarchical organization of knowledge about the self.

The final task at session 1 was to administer the self-esteem questionnaire. The child was first asked if he or she knew what a survey was. If he or she didn't, then the experimenter offered a short explanation. A sample question was then used to explain the question format. Once the child seemed to understand the question format, the experimenter read each of the thirty-six questions aloud, while the child marked the appropriate box on the answer sheet.

When the self-esteem questionnaire was completed, the child was thanked for his or her help. The experimenter also explained that she would be back again in a couple of weeks to talk to the child again for a short time. Then, the child returned to class.

Session 2. At the end of the first semester of school, each child received evaluations of his or her academic performance from the teacher in the form of a report card. This was probably an important event for most of the children, in that it served as a major source of academic feedback.

Within one week of receiving the report card, each target condition child was asked to again complete the Harter Self-Perception Profile. In this way, it was possible to ascertain the stability of self-esteem over time. The reassessment of self-esteem at session 2 also allowed for the consideration of how changes in self-esteem might be related to or mediated by self-complexity. Additionally, children in the control condition were also administered the Self-Perception Profile for the first time.

For the target children, the Self-Perception Profile was administered in the same way as at session 1, with the experimenter reading the questions aloud and the child marking the appropriate boxes on the answer sheet. The only difference was that the order of the questions was changed in order to minimize the possibility that a child might remember his or her earlier responses. In order to further minimize this possibility, it was explained to the child that "Some of these questions might sound familiar, but that's okay. Don't worry about trying to answer the questions the same way you did before. Just answer the question the way you feel now."

After completing the scale for the second time, the child was asked a set of final questions designed to assess his or her actual reactions to the report card itself. The following questions were asked, using the same five-point scale discussed earlier (1 = not at all; 5 = very very much).

"How important was getting your report card to you?"

"How surprised were you about your grades?"

"How happy were you with your grades?"

"How happy were your parents with your grades?"

The answer to the first question was designed to serve as a manipulation check of the assumption that receiving the report card was in fact a major event for the children. The second and third questions were important because how the child felt about his or her report card grades could mediate how he or she completed the second administration of the Self-Perception Profile. Finally, parental reactions to the report card might also influence the child's responses to the questionnaire at session 2.

Following these questions to the target children, each child was again thanked for his or her help with the project. Children in the target group were told that this was the end of the project, while children in the control group were told that the experimenter would be back again in a couple of weeks to talk with them again for a short time.

Session 3. At session 3, children in the control group were asked to complete the Self-Perception Profile for a second time. Again, the experimenter read the questions aloud, while the child marked the appropriate boxes on the answer sheet. As was done with the target children, the order of the questions was again changed. Again, the experimenter explained that some of the questions might sound familiar, but that the child should go ahead and answer the questions in a way that reflected how the child felt then, rather than trying to remember how he or she had answered the questions before.

When all thirty-six items had been completed, the experimenter asked the child one final question: "Okay, now I want you to think about the last couple of weeks at school. Has anything either very good or very bad happened to you during the past couple of weeks at school?"

The experimenter gave the child a few examples, such as doing either much better or much worse than expected on an exam. The child first told the experimenter whether or not anything had, in fact, happened, and then was asked to write his or her answer on a page attached to the end of the Self-Perception Profile answer sheet. If a child reported to the experimenter that no such event had happened, then he or she was instructed to simply write "Nothing" on this page.

Following this, the child was again thanked for his or her help with the project, and he or she returned to the classroom.

RESULTS

Descriptive statistics for the self-description task, self-complexity measures, and the self-esteem scales will be presented, followed by inferential statistics designed to test the four main hypotheses. Inferential statistics testing the fifth hypothesis regarding age differences will be presented throughout this section wherever relevant.

Self-description Task

The content categories used for the actual coding of each child's self-descriptive statements into content categories were created to correspond with the six self-esteem subscales from Harter's

Self-Perception Profile. Thus, each self-descriptive statement was coded according to one of the following categories: physical appearance, athletic competence, scholastic competence, behavioral conduct, social acceptance, and global self-worth. A final category for unscoreable statements was also included for any statements that did not fit into the other six categories.

The two coders, who were blind to the age and sex of the child, were expected to place a given statement into the same category. Interrater agreement for this task, based upon one-third of the data, was 86 percent. All differences were reconciled by discussion between the two coders.

Self-descriptive Statements. The mean number of statements generated by the children was 17.24, with a standard deviation of 5.99. As mentioned earlier, each child was encouraged to generate a minimum of eight statements. The fact that the mean is much higher than this indicates that the children had little trouble generating self-descriptive statements. The mean for the third graders was 17.40 (SD = 6.38), while the mean for the sixth graders was 17.07 (SD = 5.66). The number of statements generated by the two age groups was not significantly different, t(56) = 0.21, ns.

Means and standard deviations for the number of statements that fell into each of the seven coding categories are presented in table 1.1. It can be seen from the table that the athletic competence and scholastic competence categories were used quite frequently, while the global self-worth and behavioral conduct categories were used quite infrequently. This may be because an open-ended self-description task focuses one's attention on more concrete personal characteristics, such as athletic or academic accomplishments. In contrast, the child might be less likely to mention abstract, less observable characteristics such as those corresponding to the latter two categories.

In order to consider age differences in the types of self-statements made by the third and sixth graders, t-tests were performed on each of the seven coding categories; results are reported in table 1.1. Only two significant age differences emerged. Third graders generated a significantly greater number of athletic self-statements than did the sixth graders, whereas the sixth graders generated a significantly greater number of global self-worth statements than did the third graders.

Follow-up Question, Session 1. After completing the self-description task at session 1, the children were asked to indicate how "good a job" they did of describing themselves to the

Table 1.1
T-Tests by Grade on Seven Content Coding Categories

| | (Target Group) | | | |
| | Third | Sixth | | |
Category	Graders	Graders	t	p
Scholastic	3.87	4.07	−0.37	ns
competence	(1.89)	(2.31)		
Physical	0.73	1.21	−1.42	ns
appearance	(1.26)	(1.32)		
Athletic	4.70	2.57	2.99	.01
competence	(2.91)	(2.47)		
Global	0.03	0.43	−2.06	.05
self-worth	(.18)	(1.03)		
Social	1.40	2.07	−1.36	ns
acceptance	(1.67)	(2.09)		
Behavioral	0.53	0.86	−0.76	ns
conduct	(.82)	(2.19)		
Unscoreable	6.13	6.25	−0.11	ns
	(4.35)	(3.72)		

Note: The df for all t-tests were 56. Standard deviations are in parentheses.

experimenter, using a five-point scale (1 = not at all good; 5 = very very good). The average response to this question (M = 3.53, SD = .66) was significantly different from the scale midpoint (t(56) = 6.12, $p < .01$) indicating that the children generally thought they did a pretty good job of describing themselves to the experimenter. There was no significant difference between the third and sixth graders in response to this question.

Self-complexity Variables

Following the self-description task at session 1, the children performed a hierarchical sorting task using their self-descriptive statements. Their responses on that task were the basis for three of the self-complexity variables.

The total number of levels used by each child was computed by simply counting the number of hierarchical levels in his or her card sort. Although the sixth graders were expected to have higher scores on this measure than did the third graders, no significant difference was found between the two age groups.

The total number of groups constructed by each child was computed by simply counting the final number of separate groups at the end of his or her card sort. Although the third graders produced slightly more groups, their mean was not significantly different from that of the sixth graders.

The final variable computed from the child's hierarchical card sort was the complexity score, according to a formula described in Zajonc (1960):

$$\text{Complexity} = \Sigma rn$$

In this formula, n is the total number of statements at the rth level of the hierarchy. For example, if there were ten items at the first level of the hierarchy, five items at the second level, and four items at the third level, then that child's complexity score would be $(1 \times 10) + (2 \times 5) + (3 \times 4)$ or 32. The score is thus weighted to reflect the number of items at each level of the hierarchical sort. Card sorts that had more hierarchical levels produced higher complexity scores. The third and sixth graders were not significantly different in their complexity scores.

The other two self-complexity variables to be discussed were designed to focus more specifically upon the centrality of the scholastic self-statements to the child's self-concept. The fourth variable, scholastic centrality, was not expected to be different for the two age groups. However, it was expected that children having higher scholastic centrality scores would regard their scholastic performance as more important than did children with lower scores.

The scholastic centrality score was computed by first taking the total number of other self-statements that the child said would change if the scholastic competence statements were no longer true, not including other scholastic competence statements or changes. This number was then divided by the total number of scholastic statements generated by the child (total scholastic statements). In this way, the total number of self-statements that the child stated would change was corrected by the total number of scholastic statements generated by that child. This number—the numerator of the equation—was then divided by the total number of statements generated by the child (total statements generated). This was done to take into account individual differences in the number of self-descriptive statements generated by each child. Thus, the formula is as follows:

$$\text{scholastic centrality} = \frac{\Sigma \text{ changes/total scholastic statements}}{\text{total statements generated}}$$

Scores closer to one indicated higher scholastic centrality. As expected, no significant differences were found between the two age groups for this measure.

A final centrality measure, the proportion of scholastic competence statements, was also computed for use in hypothesis testing. This variable was computed by taking the total number of scholastic self-statements generated by the child, and then dividing that number by the total number of statements generated. (For use in hypothesis testing, this variable was transformed using the arcsine transformation). Again, as expected, no difference was found between the third and sixth graders for this measure.

In summary, then, no significant differences were found between the third-and sixth-grade children on any of the five self-complexity variables. This was not entirely an expected result.

Although no differences were predicted for the scholastic centrality and scholastic proportion variables, it was expected that the older children would be higher than the younger children on the other self-complexity variables.

There are a number of possible explanations for these unexpected findings. It may be that the card-sorting tasks used in the present study are not sensitive enough to detect developmental changes in self-complexity. It was hoped and expected that the hierarchical card-sorting task would be an adequate measure of cognitive complexity. Barenboim (1985) was successful in using this method with slightly older children (fourth grade and older).

Additionally, pilot work conducted for the present study also indicated that this might be a promising way of measuring cognitive complexity. The present results, however, suggest that other methods of assessing developmental changes in cognitive complexity must be devised.

Self-esteem Scales

In this section, scores from Harter's Self-Perception Profile will be discussed. As stated earlier, target group children completed the scale at sessions 1 and 2, while the control group completed the scale at sessions 2 and 3. All of the subscale scores have a range of six to twenty-four points.

Session 1: Target Group. Among the six subscale scores, the global self-worth scale had the highest scores, while the athletic competence scale had the lowest scores. Age differences were present only for physical appearance, with third graders having significantly higher scores than did the sixth graders. The sixth graders, who were most likely experiencing major changes in their bodily self-images due to the onset of puberty, may, as a result, have felt more negatively about their physical attractiveness than did the younger children. Additionally, the middle school years are typically a time when children become increasingly preoccupied with their physical appearance, particularly their attractiveness to the opposite sex (Rosenberg 1986).

Session 2, Target Group. As at session 1, the global self-worth scores were highest, while the athletic competence scores were lowest. Again, a significant age difference was found only for the physical appearance scale, with the third graders having significantly higher scores than the sixth graders.

The stability of self-esteem scores from session 1 to session 2 was also compared for each grade. For the third graders, significant changes were found for the scholastic competence, athletic competence, and behavioral conduct subscales. Scores for all three subscales increased from session 1 to session 2.

Unlike the younger children, the sixth-grade scores were quite stable from session 1 to session 2, with only the social acceptance scores showing a marginal increase ($p < .10$). Perhaps self-esteem is more stable across short periods of time for older children than for younger children, although little is known about the short-term stability of self-esteem in children.

Session 2, Control Group. As stated earlier, the control group was given the Self-Perception Profile at sessions 2 and 3, with no intervening event (such as a report card) between the two sessions. The pattern of means from the session 2 scores indicates that, as with the target group, the global self-worth scores are highest. The scholastic competence scores were lowest. There were no significant age differences between the third and sixth graders.

Session 3, Control Group. Scores from the Self-Perception Profile at session 3 were quite similar to those at session 2. Again, global self-worth scores were highest, while physical appearance scores were lowest. No significant age differences were found.

In terms of changes in self-esteem scores from session 2 to session 3, a marginally significant ($p < .07$) increase in social acceptance scores was found. No other significant changes occurred between sessions 2 and 3 for this group.

For the sixth graders in the control group, two self-esteem scores changed from session 2 to session 3. Scholastic competence scores significantly increased ($p < .01$), and the Behavioral conduct scores showed a marginally significant increase ($p < .06$). No other significant changes were found.

Target versus Control Groups. A final set of t-tests was conducted to compare the changes that occurred in self-esteem scores from one session to the next between the target and control groups. There was only one marginally significant difference ($p < .06$) between the two groups. The target group showed a somewhat greater change in behavioral conduct scores than did the control group.

In summary, then, the target group third graders did show significant changes on three of the six subscales, while the sixth graders did not. The control group, on the other hand, was quite stable during the two week period between session 2 and session 3. Finally, there were no differences of import between the target and control groups in terms of stability of self-esteem across the two week period.

Follow-up Question, Session 3. All children in the control group, following the administration of the second Self-Perception Profile at session 3, were asked to report whether anything either "very good" or "very bad" had happened to them at school since the last time they had seen the experimenter (approximately two weeks earlier). Of the twenty-eight children, ten reported that nothing had happened; fifteen reported that something good had happened (such as doing well on a test); and three reported that something bad had happened (such as doing badly on a test).

In order to consider differences between these three groups of children, a series of one-way analyses of variance was carried out. Answers to this follow-up question served as the independent variable, while the six absolute difference change scores served as the dependent variables. Only the analysis of variance for physical appearance scores was significant, $F_{(2.25)} = 9.27$, $p < .03$. The students who reported that something good had happened had higher change scores for physical appearance ($M = 2.13$) compared to the group that reported that something bad had happened ($M = 1.00$). The smallest change occurred for the group who reported that nothing had happened ($M = .40$).

For the control children, then, changes in students' perceptions of their physical appearance appeared to be related to the occurrence of some good or bad intervening event at school between sessions 2 and 3. However, this finding can most likely be attributed to chance, as there is no reasonable explanation for the link between a good or bad school event and a child's physical appearance self-esteem.

Report Cards

During the period of time between sessions 1 and 2, all of the children in both groups received their second (of four) report cards of the academic year. Because the third and sixth graders attended different schools, the formats of the report cards were different for the two groups. Thus, a composite grade score was computed separately for each child by summing his or her grades for reading, English and language, math, social studies, and science. These five subjects were courses taken at both grades.

This composite grade score was then transformed into a *z*-score, using the mean and standard deviation for all of the scores obtained from that child's age group. These *z*-scores were created for use in testing the first hypothesis, the results of which will be presented in a later section of this chapter. The relationship between these grade scores and the four follow-up questions asked of the target children at session 2 were also of interest, and will be described in the following section.

Follow-up Questions (Session 2)

As stated earlier at the end of session 2, children in the target group were asked four follow-up questions regarding their reactions to their report cards. Table 1.2 presents the means, standard deviations, and results from the t-tests of the third versus the sixth graders.

The overall mean response to the question "How happy were you with your report card?" was 4.22 (sd = .90). This mean score was significantly different from the scale midpoint ($t(56)$ = 10.33, $p < .01$) indicating that the children were generally happy with their grades. Third graders, however, reported being significantly happier with their grades than were the sixth graders.

The overall mean response to the question "How happy were your parents with the grades you received?" was 4.26 (sd = .98). Again, this number was significantly different from the scale midpoint ($t(56)$ = 10.03, $p < .01$), indicating that the children also perceived their parents as being happy with their grades. Third graders

Table 1.2
T-Tests by Grade on Four Follow-up Questions

| | (Target Group) | | | |
| | Third | Sixth | | |
Question	Graders	Graders	t	p
Happy	4.60	3.82	3.63	.01
	(0.56)	(1.02)		
Parents	4.67	3.82	3.60	.01
	(0.48)	(1.19)		
Important	4.67	4.57	0.58	ns
	(0.48)	(0.74)		
Surprised	4.27	3.39	3.01	.01
	(0.94)	(1.26)		

Note: The df for all t-tests were 56. Standard deviations are in parentheses

again, however, perceived their parents as being significantly happier than did than the sixth graders.

The overall mean response to the question "How important is getting your report card to you?" was 4.62 ($sd = .62$). This score was also significantly different from the scale midpoint ($t(56) = 19.91$, $p < .01$), indicating that the children did view the report cards as being important. Means for the third-and sixth-graders were quite similar, indicating that both age groups viewed the report card as being important.

Finally, the overall mean response to the final question—"How surprised were you with the grades you got?" was 3.84 ($sd = 1.18$). This score was again significantly different from the scale midpoint ($t(56) = 5.42$, $p < .01$), indicating that, in general, the children were surprised at the grades they received. Again, however, the third graders were significantly more surprised about the grades they received than were the sixth graders. These findings also imply that the third graders were, in fact, more pleasantly surprised by the grades they received than were the sixth graders.

In summary, the third graders had significantly higher average responses to the three questions regarding happiness about grades, parents' perceived happiness about grades, and feelings of surprise about grades. Perhaps the sixth graders were less affected by the report cards, as evidenced by their significantly lower mean responses to these questions, because of their greater cognitive capabilities as well as their greater familiarity with report cards.

Additionally, the finding that the third graders had significantly higher responses to the two questions regarding both their own and their parents' satisfaction with the report cards may be related to the general tendency of younger children to consistently overrate their own abilities (Harter 1982).

It can also be seen from table 1.2 that the third graders also had much lower standard deviations than did the sixth graders for all four follow-up questions. This is perhaps due to ceiling effects in their responses to the questions. These effects would also seem to be due to the third graders' consistently optimistic feelings regarding the report cards.

The final section will report results from the statistical tests of the first four hypotheses.

Tests of Specific Hypotheses

Hypothesis 1. The first hypothesis stated that, the more scholastic self-descriptive items generated by a child, the greater the impact of the report card on that child's self-esteem. The most direct test of this hypothesis would be to correlate the proportion of scholastic self-descriptive items with the scholastic competence difference score. Unfortunately, this correlation ($r = -.05$) was not significant for the target group as a whole.

However, significant yet quite different correlations were found for the two age groups. For the third graders, the correlation was significant but negative, ($r = -.32$, $p < .05$). For the sixth graders, on the other hand, this correlation was significant but positive ($r = .31$, $p < .05$). Thus, support was found for this hypothesis among the older children, but not for the younger children.

Hypothesis 2. The second hypothesis stated that the wider the range of self-descriptive categories used by the child (high differentiation), the less impact the report card would have on his or her scholastic competence. In order to test this hypothesis, the total number of self-descriptive categories used by a child was correlated with his or her scholastic competence difference score. This correlation was not significant for either age group, nor was it significant for the target group as a whole. Thus, no support was found for the second hypothesis.

Hypothesis 3. The third hypothesis stated that the higher the centrality of the scholastic self-descriptive items generated (that is, high scholastic centrality scores), the greater the impact of the report card on scholastic competence scores. In order to test this hypothesis, scholastic centrality scores were correlated with scholastic competence difference scores. Again, this correlation was not significant for either age group nor for the target group as a whole. This indicated a lack of support for the third hypothesis.

Hypothesis 4. The fourth hypothesis dealt with age differences, particularly with regard to the self-complexity variables. As stated earlier, results regarding age differences have been presented throughout this section where relevant. Additionally, these age differences will be discussed further in the following section.

DISCUSSION

The four major hypotheses under investigation in the present study received only weak support. Some support was found for the first hypothesis, which stated that the greater the number of scholastic competence statements used to describe the self, the greater the impact of the report card on self-esteem. However, this hypothesis was confirmed only for the sixth graders. Additionally, no relationship was found between a child's ratings of how important the report card was and the amount of change in scholastic competence scores.

The second hypothesis—that children with a wider range of self-roles would be less affected by the report card—was not supported. The third hypothesis, that children with higher scholastic centrality scores would be more affected by the report card, was also not supported.

The final hypothesis involved potential age differences in self-complexity. No age differences were found for any of the five self-complexity measures, although the sixth graders were expected to have higher scores on three of these variables. Other types of age differences did emerge, however.

First, third graders showed less stability in self-esteem over time (from session 1 to session 2) than did the sixth graders, as evidenced by changes on three of the six self-esteem subscales. Second, the third graders had significantly higher responses than did the sixth graders on three of the four follow-up questions at session 2 regarding reactions to the report card. And third, there were significant differences in the types of statements generated in the open-ended self-description task. Thus, although there were no differences in self-complexity between the two age groups, they were different in other respects.

In general, then, it must be admitted that the hypotheses under investigation in the present study were not well-supported. This lack of support could have been due to a number of unforeseen methodological problems.

One such problem might involve the age groups chosen for study. These two age groups were chosen because, according to Piaget's model of cognitive development, each group should be at a qualitatively different stage. However, the lack of age differences on the self-complexity measures would seem to indicate that measurable age-related changes in self-complexity do not occur between the third and sixth grades. Some researchers (Harter 1986a; Rosenberg 1986) have suggested that the sixth grade is a period of great transition and uncertainty for children, due to such events as the onset of puberty, an increasing awareness of the opposite sex, and so on. It may be that changes in self-complexity, as measured in the present study, do not occur until later in adolescence, after this transitional period is completed.

A second potential area of methodological problems involves the measurement of self-complexity in the present study. A simple card-sorting task, adapted from techniques used successfully with adults, was chosen to measure the complexity of children's organization of self-knowledge. In fact, pilot data collected by the author indicated that a hierarchical sorting task such as the one used in the present study would show age-related differences in self-complexity. It is clear from the current results, however, that these techniques are not always successful.

It should be noted that there was one important difference between the task used in the present study and that used to collect the pilot data. In the present study, each child was allowed to generate as many self-descriptive statements as he or she wanted, with the only stipulation being a minimum of eight items. In the pilot study, on the other hand, the children were required to generate approximately the same number of statements (about sixteen). Thus, those children in the pilot study may have had a more difficult task to perform, in that they had more items to organize than did many of the children in the present study. This may have made developmental differences in self-complexity more apparent among the pilot children.

In future research it might be better to have all children generate a larger number of self-descriptive items in order to maximize individual differences in self-complexity.

Additionally, the children in the pilot study had fewer total tasks to complete, in that they were asked only to generate the self-descriptive statements and then organize them hierarchically. Perhaps the children in the present study became fatigued because of the greater number of separate tasks which they were required to complete.

A final methodological issue involves the assumption that report-card-time constituted an important event for the children. Although responses to the follow-up questions did indicate that the children felt that the report cards were very important to them, this, nonetheless, may not have been completely true.

There may have been social desirability pressures operating in the interview situation. Perhaps the children felt that they should tell the interviewer that report cards were important, whether they really were or not. And even by the third grade, children are already quite familiar with the report card ritual, and, thus, might not be affected by one particular report card. It may also be true that the final report card of the year is viewed by children as being the most important, while those that occur earlier in the year are seen as comparatively less important.

Finally, because children also normally receive a great deal of more subtle academic feedback on a daily basis (for example, grades on tests, teacher feedback, or social comparison of academic performance with peers), they may already have a clear idea of their own scholastic competence. If so, report cards may then have had very little additional impact upon self-esteem.

In any case, and based upon the results of the present study, the report card did not seem to be an important event for these children, despite their responses to the contrary on the follow-up question. It may also be the case that children have a somewhat different interpretation of what *important* means, as compared to adults' understanding of the term.

Aside from these methodological problems, the results in the present study might also have been weak because the proposed theoretical relationship between self-esteem and self-complexity was not accurate. In this study, children's reactions to their report cards were assumed to be mediated by their levels of self-complexity. However, the relationship between self-esteem and self-complexity might actually be considerably more complicated.

It might also be the case that types of domain-specific self-esteem, other than scholastic competence, might be more strongly related to self-complexity among children at these ages. For example, among boys during the elementary school years, one's athletic competence is typically considered to be important. Thus, athletic self-esteem scores might, perhaps, show a stronger relationship for these two age groups. Clearly, this is a question that should be addressed in future research.

Finally, perhaps the hierarchical structure of the self-concept does not undergo much change with development, but, in fact, is relatively stable during the period of middle childhood and early adolescence. Although past research has indicated that hierarchical factor structures based upon instruments such as Marsh's SDQ (Marsh et. al 1984) were more stable in older than in younger children—implying that there are changes in hierarchical structures with age—there may not be large amounts of change in the structure of the self-concept between third and sixth grade (Marsh et al. 1992). If this is true, it could help explain the lack of support for the fourth hypothesis which focused on age differences in self-complexity.

Again, one might speculate that changes in the relationship between self-esteem and self-complexity do not occur until the end of adolescence, which would correspond with Linville's (1985) results in work among college-aged women.

It is also possible that there are no large individual differences in how self-knowledge is hierarchically organized. In fact, Harter has gone so far as to suggest that hierarchical models of the self-concept are useful only "to represent a conceptual model in the minds of the theorist," and that these models do not actually "define the self-concept of individual subjects" (1986a, 141). If it is true that there are no large individual differences in the hierarchical structure of the self-concept in children, this would explain the lack of support for the second and third hypotheses as well, both of which deal with the relationship between self-complexity and self-esteem.

The methodological problems encountered in this study suggest a number of future research directions to take in studying the relationship between self-esteem and self-complexity. One possible direction would be to conduct a longitudinal study of the relationship between self-esteem and self-complexity over a period of years, rather than relying on a traditional cross-sectional design such as that used in the present study. A longitudinal study would allow one to assess, for example, individual stability in self-esteem over time. Additionally, by studying the same group of subjects over a period of years, it would also be possible to assess developmental changes in self-complexity, as well as any developmental changes in the relationship between self-esteem and self-complexity. Such a study would help to clarify the hypotheses investigated in this study.

Future research is also clearly needed in the area of measurement of self-complexity variables. A few different techniques have been used with some success with adults (Linville 1985; Scott 1974). However, the tasks associated with these techniques would be too difficult for young children to carry out with their more limited verbal skills. One possible approach might be to use an entirely different sort of method, such as Damon's and Hart's (1986) clinical interview technique, which requires the children to give responses to open-ended questions such as "What kind of a person are you?"

Yet another possible strategy for assessing individual differences in self-complexity might be to first explore the measurement of self-complexity in older subjects, and then somehow alter the task for use with younger subjects. Harter (1986b), for example, has used a promising technique for looking at individual differences in self-conceptions. Her subjects are first asked to generate a series of self-descriptive roles and/or characteristics, which are then transferred to a series of round stickers. Subjects are then asked to arrange these stickers within a large circle designed to represent the self, which also includes a smaller circle designed to represent the "core" self. Although Harter's subjects were older than those children in the present study (seventh to eleventh grade), this technique is one that potentially could be modified for use with younger children.

Similarly, research which I am currently conducting concerning self-complexity in college students might also be applicable for modification and use with children. Students are first asked to generate a list of self-roles. They are then asked, on a separate page, to place these self-roles near those which relate to each other. Lines are then drawn between those roles indicating that they are related. In this way, both integration (number of lines linking the various roles) and centrality (the role with the most links to other roles) can be assessed in a relatively simple manner.

Although this instrument is still in the validation stage, the technique does appear to be a promising way of assessing individual differences in self-complexity.

Perhaps this technique could also be modified for use with younger populations. Clearly, however, the issue of how to assess individual differences in self-complexity among both younger and older student populations is one that deserves a great deal of further research.

The question of how the complexity of self-knowledge might be related to effects regarding the self has both important theoretical and practical implications. We know that the self plays an important role in information processing, social interaction, and a variety of other more specific cognitive and social behaviors. Clarifications of the relationship between the structure of the self-concept and the affect that is related to this structure would seem to be an important next step in the study of the self.

The establishment of a theoretical link between these two variables might also have important practical implications. For example, a child who is low in self-esteem could be encouraged to acquire new skills in a variety of areas, thus bolstering his or her overall self-complexity and providing the basis for more stable feelings about himself or herself. This, in turn, could lead to more positive feelings of self-esteem. Although the present study was unable to empirically support such a theoretical link between self-complexity and self-esteem, the possibility of such a relationship should continue to be investigated in future research.

REFERENCES

Ainsworth, M. D.; Blehar, M. C.; Waters, E.; and Wall, S. 1978. *Patterns of attachment: A psychological study of the strange situation.* Hillsdale, N.J.: Erlbaum.

Ames, C. 1978. Children's achievement attributions and self-reinforcement: Effects of self-concept and competitive reward structure. *Journal of Educational Psychology* 70:345–355.

Barenboim, C. 1977. Developmental changes in the interpersonal cognitive system from middle childhood to adolescence. *Child Development* 48:1467–1474.

———. 1985. Person perception and interpersonal behavior. Paper presented at the meeting of the Society for Research in Child Development. Toronto, Canada.

Bargh, J. A. 1982. Attention and automaticity in the processing of self-relevant information. *Journal of Personality and Social Psychology* 43:425–436.

Benenson, J. F., and Dweck, C. S. 1986. The development of trait explanations and self-evaluations in the academic and social domains. *Child Development* 57:1179–1187.

Bertenthal, B. I., and Fischer, K. W. 1978. Development of self-recognition in the infant. *Developmental Psychology* 14:44–50.

Bradley, G. W. 1978. Self-serving biases in the attribution process. A reexamination of the fact or fiction question. *Journal of Personality and Social Psychology* 36:56–71.

Brinthaupt, T. M., and Erwin, L. J. 1992. Reporting about the self: Issues and implications. In *The self: Definitional and methodological issues,* edited by T. M. Brinthaupt and R. P. Lipka. Albany: State University of New York Press.

Carver, C. S. 1979. A cybernetic model of self-attention processes. *Journal of Personality and Social Psychology* 37:1251–1281.

Clark, E. 1983. Meanings and concepts. In *Handbook of child psychology.* Vol. 3. Edited by J. Flavell and E. Markman. New York: Wiley. 787–840.

Coopersmith, S. 1959. A method for determining types of self-esteem. *Journal of Abnormal and Social Psychology* 59:87–94.

Damon, W., and Hart, D. 1982. The development of self-understanding from infancy to adolescence. *Child Development* 53:841–864.

———. 1986. Stability and change in children's self-understanding. *Social Cognition* 4:102–118.

Eder, R. A.; Gerlach, S. G.; and Perlmutter, M. 1987. In search of children's selves: Development of the specific and general components of the self-concept. *Child Development* 58:1044–1050.

Epstein, S. 1973. The self-concept revisited: Or a theory of a theory. *American Psychologist* 28:404–416.

Gallup, G. G. 1968. Mirror-image stimulation. *Psychological Bulletin* 70:782–793.

Gergen, K. J. 1982. From self to science: What is there to know? In *Psychological perspectives on the self.* Vol 1. Edited by J. Suls. Hillsdale, N.J.: Erlbaum. 129–149.

Gordon, C. 1968. Self-conceptions: Configurations of content. In *The self in social interaction.* Vol. 1. Edited by C. Gordon and K. J. Gergen. New York: Wiley. 13–23.

Guardo, C. J., and Bohan, J. B. 1971. Development of a sense of self-identity in children. *Child Development* 42:1909–1921.

Halpin, J. A.; Puff, C. R.; Mason, H. F.; and Marston, S. P. 1984. Self-reference encoding and incidental recall by children. *Bulletin of the Psychonomic Society* 22:87–89.

Hammen, C., and Zupan, B. A. 1984. Self-schemas, depression, and the processing of information in children. *Journal of Experimental Child Psychology* 37:598–608.

Hart, D., and Damon, W. 1986. Developmental trends in self-understanding. *Social Cognition* 4:388–407.

Harter, S. 1982. The Perceived Competence Scale for children. *Child Development* 53:87–97.

———. 1983. Developmental perspectives on the self-system. In *Handbook of child psychology*, edited by P. Mussen. Vol. 4. *Socialization, personality, and social development*. Edited by M. Hetherington. New York: Wiley. 275–385.

———. 1985. Manual for the Self-perception Profile for children. Unpublished manuscript. Denver, Colo. University of Denver.

———. 1986a. Processes underlying the construction, maintenance, and enhancement of the self-concept in children. In *Psychological perspectives on the self*. Vol. 3. Edited by J. Suls and A. G. Greenwald. Hillsdale, N.J.: Lawrence Erlbaum Associates. 137–181.

———. 1986b. Cognitive-developmental processes in the integration of concepts about emotions and the self. *Social Cognition* 4:119–151.

Hegland, S. M., and Galejs, I. 1983. Developmental aspects of locus of control in preschool children. *Journal of Genetic Psychology* 43:229–239.

Higgins, E. T. 1989. Continuities and discontinuities in self-regulatory and self-evaluative processes: A developmental theory relating self and affect. *Journal of Personality* 57:407–444.

Hull, J. G., and Levy, A. S. 1979. The organizational functions of self: An alternative to the Duval and Wicklund model of self-awareness. *Journal of Personality and Social Psychology* 37:756–768.

James, W. 1890. *The principles of psychology.* New York: Holt.

Jolley, J. M. 1982. The relationship of self to age and susceptibility to learned helplessness. Unpublished doctoral dissertation. Columbus: Ohio State University.

Jolley, J. M., and Mitchell, M. L. 1984. The hierarchical structure of self. Paper presented at the meeting of the American Psychological Association. Toronto, Canada.

Kagan, J. 1981. *The second year: Emergence of self-awareness.* Cambridge, Mass.: Harvard University Press.

Katz, P., and Zigler, E. 1967. Self-image disparity: A developmental approach. *Journal of Personality and Social Psychology* 5:186–195.

Keller, A.; Ford, L. M.; and Meacham, J. A. 1978. Dimensions of self-concept in preschool children. *Developmental Psychology* 14:483–489.

Kifer, E. 1975. Relationship between academic achievement and personality characteristics: A quasi-longitudinal study. *American Educational Research Journal* 12:191–210.

Lewis, M. 1979. The self as a developmental concept. *Human Development* 22:416–419.

Linville, P. W. 1985. Self-complexity and affective extremity: Don't put all of your eggs in one cognitive basket. *Social Cognition* 3:94–120.

———. 1987. Self-complexity as a cognitive buffer against stress-related illness and depression. *Journal of Personality and Social Psychology* 52:663–676.

Livesley, W. J., and Bromley, D. B. 1973. *Person perception in childhood and adolescence.* New York: Wiley.

Long, B. H.; Henderson, E. H.; and Ziller, R. C. 1967. Developmental changes in the self-concept during middle childhood. *Merrill-Palmer Quarterly* 13:210–215.

Mahler, M. 1972. On the first three subphases of the separation-individuation process. *International Journal of Psychoanalysis* 53:333–338.

Markus, H. 1977. Self-schemata and processing information about the self. *Journal of Personality and Social Psychology* 35:63–78.

Markus, H., and Sentis, K. 1982. The self in social information processing. In *Psychological perspectives on the self.* Vol. 1. Edited by J. Suls. Hillsdale, N.J.: Lawrence Erlbaum Associates. 41–70.

Marsh, H. W., and Hocevar, D. 1985. Application of confirmatory factor analysis to the study of self-concept: First-and higher-order factor models and their invariance across groups. *Psychological Bulletin* 97:562–582.

Marsh, H. W.; Byrne, B. M.; and Shavelson, R. J. 1992. A multidimensional hierarchical self-concept. In *The self: Definitional and methodological issues,* edited by T. M. Brinthaupt and R. P. Lipka. Albany: State University of New York Press.

Marsh, H. W.; Barnes, J.; Cairns, L; and Tidman, M. 1984. Self-Description Questionnaire: Age and sex effects in the structure and level of self-concept for preadolescent children. *Journal of Educational Psychology* 76:940–956.

Marsh, H. W.; Smith, I. D.; Barnes, J.; and Butler, S. 1983. Self-concept: Reliability, stability, dimensionality, validity, and the measurement of change. *Journal of Educational Psychology* 75:772–790.

McGuire, W. J., and Padawar-Singer, A. 1976. Trait salience in the spontaneous self-concept. *Journal of Personality and Social Psychology* 33:743–754.

Minuchin, P. P., and Shapiro, E. K. 1983. The school as a context for social development. In *Handbook of child psychology,* edited by P. Mussen. Vol. 4. *Socialization, personality, and social development,* edited by M. Hetherington. New York: Wiley. 197–274.

Mischel, W., and Patterson, C. J. 1978. Effective plans for self-control in children. In *Minnesota symposia on child psychology.* Vol. 11. Edited by W. A. Collins. Hillsdale, N.J.: Lawrence Erlbaum Associates. 199–230.

Mischel, W.; Zeiss, R.; and Zeiss, A. 1974. Internal-external control and persistence: Validation and implications of the Stanford Preschool Internal-External Scale. *Journal of Personality and Social Psychology* 29:265–278.

Montemayor, R., and Eisen, M. 1977. The development of self-conceptions from childhood to adolescence. *Developmental Psychology* 13:314–319.

Mullener, N., and Laird, J. D. 1971. Some developmental changes in the organization of self-evaluations. *Developmental Psychology* 5:233–236.

Peevers, B. H., and Secord, P. F. 1973. Developmental changes in attributions of descriptive concepts to persons. *Journal of Personality and Social Psychology* 27:120–128.

Piaget, J. 1951. *Plays, dreams, and imitation in childhood.* New York: Norton.

Piers, E. V., and Harris, D. B. 1964. Age and other correlates of self-concept in children. *Journal of Educational Psychology* 55:91–95.

Rogers, T. B.; Kuiper, N. A.; and Kirker, W. S. 1977. Self-reference and the encoding of personal information. *Journal of Personality and Social Psychology* 35:677–688.

Rosenberg, M. 1979. *Conceiving the self.* New York: Basic Books.

———. 1986. Self-concept from middle childhood through adolescence. In *Psychological perspectives on the self.* Vol. 3. Edited by J. Suls and A. G. Greenwald. Hillsdale, N.J.: Lawrence Erlbaum Associates. 107–136.

Ross, M., and Sicoly, F. 1979. Egocentric biases in availability and attribution. *Journal of Personality and Social Psychology* 37:322–336.

Ruble, D. N.; Boggiano, A. K.; Feldman, N. S.; and Loeble, J. H. 1980. Developmental analysis of the role of social comparison in self-evaluation. *Developmental Psychology* 16:105–115.

Scott, W. A. 1963. Conceptualizing and measuring structural properties of cognition. In *Motivation and social interaction*, edited by O. J. Harvey. New York: Ronald Press. 266–288.

————. 1974. Varieties of cognitive integration. *Journal of Personality and Social Psychology* 30:563–578.

Shaffer, H. R., and Emerson, P. E. 1964. The development of social attachments in infancy. *Monographs of the Society for Research in Child Development* 29(3), serial no. 94.

Shavelson, R. J.; Hubner, J. J.; and Stanton, G. C. 1976. Self-concept: Validation of construct interpretations. *Review of Educational Research* 46:407–441.

Stipek, D. J. 1981. Children's perceptions of their own and their classmates' abilities. *Journal of Educational Psychology* 73:404–410.

————. 1984. Young children's performance expectations: Logical analysis or wishful thinking? *Advances in Motivation and Achievement* 3:33–56.

Wicklund, R. A. 1975. Objective self-awareness. In *Advances in experimental social psychology.* Vol. 8. Edited by L. Berkowitz. New York: Academic Press. 233–275.

Zajonc, R. B. 1960. The process of cognitive tuning. *Journal of Abnormal and Social Psychology* 61:159–164.

STEPHEN R. SHIRK
ANDREW G. RENOUF

2

The Tasks of Self-development in Middle Childhood and Early Adolescence

There has been a proliferation of studies on the development of the self in middle childhood and early adolescence. Although the vast majority of studies focus on self-esteem, a broad range of self-constructs including self-understanding, self-awareness, self-control, self-monitoring, and self-image have been investigated. (See Harter 1983 for a comprehensive review.)

Moreover, many of these studies have documented age-related changes across a variety of self constructs. Consequently, the reviewer of development of the self in middle childhood and early adolescence is faced with a daunting task. Given the range of self-constructs, the diversity of operationalizations, and the complexity of age-related findings, can one find organization in the midst of all this variation?

Kaplan argued in 1967 that the nature of human development cannot be derived from the compilation of age trends. Contrasting development to mere change, Kaplan has maintained that the concept of development entails the notion of progress toward an ideal state.

Viewed from this perspective, a developmental model of the self involves concepts such as goals, ends, or tasks. Thus, age-related changes can be evaluated as progressive or regressive in terms of their approximation of a goal or, less teleologically, their resolution of a specific task.

We propose that greater coherence can be brought to the study of the self in middle childhood and early adolescence by considering the self in the context of pivotal socioemotional developmental tasks. As such, the first objective of this chapter is to explicate the tasks of development of the self in middle childhood and early adolescence. Based on this framework, the relevant empirical literature will be reviewed with attention to some of the methodological difficulties in studying the self during this phase of the life-span.

AN ORGANIZATIONAL FRAMEWORK FOR STUDYING THE SELF IN MIDDLE CHILDHOOD AND EARLY ADOLESCENCE

The organizational perspective conceptualizes development as a series of reorganizations around stage-salient issues (Cicchetti & Sroufe, 1978; Cicchetti, et al. 1988; Shirk 1988a; Sroufe 1979). From this perspective, each phase of development is characterized by a pivotal developmental task. Perhaps the best-known example of this approach is Erikson's epigenetic theory of development published in 1968.

According to Erikson, development proceeds through a predetermined sequence of nuclear crises. Each crisis represents a pivotal task or turning point in the development of personality. For example, the developmental task of infancy is to establish basic trust in others through interactions with one's primary caregivers. For Erikson, each task is a *crisis* not because it necessarily produces storm and stress for the developing child, but because its resolution leaves an enduring mark on the child's personality.

Recent elaborations of this perspective have emphasized the hierarchical organization of developmental tasks (Cicchetti et al. 1988; Sroufe & Rutter 1984). Because early structures are incorporated into later structures, unsuccessful mastery of early developmental tasks may result in more serious difficulties with subsequent developmental tasks.

The organizational perspective offers a number of advantages for developmentalists. First, it offers an alternative account of developmental continuity. The traditional longitudinal perspective emphasizes consistency in individual behavior over time. When development is depicted as a series of behavioral reorganizations around a sequence of specific developmental tasks, continuity can be understood as patterns of successful or unsuccessful resolutions of these diverse tasks. For example, the successful resolution of early developmental tasks increases the likelihood of successful resolution of subsequent tasks.

Second, the organizational perspective provides a framework for understanding continuities between normal and pathological development. Both adaptation and maladaptation can be understood in terms of the successful or unsuccessful negotiation of the salient developmental tasks of a given period. Thus, the basic developmental concepts of arrest, progression, and regression can be defined in relation to the resolution of particular developmental tasks. In turn, child psychopathology can be understood as the negotiation of developmental tasks gone awry (Wenar 1982).

How might one apply the organizational perspective to the study of the self in middle childhood and early adolescence? Recent elaborations of the organizational perspective have focused on infancy and early childhood. For example, in 1981, Egeland and Sroufe outlined a sequence of five developmental tasks faced by children between infancy and kindergarten. Unfortunately, for our purposes, their model ends where we must begin. However, Erikson's epigenetic model offered one source of theoretical direction for identifying the tasks of development of the self in middle childhood and early adolescence.

Mastery as a Pivotal Developmental Task of Middle Childhood

According to Erikson (1968), middle childhood is the age of industry. The principal task of this period is mastery of the tools and roles of one's given culture. As Erikson noted, children turn away from the wishes and fantasies of early childhood and harness their exuberant imaginations to the laws of concrete things. The successful negotiation of this developmental task results in a sense of competence. Whereas the main danger of this period is the emergence of a sense of inferiority, Erikson also noted that children are at risk for accepting work as the only criterion for their worthiness.

If we accept the growth of mastery and competence as one of the pivotal developmental tasks of middle childhood, then a number of subtasks of self-development follow. First, as Erikson noted, mastery of the roles and tools of one's culture requires increased accuracy in the child's social perceptions. In essence, mastery is based on veridicality rather than fantasy.

We propose that the child faces a similar challenge in the area of self-evaluation. That is, the first task of development of the self in middle childhood involves anchoring the process of self-evaluation in reality-based judgments rather than in fantasy or wish. This task implies a related challenge. The demand for increased veridicality in the apprehension of social reality, including evaluations of the self, requires the child to grasp realistic criteria for self-appraisal. The acquisition of such criteria is essential for judgments of competence. In order for the child to attain greater accuracy in self-evaluation, norms for evaluating one's behavior must be acquired.

Second, as Erikson pointed out, the salience of competence as a developmental issue is at once both a source of self-esteem and a potential threat to one's self-worth. Thus, a second task of development of the self in middle childhood involves the coordination of one's sense of self-worth with one's emerging sense of competence.

Identity as a Pivotal Developmental Task of Early Adolescence

In thinking about the central developmental task of adolescence, we again seek guidance from Erikson (1963) who found the central task of this age to be identity formation. During this period, the adolescent must integrate existing structures of knowledge and experience with emerging cognitive abilities, new and sometimes unsettling libidinal yearnings, and the awareness of impending entry into the adult world of work and love. It is a time of questioning and challenges as " . . . all sameness and continuities relied on earlier are more or less questioned again . . . " (Erikson 1963, 261).

The successful resolution of this stage is an identity encompassing the samenesses and continuities of the past. This prepares the individual to venture forth into the adult world armed with a positive sense of self and feelings of acceptance from society. The danger of this stage is role confusion or the inability to establish a continuous sense of self and positive identity rooted in the individual's own experience.

If identity formation is the central issue for adolescence, two developmental subtasks for this age suggest themselves. The first is that of conservation of self, or maintaining continuity in the face of apparent and considerable discontinuity. Identity formation can only be successful if the individual is able, not only to create a cohesive *present* self, but also to integrate into the self-concept *historical* and possible *future* selves. This requires adolescents to resolve the tension between the dramatic changes they experience, both biological and psychosocial, and their fundamental sense of continuity, of being the same person despite the changes and passage of time.

The second developmental subtask of adolescence suggested by Erikson's epigenetic model is that of maintaining positive self-esteem in the face of the vicissitudes of development and everyday life. Erikson stresses the achievement not just of identity but of a *positive* identity—one that is valued by the individual and accepted by his or her social milieu. This is necessary to maintain the impetus of optimal development, to carry the individual onto the next developmental phase equipped to successfully negotiate it. In this instance, it is useful to consider negotiation of a developmental task in nondichotomous terms. In thinking about *how* an individual negotiates a task, rather than *whether* he or she does it, we can perceive continuities between normal and atypical development, as well as appreciate some of the pitfalls inherent to growth.

Although additional tasks of self development for middle childhood and early adolescence could be identified, one advantage of the foregoing proposal is that it places aspects of self development in the context of pivotal tasks of socioemotional growth. In this respect, the development of the self is not treated as an isolated phenomenon, but it is integrated with the emergence of other behavioral systems. From an organizational perspective, development does not proceed in a piecemeal fashion. Instead, development is characterized by the reorganization of interrelated systems of affect, cognition, and behavior in relation to a series of pivotal developmental tasks (Sroufe 1979).

TASKS OF SELF DEVELOPMENT IN MIDDLE CHILDHOOD

It is tempting to view middle childhood as a plateau situated between two steep grades of development. Viewed from the perspective of socioemotional development, this period of apparent quiescence is bounded, on one side, by the vicissitudes of Oedipal strivings and, on the other, by the turbulence of impending emancipation. Even the name *latency* seems to connote the quieting of development.

Similarly, recent models of cognitive development (Case 1986; Fischer 1980), supported by a growing body of empirical evidence, offer a revisionist account of the Piagetian cognitive revolution of middle childhood. As once there was discontinuity, there is now continuity. As there was synchrony, there is now task specificity. As there was abrupt change, there is now gradual change. The drama of cognitive development in middle childhood has given way to the gradual evolution of increasingly complex cognitive skills.

Thus, from both the perspectives of cognitive and socioemotional development, middle childhood appears to be a period of relative tranquility. Yet, despite the image of middle childhood as a period of quiescence, a growing body of empirical evidence indicates that there are significant developments in the area of self-evaluation during this age period. In this section of this chapter, research will be reviewed on two lines of self development which are closely related to the pivotal socioemotional task of mastery.

The Task of Accurate Self-Evaluation

A substantial body of empirical evidence indicates that the self-evaluations of young children are often unrealistic. Perhaps the most direct evidence comes from research on children's performance expectations.

In an experimental study with preschool and school-aged children, Parsons and Ruble (1977) found that preschoolers, who are presumably less competent than are their seniors, tended to have much higher expectations about their future performance on a puzzle task than did their older peers. Of equal interest, when younger children were exposed to repeated failure on the experimental task, they did not systematically lower their expectations for success. Despite available feedback on their performance, young children continued to hold high and unrealistic expectations about their abilities.

Research by Flavell, Friedrichs, and Hoyt (1970) on children's metamemory reveals a similar pattern of findings. In their study, young children were asked to estimate how many picture names they could recall. Children were then tested on an analogous memory task. Across ages, ranging from preschool to fourth grade, children overestimated their capacities.

Moreover, many of the youngest children in the study, preschoolers and kindergartners, asserted that they could complete the task without error. In a comprehensive review of young children's performance expectations, Stipek concluded in 1984 that young children are not just inaccurate in their judgments, but they typically overestimate their competencies.

Overestimation is not limited to specific, circumscribed abilities. As Harter pointed out, it is not uncommon to find among younger children a fantasized self which possesses "a staggering array of abilities, virtues, and talents" (1988, 122). For example, Harter reported that, in one study, fully 50 percent of preschool subjects described themselves as the fastest runner in their peer group. Similarly, young children's estimations of their popularity tend to be inflated (Ausubel, Schiff & Glasser 1952). According to Harter (1988), children's inaccurate and highly inflated evaluations of self should be understood as the "normative distortion" of early childhood and the result of children's failure to differentiate wish from reality.

There is evidence that children's self-evaluations become increasingly accurate during middle childhood. In 1984, Harter and Pike examined evaluations of cognitive competence, physical competence, and social acceptance among preschoolers, kindergartners, and second graders. Accuracy was operationalized as the degree of convergence between children's evaluations of competence and teacher evaluations of the same constructs.

As Harter and Pike noted, the relatively high correlation between teacher ratings of competence and children's performance on objective tests permits the use of teacher ratings as the index of realistic evaluation. Results from this study revealed nonsignificant age trends in the degree of concordance. Overall, correlations between children's and teacher's evaluations were quite modest with values of .37, .30 and .06 for the cognitive, physical, and acceptance ratings, respectively.

It is not clear whether variation across evaluative domains is a function of differential accuracy among children or teachers. That is, teachers may be quite accurate in their appraisal of children's cognitive competencies, based on readily accessible data, but relatively less accurate in their judgments of children's peer acceptance when standardized data are not available.

However, if one considers only the domain in which teachers tend to be accurate judges—that is, cognitive competence—the results reveal only a modest degree of convergence between children's and teacher's evaluations in early childhood. Stipek (1981) found a similar pattern of results with kindergartners and young school-aged children. Children in kindergarten through third grade rated their own and their classmates "smartness." Among kindergartners and first-graders, self-evaluations were unrelated to either teacher ratings or to ratings which they received from peers. In contrast, ratings by second- and third-graders were related to both teacher and peer ratings. These results suggest that entry into middle childhood involves the gradual development of increasingly accurate self-evaluation, at least in the intellectual domain.

The trend toward increasing accuracy appears to continue into middle childhood. Harter (1982) examined the relationships between children's evaluations of competence and both teacher evaluations and children's scores on standardized achievement tests. Children ranged in grade level from third to ninth. For perceived cognitive competence, correlations between children's evaluations and teacher evaluations steadily increased between third and sixth grade. A similar pattern emerged for the relationship between children's evaluations and their actual performance on standardized cognitive tests. After a significant but temporary drop at seventh grade, the relationship between perceived and actual competence rises during early adolescence.

As Harter concluded, these results suggest that children become increasingly able to evaluate their competencies during middle childhood. The temporary decline in late childhood suggests that the transition to early adolescence may pose new challenges to self-evaluation.

Is there evidence to support the claim that children's increasing self-evaluative accuracy is the result of their emerging ability to differentiate wish and reality? Stipek (1984) demonstrated that children's unrealistic and inflated performance expectancies can be intruded upon by personal desires.

Stipek hypothesized that young children have higher expectations for their own performances than for the performances of others because they have a stronger wish for their own success. However, if the desirability of the other child's success is increased, then one should see corresponding elevation in the first child's expectancies for the other child's performance.

In an experimental study, Stipek (1984) had children estimate the performance of a target child under two conditions of desirability. In the experimental condition, children were offered rewards contingent on the other child's performance (high desirability). In the control condition, no rewards were mentioned. Consistent with the hypothesis, the expectancies of preschool children varied as a function of incentive value. Investment in the other child's performance elevated performance expectancies. These results suggest that young children fail to differentiate their desires from their judgments.

Harter (1988) attempted to determine at what level of consciousness younger children's wishful thinking influences their reports of competence. Using a picture technique that encourages children to distinguish between their real self and their wished-for self, Harter hypothesized that children might respond more accurately, especially if their distortions are more consciously determined, because the experimental conditions made it more socially acceptable to be realistic about their competencies. Results from two samples—one with children who overrate their scholastic abilities and one with physically handicapped children—indicated that a subset of children altered their judgments as a result of the experimental conditions. Such children appeared to inflate their self-evaluations as part of a more conscious attempt at self-preservation.

By contrast, for a large number of children, the experimental procedure had no effect on their highly elevated reports of competence. These children continued to have difficulty differentiating realistic self-evaluations from idealized self-evaluations. One possibility is that these children needed to deny their own vulnerabilities (Harter 1988).

The lack of differentiation appeared to involve a defensive process and possibly reflected emotional maladjustment. In this context, it is interesting to note that Katz, Zigler, and Zalk (1975) found one group of emotionally disturbed children—children with externalizing, action-oriented symptoms—had relatively undifferentiated real and ideal views of themselves.

Perhaps the most systematic evidence for increasing differentiation between wish and reality in self-evaluation comes from the work of Zigler and his colleagues on the development of self-image disparity. According to this group (Achenbach & Zigler 1963; Katz & Zigler 1967; Phillips & Zigler 1980), children's capacity to distinguish realistic self-evaluations from ideal self-evaluations is a function of cognitive differentiation.

In essence, as children mature, they move from global, undifferentiated evaluations of self to evaluations reflecting more categories and finer distinctions. Differentiation of the self-image, in this case, into real and ideal images, follows the same developmental pattern as any developing symbolic construction (Glick & Zigler 1985). Moreover, with increasing development, the capacity to experience guilt increases as a function of the child's growing ability to internalize social norms and demands (Zigler & Phillips 1960). Comparisons of one's own performance with internalized social norms results in more realistic, and less inflated, self-evaluations (Phillips & Zigler 1980).

Katz and Zigler showed in 1967 that self-image disparity—the discrepancy between real and ideal self-evaluations—increases during middle childhood and early adolescence. Of particular importance for the cognitive differentiation hypothesis, children at higher levels of conceptual development, as reflected by higher mental ages, showed greater self-image disparity than did children at lower levels of conceptual development.

Zigler, Balla, and Watson replicated these results in 1972, and found that children at higher mental ages actually had lower real self-images than did children at lower mental ages. Similarly, Leahy and Huard (1976) demonstrated that egocentric children, lacking the ability to differentiate social perspectives, have smaller disparities between real and ideal self-images than do nonegocentric children. In sum, these results suggest that increasing differentiation of the child's cognitive system during middle childhood provides the basis for distinguishing wish from reality and possibly for more realistic self-evaluations.

There are other developmental processes that may account for increasing accuracy in self-evaluation in middle childhood. One method for evaluating one's abilities and behaviors is to make comparisons with a normative standard. In everyday social interaction, this process usually takes the form of social comparisons with an immediate reference group, such as one's peers. Research by Ruble and her colleagues (Ruble, Feldman & Boggiano 1976; Ruble, Boggiano, Feldman & Loebl 1980) suggests that the use of social comparison information in the process of self-evaluation does not emerge until middle childhood.

In one study, Ruble and colleagues (1980) asked open-ended questions about the determinants of self-evaluation to a sample of kindergarten, second-, and fourth-grade children. Their results revealed a much stronger tendency for fourth-graders to refer to social comparison information. Although the use of social comparison information may not become salient until middle childhood, Harter and Pike (1984) found that the use of such information may vary as a function of evaluative domain.

It is interesting to note that the emergence of social comparison processes may entail costs for some children. Although social comparison processes may lead to increasing accuracy in self-evaluation for most children, for some children this developmental achievement can introduce new problems. In 1983, Matthews and Siegel examined social comparison processes in children who are characterized by Type A behavior, that is, by a chronic struggle to achieve ever-escalating but poorly defined goals, and those who are not characterized by strongly driven, achievement behavior. Matthew's and Siegel's results suggest that the social comparison processes of Type A children fuel their competitive achievement strivings.

In contrast to less driven children, Type A children compared their performances to the top performer even when an explicit performance standard was provided. For some children, a developmental achievement, the capacity to make social comparisons in order to evaluate one's competencies, is transformed into a developmental hazard. In this case, maladaptation can be understood as the negotiation of a developmental task gone awry.

Another developmental process that may contribute to increasing accuracy in self-evaluation during middle childhood is the child's growing capacity for self-reflection. From the perspective of self-perception theory (Bem 1967), self-evaluations are derived from observations of one's own behavior over time. There is substantial evidence that indicates that children's capacity to take perspective on their own thoughts, feelings, and behavior increases dramatically during middle childhood and early adolescence (Chandler & Greenspan 1972; Edelstein, Keller & Whalen 1984; Selman 1980; Selman & Byrne 1974). The development of perspective-taking ability provides the cognitive basis for more systematic self-observation during this age period. Interestingly, this developmental achievement also entails costs for some children in the form of acute self-consciousness (Elkind & Bowen 1979).

Finally, increased self-evaluative accuracy in middle childhood is not entirely internally determined. Although cognitive changes undoubtedly contribute to the child's growing realism, the social environment also plays an important role. Eccles, Midgley, and Adler (1984) suggested that ability grouping and other forms of evaluative feedback become increasingly salient as the child progresses through elementary school. Moreover, during this period, children may rely less heavily on input from parents who may exaggerate their abilities and more heavily on feedback from teachers and peers who may be more realistic. In this connection, Stipek (1984) showed that increasing the salience of performance feedback results in more realistic self-evaluations.

The low to moderate correlations of children's self-evaluations with other's evaluations of them and with objective performance criteria raise a serious methodological question for studying the self in middle childhood. Are children reliable reporters of their own characteristics during this age period? One might elude this problem by arguing that, as long as the object of inquiry is the child's perceptions, then issues of veridicality and reliability are largely irrelevant. However, if one is concerned with the assessment of internal constructs with potential predictive power, such as self-esteem or perceived competence, then the issue of valid reporting is critical.

For example, if children inflate their reports of competence or elevate their reports of self-esteem when their actual sense of competence or self-esteem is less than robust, predictive relations between these constructs and social behavior will be difficult to discern. For example, Harter (1988) found different patterns of relationships between perceived competence and competence behavior for accurate and inaccurate reporters. Such problems have led some to seek alternate methods of assessing the self without relying on self-report (Waters et al. 1985).

A number of factors may conspire to make it difficult for children to reliably report their own characteristics. In addition to the cognitive processes which we have already considered, such as the inability to differentiate wish and reality, failure to use social comparison and other normative information, and the lack of perspective-taking skills, emotional processes may interfere with children's self-reports of their abilities and behaviors. Shirk and Rossman (1989) found that the degree of discrepancy between child and parent evaluations of problem behaviors was related to indices of child maladjustment. In general, children who were less well-adjusted, as reflected by greater anxiety, higher levels of denial as a coping strategy, and more behavior problems, diverged more widely from their parents' perspectives than did their well-adjusted peers. These results suggest that emotional processes may contribute to individual differences in the accuracy of self-evaluations and are consistent with Harter's conclusion (1987b) that defensive processes contribute to self-evaluative inaccuracy among a subset of children.

It is likely that maladjustment and defensive processes only serve to exacerbate the main problem with self-reports during middle childhood. That is, children are reluctant reporters of negative traits, states, and other potentially socially unacceptable characteristics. For example, Kagan (1989) reported that children with a reading disability or low popularity refused to acknowledge their difficulties in self-reports, but acknowledged their problems through empathetic responses to a filmed model.

Other evidence supporting this position is found in the work of Brody and Carter (1982). They systematically compared seven-, nine-, and eleven-year-old children's emotional attributions to themselves as protagonists in affect-laden stories with their emotional attributions to ambiguous characters in the same stories. The results indicated that children attributed greater and more intense negative affect to the ambiguous figure than to themselves. Children appeared to censure situationally appropriate negative affect when attributing it to themselves while acknowledging these feelings when attributing them to others.

There is also some evidence that children's tendency to keep their distance from negative affect may decrease with age. Comparing five- and seven-year-olds, Glasberg and Aboud (1982) found that younger children denied sad experiences more than did older children and were less likely to see sadness as part of their emotional disposition. Because of the narrow age range examined, it is not clear whether this trend continues through middle childhood. An equally important issue for the study of the self in middle childhood is to what degree children maintain comparable distance from the report of other negative characteristics, such as low self-esteem, perceived incompetence, and problem behaviors.

Competence and Self-worth

Erikson (1968) was not the first to underscore the significance of competence for self-evaluation. Much earlier in the history of psychology, James (1890) proposed that the fit between one's achievements and one's aspirations was critical for the process of self-evaluation. Although this relationship might be fundamental throughout the life span, from an organizational perspective, the growth of competence and mastery is a salient developmental issue in middle childhood and should figure pivotally in the process of self-evaluation during this age period. As Erikson noted in 1968, the salience of competence as a developmental issue is, at once, both a source of and potential threat to self-worth. From this perspective, a second task of self development in middle childhood involves the coordination of one's sense of self-worth with one's emerging sense of competence.

It is important to note that there is an enduring controversy over the conceptualization of self-esteem (Marsh, Byrne & Shavelson 1992). Two major models appear to inform the conceptualization and measurement of this construct.

The first might be termed the additive model in which self-esteem or self-worth is conceptualized as the sum of specific self-evaluative judgments. There are both unidimensional and multidimensional versions of this model. In the former, self-esteem is derived by summing across a heterogeneous pool of specific self-evaluations (Coopersmith 1967). In the later, self-esteem is the additive product of specific self-evaluations from a variety of coherent self-evaluative domains (Epstein 1973).

In contrast to this approach is the gestalt model in which global self-esteem refers to an evaluation of and affective orientation to the self as a whole (Rosenberg 1979). Although global self-esteem—that is, one's sense of worth as a person—may be related to specific self-evaluations, it cannot be reduced to them. As Harter (1985a) pointed out, this approach is in keeping with the gestalt notion that the whole is different from the sum of the parts. One major advantage of this approach is that it provides a way for investigating the contribution of specific self-evaluations to the individual's experience of self-worth.

Harter (1982, 1986) has argued that the concept of global self-worth is not in the cognitive repertoire of children until entry into middle childhood. Drawing on cognitive-developmental theory, Harter has maintained that, because young children lack a generalized concept of personhood, meaningful judgments about their worth as individual persons are difficult to obtain prior to about age eight. Research on the development of self-knowledge indicates that children's conceptualizations of self undergo important transformations during middle childhood. These include the emergence of psychological rather than physicalistic concepts of self (Selman 1980); the development of generalized, trait conceptions of self (Peevers & Secord 1973); and the emergence of conceptions of individuality (Guardo & Bohan 1971). These changes signal the child's emerging capacity to move beyond limited considerations of specific, concrete attributes to meaningful judgments about himself or herself as a person.

Consistent with this position, Harter (1986) found that a separate factor defining self-worth did not emerge in the self-evaluations of children with lower mental ages—that is, mental ages equivalent to preschool and younger school-age children. Moreover, items referring to general self-worth did not load systematically on any single factor. In contrast, research with children older than the age of eight clearly indicates that such children make both specific judgments about their competencies *and* global appraisals of their self-worth (Harter 1982).

In keeping with the salience of competence as a pivotal developmental issue in middle childhood, children's evaluations of their competencies become increasingly differentiated during this period.

In research with preschool and younger school-age children (six- and seven-year-olds), Harter and Pike (1984) found that a two-factor solution accounted for the self-evaluations of these children. Younger children did not meaningfully distinguish domains of competence. Instead, the first factor to emerge was a general competence dimension defined by both evaluations of physical and cognitive skills. However, young children did distinguish evaluations of competence from judgments of social acceptance (Harter & Pike 1984).

In contrast to younger children, older children did not view their competencies in a unidimensional manner. Instead, evaluations of cognitive, social, and physical competencies were clearly differentiated (Harter 1982). More recent work by Harter and her colleagues indicates that older children also make differentiated judgments about their physical appearance and behavioral conduct (Harter 1985a). This pattern of increasing differentiation appears to continue throughout adolescence (Mullener & Laird 1971. See also chapter 1 of this volume.)

There is little doubt that the differentiation of competence judgments during middle childhood reflects the overall differentiation of the child's cognitive system. For example, research with retarded children reveals less differentiation of self-evaluations of competence when compared with nonretarded peers (Harter 1987a). However, there is also indirect evidence to suggest that the salience of competence as a developmental task also contributes to increasing differentiation of evaluations of competence. Research with learning disabled children, for whom scholastic competence is made increasingly salient by virtue of their disabilities, systematically distinguishes broad, trait-like judgments of cognitive competence from evaluations of specific academic skills (Renick 1987). In this case, it appears that the salience of scholastic tasks leads to highly differentiated judgments of cognitive competencies.

Given the importance of mastery in middle childhood, one might expect self-worth to be closely yoked to children's perceptions of their competencies. As Erikson noted, mastery is both a source of and potential threat to self-worth in middle childhood. In fact, Harter found in 1982 that global self-worth is significantly correlated with evaluations of cognitive, social, and physical competence. However, the magnitude of these relationships is moderate (.42 − .53).

Although self-worth is significantly related to perceived competence, given the interrelationships among these domains, it is evident that straight-forward evaluations of competence do not account for all the variance in self-worth. Drawing on the work of James in 1890, Harter proposed that the relationship between self-worth and perceived competence is somewhat more complex. Rather than conceptualizing self-worth to be a direct function of self-evaluations of specific competencies, Harter (1985a) suggested that the importance of specific domains of competence also contribute to the relation between evaluations of competence and self-worth.

To paraphrase James, self-worth reflects the ratio of one's successes to one's pretensions. Harter operationalized this formula in terms of the congruence between one's perceived competencies in a given domain and the importance of the domain. Research with older children and early adolescents reveals a strong relationship between self-worth and the degree of congruence between perceived competence and importance of a competence domain (Harter 1987b).

For example, children with a high level of discrepancy between importance ratings and perceived competence ratings evidence relatively low levels of self-worth. Moreover, it is interesting to note that children with low self-worth appear to have difficulty discounting the importance of cognitive competence. That is, across varying levels of self-worth, cognitive competence is consistently rated as important (Harter 1985a). This finding suggests that mastery in the cognitive domain is highly salient to school-age children, and that it is difficult to discount as an important contributor to their overall sense of self-worth.

Harter's research indicates that a substantial amount of variability in self-worth can be explained by the relationship between perceived competence and the importance of the competence domain. However, a better test of the centrality of perceived competence to self-worth would be to compare the relative contribution of competence evaluations and other types of self-evaluations. The addition of evaluations of physical appearance and behavioral conduct to Harter's original measure allows for such a comparison. As Harter has pointed out (1985b), while the original scale (Perceived Competence Scale for Children) focused on children's judgments of competence, the revised scale (Self-Perception Profile for Children) includes evaluations of adequacy which do not necessarily involve competence in specific skills.

In an effort to address the question of the relative contribution of specific domains of self-evaluation to global self-worth, Harter (1987b) calculated separate correlations between global self-worth and the discrepancy scores—the degree of congruence between importance and competence ratings—for each domain. Contrary to expectation, the competence domains were not the best predictors of global self-worth for school-aged children. Instead, the self-evaluation of physical appearance contributed the most to self-worth in middle childhood and early adolescence.

Moreover, competence judgments were not the next most important contributor to self-worth in either age group. For both school-aged children and young adolescents, social acceptance followed physical appearance as the next most important contributor. This pattern of findings suggest that competency may play less of a role in global self-worth than one might expect if mastery is such a salient developmental issue in middle childhood. Instead, physical appearance and social acceptability appear to be more powerful determinants of self-worth during this age period.

It should be noted that this is not equivalent to saying that perceived competence is unimportant for global self-worth in middle childhood. In fact, evaluations of competence were significantly related to global self-worth. However, in comparison to judgments of physical appearance and social acceptability, perceived competence exerts less of an influence on self-worth. Although Erikson maintained that children are at risk for overemphasizing work as the sole criterion for measuring their worth, these results suggest that self-worth may be more closely tied to attractiveness.

These results raise an interesting question about the pivotal developmental tasks of middle childhood. The relative importance of physical appearance and social acceptability suggests that the negotiation of social relationships, particularly peer relationships, is also quite salient to school-age children. One possibility is that these results reflect the so-called "secular trend." That is, when one looks across cohorts, there is evidence to suggest that developmental milestones such as onset of puberty, are being reached earlier in the life span.

Consequently, issues that were once thought to be highly salient to young adolescents—in this case, a preoccupation with physical appearance—are now relevant to younger children. Although this interpretation is intriguing, it should be noted that Harter (1987b) has found a strong relationship between physical appearance and self-worth across a broad range of the life span. Perhaps the simplest explanation is that children are faced with multiple developmental tasks at different age periods.

In 1982, Gilligan criticized Erikson for overemphasizing issues of industry and mastery over issues related to social relationships. However, in defense of Erikson, the age of industry was also described as a socially "most decisive stage" (Erikson 1968, 126). For Erikson, mastery involves the ability to work with others. Given the significance of physical appearance and social acceptability, it appears that another pivotal task of middle childhood is the negotiation of social relationships.

TASKS OF SELF DEVELOPMENT IN EARLY ADOLESCENCE

The traditional formulation of adolescence as a difficult time of transition has been part of our cultural consciousness since Hall (1904) first characterized the age as one of "storm and strife." Given the dramatic biological and psychosocial changes occurring at this age, spurred by puberty, school transitions, and cognitive advances, Hall's description would seem to be reasonable. More recently, however, some theorists have challenged this notion questioning whether there is an adolescent crisis (Offer 1969; Savin-Williams & Demo 1984; Simmons & Blyth 1987. See also chapter 4 of this volume.). Our own position is that adolescence (as implied by the organization of this chapter and volume) covers at least two distinct developmental phases—early and late adolescence—and each has its own unique set of challenges.

For instance, it is the early adolescent who must deal with pubertal changes, while issues of career and adult roles are more salient for the late adolescent. Although adolescence encompasses a number of significant and difficult challenges, there will only be a limited number that require resolution at any one time. Furthermore, these challenges may be subsumed under the general category of *issues of identity formation.*

It is within this context that we consider the particular tasks associated with identity formation in early adolescence. As stated earlier, we understand those to be conservation of self and maintenance of positive self-esteem. In this section, we will examine these two developmental subtasks of early adolescence and argue that the resolution of these tasks has important implications for further development and, especially, for mental health.

Continuity and Conservation of the Self

Conservation of self, or an individual's ability to maintain a sense of personal sameness across the life span, is an intuitively appealing concept. The strongest evidence in support of it must surely be our own subjective experience of the self's continuity. Yet this sense is, by no means, a given across the life span. In fact, it must be created in a world in which change is the only constant. So then, how does one *conserve* a sense of personal sameness in the face of development? At least two potential processes are possible.

The first is the cognitive ability to consider and track within one's own life enduring facets of personality, such as temperament and attachment patterns. Although concrete-operational thinking provides the basis for conservation in concrete domains—such as conservation of volume—it is likely that formal operational thought facilitates the developing adolescent's ability to conserve more abstract aspects of identity, such as traits or other psychological characteristics.

Similarly, the capacity to perceive relations between distal events and the present, a prerequisite for experiencing continuity over time, increases with cognitive development (Shirk 1986b). The second is the actual experience of continuity. For example, to the degree that identity is an interpersonal process, continuity in relationships which provide consistent feedback to the self may represent an important source of conservation. In fact, it is not uncommon to hear distressed individuals talk about extracting themselves from old relationships in order to experience themselves in new ways.

One question for researchers in this area might then be which continuities must be experienced and under what conditions? That is, are particular domains of continuity, for example continuity in significant relationships or in self-esteem, more central than are others for conservation of the self? (The relationship between self-consistency and self-esteem will be further discussed later in this section.) Or must a person experience a certain level of continuity independent of particular domain to reach a sort of critical mass for conservation of the self to be attained? One approach to studying this issue would be to examine self-concept in children in which there have been significant discontinuities in various domains—for example, children who have experienced numerous geographic relocations, disruptions in significant relationships due to divorce or death, or children who have become physically disabled prior to puberty. This method again highlights the issue of pathology existing along a continuum of developmental adaptation. Studying development in the face of obstacles or instances in which development has clearly gone awry often sheds light on normal processes.

Change, as a fundamental characteristic of existence, is why conservation of self is such an apt metaphor. The important issue is not so much the *stability* of self-concept, which implies no change, but rather the *continuity*, or how change is linked to existing structures. The ability to conserve in various domains—for example mass, volume, or identity—requires the individual to ignore extraneous dimensions and focus on the defining one.

Thus, in the Piagetian conservation of liquids task, the conserving child must ignore the unequal heights of water in the different beakers and, through reversibility, equate the two volumes of water. Likewise, in the conservation of self, the individual must ignore the changes in physical size and shape, knowledge base, thought processes, and social roles and expectations, and remain focused on the phenomenology of continuity. This phenomenology must, in turn, be integrated with the very real changes that occur.

Consistent with our choice of developmental tasks during early adolescence, Rosenberg (1979) found the period of greatest self-concept disturbance is between ages eleven and fourteen. During this period, as compared to late childhood or late adolescence, Rosenberg found higher levels of self-consciousness and self-concept instability, and lower levels of self-esteem. Shirk (1987) found a similar trend in a measure of self-doubt, although those data indicated self-doubt to be greater in late childhood and early adolescence as compared to late adolescence. Given, however, that age and developmental stage are seldom perfectly correlated, we see this as generally supporting the notion of greatest self-concept disturbance in early adolescence.

Others (Offer 1969) have also found early adolescence to be the most tumultuous or disruptive age period from the viewpoint of both adolescents and parents. Thus, it appears that early adolescence is a period when issues of continuity in the self-concept are more salient to the individual.

Researchers have linked this instability in self-concept to various processes and transitions typically occurring in early adolescence such as changes in person-perception and self-understanding (Barenboim 1981; Damon & Hart 1982; Leahy & Shirk 1984), puberty (Rosenberg 1979), and school transitions (Rosenberg 1985; Simmons 1987). In the case of person-perception and self-understanding, for instance, Barenboim in 1981 and Damon and Hart in 1982 have reached similar conclusions in regard to developmental trends.

Barenboim found a developmental progression in children's understanding of others from comparisons based on overt behaviors in middle childhood to comparisons based on psychological constructs in early adolescence. In reviewing the literature, Damon and Hart reached similar conclusions about developmental trends in self-understanding; that is, a progression from understanding based on behaviors, physical attributes, and physical competencies in middle and late childhood to one based on psychological traits and more abstract skills such as communication or social skills in early adolescence.

These changes, along with the others due to puberty and school transitions, map out the challenges to conservation of self during this age period. Despite these obstacles, most children do successfully negotiate the task. Here again, it is useful to consider the concept of continuity versus stability. The self-concept may be continuous and still be mutable, or subject to change. In essence, what has been documented empirically needs to be experienced directly by the adolescent. That is, change can occur in self-concept without destroying links to previous states. After an initial period of disturbance, the adolescent is able to consolidate self-understandings and evaluations through his or her increasing abilities to abstract psychological traits from seemingly disparate behaviors and skills.

Although self-esteem is only one component of the self-concept, an examination of self-esteem sheds light on the issue of continuity versus stability of the self. As stated earlier, many researchers now challenge the traditional notion of adolescence as a period of *Sturm und Drang* and have failed to find decreases in self-esteem during this time (Harter 1986; Nottelmann 1987; Rosenberg 1986; Simmons 1987. See also chapter 4 of this volume.).

In research with middle-school children, Renouf (1989) found a correlation of .52 (p<.001) between two assessments of self-esteem over a twelve-month period. This indicates some stability. Other researchers have found a small but significant increase over the course of adolescence after an initial decrease (Harter 1986; McCarthy & Hoge 1982; O'Malley & Bachman 1983; Savin-Williams & Demo 1984; Simmons, Rosenberg & Rosenberg 1973).

The aforementioned research provides, we believe, evidence for both the continuity and mutability of self-esteem. Support for the construct's continuity comes from the strong relationships found between measures of self-esteem over a period of time. Support for its mutability comes, not only from findings of a decrease in late childhood and early adolescence followed by gradual increase during adolescence, but also from the same correlations demonstrating continuity. These correlations range from approximately .50 to .70, which, although indicating significant stability, also account for only 25 to 50 percent of the variance.

In addition, there is the issue of developmental versus individual differences approaches to studying the self-concept. Although self-esteem appears stable or gradually improving on average, there may exist groups of children who are experiencing change in their self-esteem, this change being obfuscated by averaging across samples. Research by Renouf in 1989 suggests this may indeed be the case.

In our middle-school sample, we found no significant change in mean scores of self-esteem over a year's period. Further analyses revealed, however, that 35 percent of the children were stable in their level of self-esteem; 39 percent decreased in level of self-esteem; and 26 percent increased in level of self-esteem. This suggests to us that, although the developmental trend may be gradually increasing self-esteem during early adolescence, within that trend do exist groups who experience significant changes in either direction.

Associated with the issue of the continuity versus stability of the self-concept is that of a trait versus state conceptualization of the construct. Like most dichotomies, this one is misleading as it presumes no middle road. Again, the example of self-esteem will serve as a useful illustration.

Although our argument for self-esteem as continuous would appear to advocate a trait approach, we understand the construct to be far too dynamic to be so defined. In part, this dynamic quality may be due to an interaction between global self-esteem and domain-specific self-esteem. That is, previous researchers utilizing factor-analytic techniques have found that global self-esteem forms a separate factor from the individual domains (Harter 1982; Marsh & Shavelson 1985; Marsh et al. 1992). None of these domains predicts global self-esteem very well, nor does any form of aggregate of domains.

Although no particular domain may be a good predictor overall, at any one time the domain most salient to the individual—and thus the most important—may have the greatest impact on his or her self-esteem. For instance, for the young adolescent at her first school dance, social competence may be so overwhelmingly salient that being able to talk appropriately to a member of the opposite sex will have a significant, although ultimately temporary, impact on her global self-esteem.

What we suggest here is that interacting with an underlying and continuous sense of self-esteem is a moment-to-moment, fluctuating self-esteem determined by the shifting dominance of individual domains according to particular context. In fact, Rosenberg (1985) speculated about just such a distinction between the *barometric* self-concept and the *baseline* self-concept. The barometric self-concept refers to the moment-to-moment fluctuations in self-concept which an individual experiences, while the baseline self-concept refers to the underlying self-concept that changes slowly and over an extended period of time.

It is interesting to consider the relationship between self-esteem and the conservation of self. In systematic research examining the structure of the self-concept in middle childhood through adolescence, Elliot proposed that self-esteem provides the motivation to maintain or change the self-concept (Elliot 1982, 1984, 1986, 1988; Elliot, Rosenberg & Wagner 1984). He argued that young people with low self-esteem are unhappy with who they are and " . . . would generally prefer to change in order to think better of themselves, and hence, their self-concepts would then tend to be less consistent." (Elliot 1986, 209).

On the other hand, those with high self-esteem, being satisfied with who they are, would be motivated to maintain their existing sense of self. Using structural equation modeling techniques, Elliot (1986) found that self-esteem has a direct causal effect on self-consistency during middle childhood through adolescence. Elliot also found this relationship becomes increasingly mediated with age by other theoretically derived components of the self-concept (self-consciousness, tendency to fantasize about the self, and presentation of a false self).

Stern suggested in 1985 that the basis of self-consistency is the stability within individuals of the subjective experience of affect. He argued that the individual phenomenology of physiological arousal and psychic experience associated with particular affective states remains constant across the life span, and this phenomenology forms the foundation upon which self-consistency is built. If this is the case, then self-esteem, which has a large affective component, may well contribute toward self-consistency to the extent that self-esteem is continuous. At the very least, the valence of emotion associated with an individual's self-esteem (positive or negative) is likely to remain relatively stable, thus providing continuity in experience of the self that may contribute to a sense of self-consistency.

Although this line of research appears promising, Elliot's conclusions are still tentative. Wells and Sweeney, for instance, found in their 1986 research on bias in self-assessment that self-consistency is causally prior to self-esteem. This work, however, was done with people in late adolescence at an age in which Elliot found a more mediated effect on self-esteem of self-consistency. Furthermore, Elliot's hypothesis that individuals with low self-esteem would be more open to changing their self-concept in order to improve it may not adequately explain all the data.

For example, Fitch (1970) found that people with low self-esteem were more likely than those with high self-esteem to make attributions about failure that were consistent with their poor self-image. In this case, it would appear that self-consistency preceded self-esteem. The question of the relationship between self-esteem and self-consistency and causal priority is an important one in further expanding our understanding of the self-concept and seems by no means resolved. Additional work in this area would not only fill the existing gap in theory, but may also have significant clinical implications as it would indicate treatment priorities in working with children and adolescents where self-esteem and self-consistency are salient issues.

Maintenance of Self-esteem

If a primary developmental task during early adolescence is the maintenance of self-esteem, how is this different from any other period in the life span? Although maintenance of self-esteem is certainly an important task at any point during the life span, we suggest that it is particularly difficult during early adolescence. Challenges to self-esteem can be understood as falling into two categories: developmental transitions and the vicissitudes of life. Although both have profound effects on self-esteem, it is the former which distinguishes early adolescence as an especially vulnerable period.

The developmental transitions referred to here are the same challenges to conservation of self discussed earlier, that is, biological, social, and cognitive. The role these transitions play in self-esteem, however, is more complicated.

For instance, research indicates that it is not so much the transition to puberty that is damaging to self-esteem but rather early maturation which is damaging to some children, predominantly girls (Simmons & Blyth 1987; Simmons, et al. 1979). Consequently, it is not the transition to puberty per se that is damaging, but rather the timing in relation to one's cohort. Early transitions appear to be related to higher risk. Similar findings have been reported for school transitions (Rosenberg 1986; Simmons & Blyth 1987; Simmons et al. 1987).

Children who make the transition to a new school at an earlier age, for instance the transition to junior high school in seventh grade, appear to be more negatively impacted than are those entering high school in ninth grade. Again, however, it appears that girls' self-esteem is more vulnerable to the earlier change than is that of boys. These findings on differential responses to transition led Simmons (1987) to propose an arena-of-comfort hypothesis.

Essentially, if change is too discontinuous, for instance happening too early or suddenly, or if too many changes are experienced simultaneously, then the transition to adolescence will have a negative impact on self-esteem. Simmons and colleagues (Simmons 1987; Simmons & Blyth 1987; Simmons et al. 1979) have found this applied only to girls. They do not, however, report whether there were subsets of their male samples who responded similarly to multiple or premature changes.

While Renouf's (1989) findings do not directly address this question, he did discover boys whose self-esteem decreased during middle school, suggesting that average trends may not be completely representative. Again, this highlights the importance of both developmental and individual differences research. Although the developmental trend may indicate that girls are more vulnerable to decreases in self-esteem at this age, it does not necessarily hold that all boys are exempt from such decreases.

Another transition in the social arena during early adolescence is that of social roles and areas of competency. Harter (1982, 1988), for instance, has found that the number of domains important to self-esteem increases from five in middle and late childhood to eight in adolescence. The new domains include job competence, romantic appeal, and close friendships, implying that new skills need to be acquired and coordinated. The acquisition of new skills, however, presents not only the opportunity for new successes but also new failures, and as such, represents additional challenges to the early adolescent's self-esteem.

Advances in cognitive abilities during early adolescence also carry with them challenges to the individual's self-esteem. For example, Selman delineated in 1980 a developmental sequence of self-awareness in which the early adolescent achieves an awareness of his or her own self-awareness. This new order of self-reflexivity engenders the increased self-consciousness one so often encounters in young adolescents (Rosenberg 1979; White 1972) and can negatively affect their self-esteem. Increased self-awareness (Selman 1980); increased sense of one's agency (Broughton 1978); the ability to think in terms of single abstractions or psychological traits yet not be able to integrate multiple ones (Barenboim 1981; Fischer 1980)—all represent both new resources and pitfalls for the early adolescent that may directly impact on his or her self-esteem.

Finally, the normative reorganization of parent-child relationships in early adolescence poses an additional challenge to the maintenance of self-esteem. A critical aspect of family development involves an adjustment to the adolescent's changing status in the family. Robin suggested in 1981 that families who have difficulty with this transition are often characterized by high levels of parent-adolescent conflict. Such conflict can compromise parental support of the contentious adolescent. Some researchers have implicated, in addition to competency, the importance of social support to self-esteem (Harter 1986; Rosenberg 1979). Harter, in particular, has developed a systematic program of research focusing on self-esteem that provides strong empirical support for this two-pronged theoretical approach. Her work indicates that positive regard from significant others, specifically parents and peers, contributes significantly to the maintenance of self-esteem (Juhasz 1992). In fact, Harter's work (1986, 1987a) indicates that the contributions of social support and competency to self-esteem are equal in degree and relatively independent of each other. Thus, increases in parent-adolescent conflict which could entail decreases in parental support represent an additional challenge to the maintenance of self-esteem in early adolescence.

Not only do developmental transitions impact on an individual's self-esteem, but so do the vicissitudes of life. If we conceive of self-esteem as being a result of both competencies in important areas and social support, then any event impacting these two areas will also make itself felt on self-esteem.

For example, the illness or death of a significant other or divorce of one's parents would all lead to decreases in social support available to the early adolescent. Likewise, the adolescent who becomes disabled, suffers physical trauma, or becomes chronically ill will probably experience the loss of some competencies which may impact on his or her self-esteem. Finally, Rosenberg suggested in 1979 that contextual dissonance may have a negative impact on self-esteem. By this, he meant some central feature of the individual—such as race, gender, religion, or socioeconomic status—is different from that of others in the social milieu. Thus, a geographic move, loss of family income, or some other change that affects the social environment may also impact self-esteem.

Given these challenges to self-esteem, what happens when the maintenance of self-esteem goes awry? Although some have argued that research has over-emphasized self-esteem at the expense of other components of self-concept (Rosenberg 1979, 1985), we feel that much of this attention has been deserved because of the functional value of self-esteem. Many theorists have claimed the maintenance and enhancement of self-esteem to be central to an individual's motivational system (Harter 1986; James 1890; Kaplan 1975; Rosenberg 1979; Schwartz & Stryker 1971; Snygg & Combs 1949). We have not found a dissenting voice.

Once again, Harter's work provides us with a systematic approach to this issue. Her 1986 model stresses the mediational role self-esteem plays between social support and competency on the one hand, and affect and motivation on the other. Although Harter's research has found a small direct relationship between self-esteem and motivation, it is primarily through its strong impact on affect that self-esteem influences motivation. These relationships have held up in replications with children in middle childhood through early adolescence (Harter 1986; 1987a).

A second function of self-esteem often cited in the literature is that of maintaining mental health (Harter 1987a; Kaplan & Pokorny 1969; Rosenberg 1979, 1985). Although low self-esteem has been linked with anxiety (Bachman 1970), irritability and aggression (Lochman & Lampron 1986; Rosenberg 1985), and low life-satisfaction (Campbell 1981), it is most frequently associated with depression (American Psychiatric Association 1987; Battle 1987; Beck 1975; Freud [1917] 1968; Harter 1988; Kaslow, Rehm & Siegel 1984; Nolen-Hoeksema, Girgus & Seligman 1986; Poznanski 1982; Renouf 1989).

The Diagnostic and Statistical Manual of Mental Disorders (American Psychiatric Association 1987) lists low self-esteem as only a secondary symptom of depression, yet theorists have given it a more central role, suggesting it may be a primary symptom along with depressed affect (Beck 1975; Harter 1988; Kovacs et al. 1984a). Beck and Kovacs have suggested that negative perceptions of the self are part of the cognitive triad (Beck 1967, 1975; Kovacs & Beck 1977; Kovacs et al. 1984a)—construing experiences in a negative way, viewing the self in a negative light, and having negative expectancies for the future—that are both causal and pathognomonic factors of depression. This model was originally developed with depressed adults (Beck 1967, 1975) but has been extended to include children and adolescents (Kovacs & Beck 1977; Kovacs et al. 1984a, 1984b). The model's cognitive-behavioral foundations lead to the essentially adevelopmental premise that basic processes involved in depression remain the same across the life span.

Other researchers have examined the role of self-esteem in depression from a developmental perspective, using data from children, rather than adults, as their starting point (Battle 1987; Harter 1986, 1988; Harter & Marold 1986; Kaslow, Rehn & Siegel 1984; Renouf 1989). These researchers have consistently found correlations ranging from .72 to .83 between low self-esteem and depression (Battle 1987; Kaslow, Rehm & Siegel 1984) or depressed affect (Harter & Marold 1986; Renouf 1989).

In our own data from a middle school sample (Renouf 1989), we found a correlation of .81 between low self-esteem and depressed affect. Furthermore, we found no children in our sample who reported depressed affect and high self-esteem, but a few children (1 percent) who reported low self-esteem and positive affect. Factor-analytic and regression techniques revealed that depressed affect and low self-esteem are virtually impossible to tease apart statistically, although it has been demonstrated that children do discriminate between the two variables as we measured them (Harter 1987a). This suggests to us that self-esteem and affect are distinct constructs phenomenologically for young people in middle-childhood and early adolescence, although intimately linked in their experience of depression.

These data and other correlational studies beg the question of causal order. Seligman and colleagues' "Learned Helplessness" theory of depression (Abramson, Seligman & Teasdale 1978; Nolen-Hoeksema, Girgus & Seligman 1986; Seligman 1975; Seligman & Peterson 1986) postulates that global, stable, and internal attributions about negative events constitute a depressive cognitive style as well as a primary etiological factor. Indeed, these researchers and others have marshaled an impressive body of work supporting this theory in child and adolescent depression (Kaslow, Rehm & Siegel 1984; McCauley et al. 1988; Nolen-Hoeksema, Girgus & Seligman 1986; Seligman & Peterson 1986; Seligman et al. 1984). According to this model, low self-esteem is a consequence of internal attributions about events with negative outcomes and, thus, is not a primary causal factor of depression in young people.

There is a growing body of research, however, which indicates that low self-esteem is causally *prior* to a depressive attributional style (Brewin 1986; Feather 1987; Tennen & Herzberger 1987; Tennen, Herzberger & Nelson 1987). Although this work has been done primarily with adults, it is highly suggestive in regard to the role of self-esteem in depression during middle-childhood and early adolescence. If, in fact, it is the case that low self-esteem leads to a depressive attributional style in children and adolescents, not only would it delineate the processes linking low self-esteem to depression, but it would also further demonstrate the importance and centrality of self-esteem to mental health.

CONCLUSION

The proliferation of theory and research on the development of the self in middle childhood and early adolescence reflects the multidimensional nature of this construct. By studying the self from an organizational perspective, specific aspects of self development become figural against the background of stage-salient, socioemotional tasks. Based on Erikson's epigenetic model, mastery and identity represent stage-salient developmental issues for middle childhood and early adolescence. Given these pivotal developmental tasks, four subtasks of self-development have been identified: accuracy in self-evaluation, coordination of self-worth with perceived competence, conservation of the self, and the maintenance of self-esteem. One advantage of this approach is that aspects of self development are viewed in the context of other developing systems rather than in isolation.

It is interesting to consider the implications of this framework for studying the self in other phases of the life span. For example, consider one of the stage-salient tasks of early adulthood, that of intimacy versus isolation.

When the development of the self is viewed in this context, social dimensions of the self—such as the differentiation and management of private and public selves—figure prominently. Although Erikson's epigenetic model represents a starting point, the first task of an organizational approach would be to identify the salient socioemotional issues for each stage of development. Once identified, these issues will provide the researcher with an organizing heuristic. It is only when viewed in the context of larger developmental trends—specifically the stage-salient tasks of socioemotional development—that central versus peripheral aspects of self development can be meaningfully discriminated.

REFERENCES

Abramson, L. Y.; Seligman, M. E. P.; and Teasdale, J. D. 1978. Learned help-lessness in humans: Critique and reformulation. *Journal of Abnormal Psychology* 87:49–74.

Achenbach, T., and Zigler, E. 1963. Social competence and self-image disparity in psychiatric and nonpsychiatric patients. *Journal of Abnormal and Social Psychology* 67:197–205.

American Psychiatric Association. 1987. *Diagnostic and statistical manual of mental disorders.* 3d ed. Revised. Washington, D.C.: Authors.

Ausubel, D.; Schiff, H.; and Glasser, E. 1952. A preliminary study of the developmental trends in socioempathy: Accuracy of perception of own and others' sociometric status. *Child Development* 23:111–128.

Bachman, J. G. 1970. *Youth in transition.* Vol. 2. *The impact of family background and intelligence on tenth-grade boys.* Ann Arbor, Mich.: Survey Research Center, Institute for Social Research.

Barenboim, C. 1981. The development of person perception in childhood and adolescence: From behavioral comparisons to psychological constructs to psychological comparisons. *Child Development* 52:129–144.

Battle, J. 1987. Relationship between self-esteem and depression among children. *Psychological Reports* 60:1187–1190.

Beck, A. T. 1967. *Depression: Clinical, experimental, and theoretical aspects.* New York: Hoeber.

———. 1975. *Depression: Causes and treatments.* Philadelphia: University of Pennsylvania Press.

Bem, D. 1967. Self-perception: An alternative interpretation of cognitive dissonance phenomena. *Psychological Review* 74:183–200.

Brewin, C. R. 1986. Internal attribution and self-esteem in depression: A theoretical note. *Cognitive Therapy and Research* 10:469–475.

Brody, L., and Carter, A. 1982. Children's emotional attributions to self versus other: An exploration of an assumption underlying projective techniques. *Journal of Consulting and Clinical Psychology* 50:665–671.

Broughton, J. 1978. Development of concepts of mind, self, reality, and knowledge. In *Social cognition,* edited by W. Damon. San Francisco: Jossey Bass.

Campbell, A. 1981. *The sense of well-being in America.* New York: McGraw-Hill.

Case, R. 1986. *Intellectual development: Birth to adulthood.* New York: Academic.

Chandler, M., and Greenspan, S. 1972. Ersatz egocentrism: A reply to Borke. *Developmental Psychology* 9:326–332.

Cicchetti, D., and Sroufe, A. 1978. An organizational view of affect: Illustration from the study of Down's syndrome infants. In *The development of affect,* edited by M. Lewis and L. Rosenblum. New York: Plenum.

Cicchetti, D.; Toth, S.; Bush, M.; and Gillespie, J. 1988. Stage-salient issues: A transactional model of intervention. In *New directions in child development,* edited by E. Nannis and P. Cowen. San Francisco: Jossey Bass. 123–145.

Coopersmith, S. 1967. *The antecedents of self-esteem.* San Francisco: Freeman.

Damon, W., and Hart, D. 1982. The development of self-understanding from infancy through adolescence. *Child Development* 53:841–864.

Eccles, J.; Midgley, C.; and Adler, T. 1984. Grade-related changes in the school environment: Effects on achievement motivation. In *Advances in motivation and achievement.* Vol. 3. Edited by J. Nicholls. Greenwich Conn.: JAI Press. 283–331.

Edelstein, W.; Keller, M.; and Wahlen, K. 1984. Structure and content in social cognition: Conceptual and empirical analyses. *Child Development* 55:1514–1526.

Egeland, B., and Sroufe, A. 1981. Developmental sequelae of maltreatment in infancy. In *New directions in child development,* edited by R. Rizley and D. Cicchetti. San Francisco: Jossey Bass.

Elkind, D., Bowen, D. 1979. Imaginary audience behavior in children and adolescents. *Developmental Psychology* 15:38–44.

Elliot, G. C. 1982. Self-esteem and self-presentation among the young as a function of age and gender. *Journal of Youth and Adolescence* 11:135–155.

———. 1984. Dimensions of the self-concept: A source of further distinctions in the nature of self-consciousness. *Journal of Youth and Adolescence* 13:285–309.

————. 1986. Self-esteem and self-consistency: A theoretical and empirical link between two primary motivations. *Social Psychology Quarterly* 49:207–218.

————. 1988. Gender differences in self-consistency: Evidence from an investigation of self-concept structure. *Journal of Youth and Adolescence* 17:41–57.

Elliot, G. C.; Rosenberg, M.; and Wagner, M. 1984. Transient depersonalization in youth. *Social Psychology Quarterly* 47:115–129.

Epstein, S. 1973. The self-concept revisited or a theory of a theory. *American Psychologist* 28:405–416.

Erikson, E. 1968. *Identity, youth, and crisis.* New York: Norton.

Erikson, E. 1963. *Childhood and society.* 2d ed. New York: Norton.

Feather, N. T. 1987. The rosy glow of self-esteem: Depression, masculinity, and causal attributions. *Australian Journal of Psychology* 39:25–41.

Fischer, K. W. 1980. A theory of cognitive development: The control and construction of hierarchies of skills. *Psychological Review* 87:477–531.

Fitch, G. 1970. Effects of self-esteem, perceived performance, and choice on causal attributions. *Journal of Personality and Social Psychology* 16:311–315.

Flavell, J.; Friedrichs, A.; Hoyt, J. 1970. Developmental changes in memorization processes. *Cognitive Psychology* 1:324–340.

Freud, S. [1917] 1968. Mourning and melancholia. In *The standard edition of the complete works of Sigmund Freud.* Vol. 14. Edited by J. Strachey. London: Hogarth Press.

Gilligan, C. 1982. *In a different voice.* Cambridge, Mass.: Harvard University Press.

Glasberg, R., and Aboud, F. 1982. Keeping one's distance from sadness: Children's self-reports of emotional experience. *Developmental Psychology* 18:287–293.

Glick, M., and Zigler, E. 1985. Self-image: A cognitive-developmental approach. In *The development of the self,* edited by R. Leahy. New York: Academic Press.

Guardo, C., and Bohan, J. 1971. Development of sense of self-identity in children. *Child Development* 42:1909–1921.

Hall, G. S. 1904. *Adolescence.* New York: Appleton.

Harter, S. 1982. The perceived competence scale for children. *Child Development* 53:27–97.

————. 1983. Developmental perspectives on the self-system. In *Handbook of child psychology: Social and personality development*, Vol. 4, edited by M. Hetherington. New York: Wiley.

————. 1985a. Competence as a dimension of self-evaluation: Toward a comprehensive model of self-worth. In *The development of the self*, edited by R. Leahy. New York: Academic.

————. 1985b. *Manual for the self-perception profile for adolescents.* Denver, Colo.: University of Denver.

————. 1986. Processes underlying the construction, maintenance, and enhancement of the self-concept in children. In *Psychological perspectives on the self*, Vol. 3, edited by J. Suls and A. G. Greenwald. Hillsdale, N.J.: Lawrence Erlbaum Associates.

————. 1987a. Causes, correlates, and the functional role of global self-worth: A life span perspective. In *Perceptions of competence and incompetence across the life span*, edited by J. Kalligan and R. Sternberg. New Haven, Conn.: Yale University Press.

————. 1987b. The determinants and mediational role of global self-worth in children. In *Contemporary topics in developmental psychology*, edited by N. Eisenberg. New York: Wiley.

————. 1988. Developmental and dynamic changes in the nature of the self-concept. In *Cognitive development and child psychotherapy*, edited by S. Shirk. New York: Plenum. 119–160.

Harter, S., and Marold, D. 1986. Risk factors related to child and adolescent suicidal ideation. Unpublished manuscript, University of Denver; Denver, Colorado.

Harter, S., and Pike, R. 1984. The pictorial scale of perceived competence and social acceptance for young children. *Child Development* 55:1969–1982.

James, W. 1890. *The principles of psychology.* New York: Holt, Rinehart & Winston.

Juhasz, A. 1992. Significant others in self-esteem measurement: Methods and problems in measurement. In *The self: Definitional and methodological issues*, edited by T. M. Brinthaupt and R. P. Lipka. Albany: State University of New York Press.

Kagan, J. 1989. *Unstable ideas: Temperament, cognition, and self.* Cambridge, Mass.: Harvard University Press.

Kaplan, H. B. 1967. Meditations on genesis. *Human Development* 10:65–87.

———. 1975. *Self-attitudes and deviant behavior.* Pacific Palisades, Calif.: Goodyear Publishing.

Kaplan, H. B., and Pokorny, A. D. 1969. Self-derogation and psychosocial adjustment. *Journal of Nervous and Mental Disease* 149:421–434.

Kaslow, N. J.; Rehm, L. P.; and Siegel, A. W. 1984. Social-cognitive and cognitive correlates of depression in children. *Journal of Abnormal Child Psychology* 12:605–620.

Katz, P., and Zigler, E. 1967. Self-image disparity: A developmental approach. *Journal of Personality and Social Psychology* 5:186–195.

Katz, P.; Zigler, E.; and Zalk, S. 1975. Children's self-image disparity: The effects of age, maladjustment, and action-thought orientation. *Developmental Psychology* 11:546–550.

Kovacs, M., and Beck, A. T. 1977. An empirical-clinical approach toward a definition of childhood depression. In *Depression in childhood: Diagnosis, treatment, and conceptual models*, edited by J. G. Schelterbrandt and A. Raskins. New York: Raven Press.

Kovacs, M.; Feinberg, T. L.; CrouseNovak, M. A.; Paulauskas, S. L.; and Finkelstein, R. 1984a. Depressive disorders in childhood I. A longitudinal prospective study of characteristics and recovery. *Archives of General Psychiatry* 41:229–237.

———. 1984b. Depressive disorders in childhood II. A longitudinal study of the risk for subsequent major depression. *Archives of General Psychiatry* 41:643–649.

Leahy, R., and Huard, C. 1976. Role taking and self-image disparity in children. *Developmental Psychology* 12: 504–508.

Leahy, R. L., and Shirk, S. R. 1984. The development of social cognition: Conceptions of personality. In *Annals of child development*, edited by G. Whitehurst. Greenwich, Conn.: JAI Press.

Lochman, J. E., and Lampron, L. B. 1986. Situational social problem-solving skills and self-esteem of aggressive and nonaggressive boys. *Journal of Abnormal Child Psychology* 14:605–617.

Marsh, H. W. and Shavelson, R. J. 1985. Self-concept: Its multifaceted, hierarchical structure. *Educational Psychologist* 20:107–125.

Marsh, H.; Byrne, B.; and Shavelson, R. 1992. A multidimensional, hierarchical self-concept. In *The self: Definitional and methodological is-*

sues, edited by T. M. Brinthaupt and R. P. Lipka. Albany: State University of New York Press.

Matthews, K., and Siegel, J. 1983. Type A behaviors by children, social comparison and stands for self-evaluation. *Developmental Psychology* 19:135–140.

McCarthy, J. D., and Hoge, D. R. 1982. Analyses of age effects in longitudinal studies of adolescent self-esteem. *Developmental Psychology* 23:441–450.

McCauley, E.; Mitchell, J. R.; Burke, P.; and Moss, S. 1988. Cognitive attributes of depression in children and adolescents. *Journal of Clinical and Consulting Psychology* 56:903–908.

Mullener, N., and Laird, J. 1971. Some developmental changes in the organization of self-evaluations. *Developmental Psychology* 5:233–236.

Nolen-Hoeksema, S.; Girgus, J. S.; and Seligman, M. E. P. 1986. Learned helplessness in children: A longitudinal study of depression, achievement, and explanatory style. *Journal of Personality and Social Psychology* 51:435–442.

Nottelmann, E. D. 1987. Competence and self-esteem during transition from childhood to adolescence. *Developmental Psychology* 23:441–450.

Offer, D. 1969. *The psychological world of the teen-ager.* New York: Basic Books.

O'Malley, P. M., and Bachman, J. B. 1983. Self-esteem: Change and stability between ages 13 and 23. *Developmental Psychology* 19:257–268.

Parsons, J., and Ruble, D. 1977. The development of achievement related expectancies. *Child Development* 48:1075–1079.

Peevers, B., and Secord, P. 1973. Developmental changes in attributions of descriptive concepts to persons. *Journal of Personality and Social Psychology* 27:120–128.

Phillips, D., and Zigler, E. 1980. Children's self-image disparity: Effects of age, socioeconomic status, ethnicity, and gender. *Journal of Personality and Social Psychology* 39:689–700.

Poznanski, E. O. 1982. The clinical phenomenology of childhood depression. *American Journal of Orthopsychiatry* 52:308–313.

Renick, M. 1987. Measuring the relationship between academic self-perceptions and global self-worth. The Self-Perception Profile for

Learning Disabled Children. Poster presented at meetings of the Society for Research in Child Development. Baltimore.

Renouf, A. G. 1989. Correlates of depressed affect and self-esteem in children: Implications for early adolescent depression. Unpublished master's thesis. University of Denver, Colorado.

Robin, A. 1981. A controlled evaluation of problem-solving communication training with parent-adolescent conflict. *Behavior Therapy* 12:593–609.

Rosenberg, M. 1979. *Conceiving the self*. New York: Basic Books.

————. 1985. Self-concept and psychological well-being in adolescence. In *The development of the self*, edited by R. Leahy. New York: Academic Press.

————. 1986. Self-concept from middle childhood through adolescence. In *Psychological perspectives on the self*, Vol. 3, edited by J. Suls and A. Greenwald. Hillsdale, N.J.: Lawrence Erlbaum Associates.

Ruble, D.; Feldman, N.; and Boggiano, A. 1976. Social comparison between young children in achievement situations. *Developmental Psychology* 12:192–197.

Ruble, D.; Boggiano, A.; Feldman, N.; and Loebl, J. 1980. Developmental analysis of the role of social comparison in self-evaluation. *Developmental Psychology* 16:105–115.

Savin-Williams, P. C., and Demo, D. H. 1984. Developmental change and stability in adolescent self-concept. *Developmental Psychology* 20:1100–1110.

Schwartz, M., and Stryker, S. 1971. *Deviance, selves, and others*. Washington, D.C.: American Sociological Association.

Seligman, M. E. P. 1975. *Helplessness: On depression, development, and death*. San Francisco: Freeman.

Seligman, M. E. P., and Peterson, C. 1986. A learned helplessness perspective on childhood depression: Theory and research. In *Depression in young people: Clinical and developmental perspectives*, edited by M. Rutter, C. E. Izard, and P. B. Read. New York: Guilford Press.

Seligman, M. E. P.; Peterson, C.; Kaslow, N. J.; Tanenbaum, R. L.; Alloy, L. B.; and Abramson, L. Y. 1984. Explanatory style and depressive symptoms among school children. *Journal of Abnormal Psychology* 93:235–238.

Selman, R. 1980. *The growth of interpersonal understanding.* New York: Academic.

Selman, R., and Byrne, D. 1974. A structural developmental analysis of levels of role-taking in middle childhood. *Child Development* 45:803–808.

Shirk, S. R. 1987. Self-doubt in late childhood and early adolescence. *Journal of Youth and Adolescence* 16:59–68.

————. 1988a. The interpersonal legacy of physical abuse of children. In *Abuse and victimization across the life-span,* edited by M. Straus. Baltimore: Johns Hopkins. 57–81.

————. 1988b. Causal reasoning and children's comprehension of therapeutic interpretations. In *Cognitive development and child psychotherapy,* edited by S. Shirk. New York: Plenum. 53–115.

Shirk, S. R. and Rossman, R. 1989. Discrepancies between parents' and children's appraisals of problem behaviors. Paper presented at meetings of Society for Research on Child Development. Kansas City.

Simmons, R. G. 1987. Self-esteem in adolescence. In *Self and identity: Perspectives across the life span,* edited by T. Honess and K. Yardley. New York: Routledge and Kegen Paul.

Simmons, R. G., and Blyth, D. A. 1987. *Moving into adolescence: The impact of pubertal change and school context.* Hawthorne, N.Y.: Aldine.

Simmons, R. G.; Rosenberg, F.; and Rosenberg, M. 1973. Disturbance in the self-image at adolescence. *American Sociological Review* 38:553–568.

Simmons, R. G.; Blyth, D. A.; Van Cleave, E. F.; and Bush, D. M. 1979. Entry into early adolescence: The impact of school structure, puberty, and early dating on self-esteem. *American Sociological Review* 44:948–967.

Snygg, D., and Combs, A. W. 1949. *Individual behavior: A new frame of reference for psychology.* New York: Harper.

Sroufe, A. 1979. The coherence of individual development. *American Psychologist* 34:834–841.

Sroufe, A., and Rutter, M. 1984. The domain of developmental psychopathology. *Child Development* 55:17–29.

Stern, D. N. 1985. *The interpersonal world of the infant.* New York: Basic Books.

Stipek, D. 1984. Young children's performance expectations: Logical analysis or wishful thinking? In *Advances in motivation achievement*, Vol. 3, edited by J. Nicholls. Greenwich, Conn. JAI Press. 33–56.

————. 1981. Children's perceptions of own and classmates' ability. *Journal of Educational Psychology* 73:404–410.

Tennen, H., and Herzberger, S. 1987. Depression, self-esteem, and the absence of self-protective attributional biases. *Journal of Personality and Social Psychology* 52:72–80.

Tennen, H.; Herzberger, S.; and Nelson, H. F. 1987. Depressive attributional style: The role of self-esteem. *Journal of Personality* 55:631–660.

Waters, E.; Noyes, D.; Vaughn, B.; and Ricks, M. 1985. Q-sort definitions of social competence and self-esteem: Discriminant validity of related constructs in theory and data. *Developmental Psychology* 21:508–522.

Wells, L. E., and Sweeney, P. D. 1986. A test of three models of bias in self-assessments. *Social Psychology Quarterly* 49:1–10.

Wenar, C. 1982. Developmental psychopathology: Its nature and constructs. *Journal of Clinical Child Psychology* 11:192–201.

White, R. W. 1972. *The enterprise of living: Growth and organization in personality*. New York: Holt, Rinehart & Winston.

Zigler, E.; Balla, D. S.; and Watson, N. 1972. Developmental and experiential determinants of self-image disparity in institutionalized and non-institutionalized retarded and normal children. *Journal of Personality and Social Psychology* 23:81–87.

Zigler, E., and Phillips, L. 1960. Social effectiveness and symptomatic behaviors. *Journal of Abnormal and Social Psychology* 61:231–238.

PART II: LATE CHILDHOOD AND ADOLESCENCE

RICHARD P. LIPKA
DAVID P. HURFORD
MARY JO LITTEN

3

Self in School: Age and School Experience Effects

INTRODUCTION

The purpose of this chapter is to make the argument that educational researchers who study the self have relied too heavily upon research designs that are insensitive to the chronological age (CA) and school-experience issue. To highlight this issue, attention will be paid to the research explicating the impact upon the self as one makes the transition from one school type to another—for example, elementary school to middle school or junior high school to high school.

The chapter will be organized into the following four sections: (1) a brief review of the extant transition literature to demonstrate the status quo within the research community; (2) a review of work undertaken by developmental psychologists who have generated frameworks to explore the CA/school-experience level issue; (3) a discussion of a design which we believe might be useful to researchers who examine the self in school settings; and (4) a discussion of a longitudinal study by the authors of this chapter that clearly articulates the need for the issues to be disentangled.

THE STATUS QUO

Kelley (1962) and Mead (1934) suggested that the self develops almost entirely as a result of interaction with others. This thinking implies that, while both the environment and the individual play a role in the development of the self, the environment is more powerful as it provides the contexts in which behaviors are embedded. Thus, analyses of these various contexts are necessary to understand the multifaceted hierarchial nature of the self (Wells & Stryker 1988).

The environmental theory is further refined by the idea that we screen our environment by paying attention to those persons whom we consider to be *significant others* (Beane & Lipka 1986; Juhasz 1992). As we play out our roles in specific situations, we receive feedback from others and use it to modify our self-perceptions. The revised or refined sense of self is then tested in new situations as we search for new and potentially validating feedback from the environment.

For young people, the school serves as one of the most powerful of environments. Most elementary-age children experience school through the framework of the self-contained classroom in which a single teacher may get to know them well and view them holistically and humanistically (Willower, Eidell & Hoy 1967). The immediate peer group and significant others may be limited to a particular group with which the vast majority of time is spent.

The transition to the junior high school and high school presents a much more complex situation. The transescent—that is, the ten- to fourteen-year-old—and adolescent are most often forced to deal with a larger and less familiar peer group, many teachers, and a more competitive reward system. Teachers often have less opportunity to get to know learners and are frequently oriented to custodial views of teaching and learning. In these latter environments, the sense of self may thus be subject to confusion or dissonance.

Studies conducted by the Eccles group published in 1987 (Eccles, Wigfield, Reuman & MacIver 1987; Reuman 1984; Reuman, MacIver, Eccles & Wigfield 1987; Wigfield, Eccles, Flanagan, Miller, Reuman, Yee & Lange 1987) demonstrate both within year (fall to spring) and between year declines in global self-esteem with the lowest score being in the fall immediately after the transition to the junior high.

Reuman's initial work in 1984 demonstrated this transitional decline for self-concept of math ability. However, his more recent work (Reuman et al. 1987) suggests that different within-class environments impact upon students in differing ways. Thus, to aggregate across all students (which showed transitional decline) is a very risky venture—at least in terms of self-concept of math ability.

In an exhaustive review of the literature on the link between age-related changes in motivational orientations and the impact of classroom processes on student motivation, Eccles, Midgley, and Adler concluded in 1984 that age was a key player in the findings. They summarized their findings by stating "although there are changes in both school environment and student beliefs across grade levels, typically the changes are confounded with age level" (1984, 321); and that the "effects of increasing age and changing school environment cannot be disentangled" (1984, 321).

The school transition issue has not escaped the attention of the sociological research community. Simmons and her colleagues (Blyth, Simmons & Carlton-Ford 1983; Simmons & Blyth 1986; Simmons, Carlton-Ford & Blyth 1987) have utilized Rosenberg's (1965) self-esteem measure to examine the transition from elementary school to the junior high. The studies have yielded mixed findings for gender with females showing a decrease and males showing an increase in self-esteem across the junior-high transition. The exception to this generalized finding appears in Simmons's and her colleagues' work in 1987 as the larger and more ethnically heterogeneous the school, the lower the self-esteem for both males and females.

Simmons and Blyth (1987) talk about "on-time" versus "off-time," with their variable of interest being the attainment of puberty earlier or later than one's average peer. However, they are not willing to explore the age variable further as is made clear in their research design (Simmons & Blyth 1987, figure 2.1, 24) where the ages are averages to the nearest whole year for each of the grade levels of record.

In summary, for two of the most productive transitions research groups, Eccles and her colleagues realized the importance of the age variable but cannot see a way to disentangle its influence. Simmons and her colleagues, on the other hand, choose to ignore it as a variable of interest by creating an average age per grade level.

THE FRAMEWORK

A fundamental difficulty in the developmental research arena concerns the confounding of differences in behavior due to age, an individual's cohort, and the time during which the measures are made. The basis of the confounding between age, cohort, and time of measurement is that, although the three make separate contributions to the developmental data, only two of the variables are free to vary at any given time. The variables are simply not independent of each other. If any of the two variables are known, then the third variable is also known.

These confounds regarding the effects due to age, cohort, and time of measurement have been recognized for quite some time (Kessen 1960; Kuhlen 1940) and have been a very sensitive issue in developmental inquiry. For the developmentalist to be able to make statements regarding how individuals may change as a function of age, he or she must be able to distinguish the effects of aging from those of the individual's environmental constraints or supports and the peculiarities that may have existed at the different times of measurement. If the researcher is unable to do this, then it is impossible to make conclusions about development or aging.

When a cross-sectional design is used to investigate developmental issues, any differences that are found may be due to changes in behavior that have occurred as a function of age or to the cohort framing the individual's development. For example, an individual who was born in 1910 was raised in a culture that was much less educated academically, nutritionally, and in matters that concerned exercise and health. Implying that individuals who were born in 1980 will behave as did those individuals born in 1910 when they, too, become eighty years of age may be completely inappropriate. Each cohort is likely to know more about growing older than did the preceding cohort. If this is truly the case, then each generation should be more adept at a variety of tasks than was the preceding generation at their respective ages.

The longitudinal design faces similar types of shortcomings. Specifically, any differences that are found using a longitudinal design may be due to changes in behavior that have occurred as a function of age or changes in the environment that occurred when the data were collected. The time-lag design, which examines behavior from different cohorts all at the same age, has cohort and time of measurement confounded. To address these limitations, Schaie (1965) proposed a general developmental model that requires simultaneous considerations of the components of age, time, and cohort differences. The consideration takes the form of three sequential strategies: cohort-sequential, time-sequential, and cross-sequential. It also requires a data matrix of at least three cohorts and three time of measurements. While the Schaie model of 1965 has been criticized in the literature (Baltes 1968; Nesselroade & Baltes 1974), it clearly has won acclaim in the developmental community, in that ". . . the issue of cohort or time effects on age functions is a most fundamental one that needs to be reckoned with whenever the search is for the form and direction of developmental change" (Nesselroade & Baltes 1974, 7).

Schaie has recommended that at least two of the three sequential designs should be used to tease apart the confounding, and he suggests that the cross-sequential and the time-sequential designs are the two that should be used.

To analyze the data that have been generated with the sequential designs, Schaie proposed that a series of analyses of variance be conducted. As has been noted by Adam (1977, 1978) and others (Baltes 1968; Buss 1973; Horn & Donaldson 1976, 1977; Wohlwill 1970), several difficulties arise when analysis of this complicated design is attempted. Most notable are the problems associated with linearity.

Although the use of the entire model seems warranted by Schaie, careful inspection of the results of the analyses produced by the full model indicates that the model does not disentangle age, cohort, and time of measurement as Schaie proposed (Adam 1977). The trifactor model produces redundant effects in that any of the two sequential designs produces the information of the third. Because of this situation, Baltes (1968) proposed the use of a bifactor model. According to Baltes, varying the time of measurement cannot separate the effects of environment and maturation. He also suggested that the influence of time of measurement (T) could be redefined by age (A) and cohort (C) effects ($T = A + C$).

Schaie's trifactor model can now be described by a bifactor model. Baltes proposed that a two-factor analysis of variance with age and cohort as factors could be used to tease apart the effects of age and cohort and to examine the interaction of age and cohort.

The same issues face the researcher of children's self-concept in school settings. However, in this case, age, grade, and time of measurement are the variables that are confounded. Both research into the self and educational research is replete with studies cast in cross-sectional design as a way of unearthing the changes that occur with age (Wylie 1979. See also chapter 4 of this volume).

In short, people of different ages—usually different grade levels are offered as synonymous with different ages—are gathered together and given tests, questionnaires, or interviews appropriate for the hypotheses under test. However, as noted by Schaie (1965), age and time of birth (cohort) are confounded in a cross-sectional study. What is being attributed to an age difference may, in reality, be partly or entirely due to changes in the environment and content of our culture. As stated by Botwinick regarding the confounding of age and cohort in developmental changes in intelligence:

> The confounding of cohort and age is most apparent in cross-sectional studies, i.e., studies in which two or more age (cohort) groups are compared during the single period of the examination. The age groups are compared in intelligence and other test performances, with the knowledge that the quality and quantity of formal education has been different for old and young. Age groups are compared although researchers know that so many of today's sources of cognitive stimulation were unknown generations ago. Social patterns, values, and attitudes were different . . . —how can people of different ages be compared? (1973, 365)

A more powerful design for studying age changes is the longitudinal design (Dusek & Flaherty 1981; Kohr 1974). While clearly superior to the cross-sectional design for examining age-change data, it, too, has a risk in that it is cohort-specific and requires the researcher to generalize age differences over time from one cohort to another (Schaie 1965).

For those of us who conduct our research in school settings, Goulet's conceptualization of the age school-experience issue in 1975 is a most important referent. It is Goulet's contention that most educational researchers utilize designs that are insensitive to short-term influences of educational experiences and the long-term cumulative influences of schooling. The key element is the utilization of the time-lag method to explicate the effects of school experiences. In brief, the time-lag design requires the testing of subjects with different birth dates at the same chronological age. Multiple times of testing within a school year would allow for within-grade contrasts while sampling from adjacent grades would permit between-grade contrasts.

> For example, within grade contrasts would be especially appropriate when the researcher is interested in cross-seasonal behavioral changes in the children. For example, the amount of time spent in study may vary with the season of the year or the proximity to important holidays (e.g., Christmas). Similarly, between-grade contrasts for matched-CA samples at the end of one grade and the beginning of another may provide information concerning the (non-CA related) impact of changing school grades on children's behavior. (Goulet 1975, 511)

Figure 3.1 represents a graphic explanation of just such a design effort.

Figure 3.1
Diagramatic Representation of the Goulet Design
as Applied to Self-esteem.

Times of Testing

Chronological Age	Sept.	Jan.	May	Sept.	Jan.	May
	Grade 5			Grade 6		
10-2	A1 S1		I			
10-6	A2 S1[a]	A2 S2[b]	II			
10-10	A3 S1[c]	A3 S2[d]	A3 S3[e]	III		
11-2		A4 S2[f]	A4 S3[g]	A4 S4[h]	IV	
11-6			A5 S3[i]	A5 S4[j]	A5 S5[k]	
11-10				A6 S4[l]	A6 S5[m]	A6 S6
12-2					A7 S5	A7 S6
12-6						A8 S6

Rectangle I (*a, b, c, d*) would yield information about growth or decline of the self during the first four months of the school year in grade five as represented by $\frac{\bar{X}_b+\bar{X}_d-\bar{X}_a+\bar{X}_c}{2}$.

Rectangle II (*d, e, f, g*) would yield information about growth or decline of the self during the last four months of the school year in grade five as represented by $\frac{\bar{X}_e+\bar{X}_g-\bar{X}_d+\bar{X}_f}{2}$.

Rectangle III (*g, h, i, j*) allows information about growth or decline of the self during the latter part of grade five and the early part of grade six to be estimated as represented by $\frac{\bar{X}_h+\bar{X}_j-\bar{X}_g+\bar{X}_i}{2}$.

Another way of stating this is that rectangle III will present an estimate of the growth or decline of the self for the transition from elementary (grade five) to middle school (grade six).

Equally important, a reordering of the contrasts would also permit an estimate of the CA function. For example, utilizing rectangle IV as represented by $\frac{\bar{X}_l + \bar{X}_m - \bar{X}_i + \bar{X}_k}{2}$ would provide us with the CA function for the first period of schooling in grade six. Further, orienting rectangle III in this manner $\frac{\bar{X}_i + \bar{X}_i - \bar{X}_g + \bar{X}_h}{2}$ would provide an estimate of the CA function for the transition from elementary to middle school.

Further, the design will allow for cumulative influences of schooling to be estimated across grades by adding the differences in performance for matched CA samples over different times of the school year for subjects in different grades (Goulet 1975). Doubling or tripling of the sample size would allow for separate male-female analyses and perhaps unearth patterns of gender differences such as those found by Simmons and her colleagues. Whereas the interest of the present researchers is self-concept and self-esteem, there are virtually no limitations to the dependent measures that could be utilized within the design.

THE KANSAS STUDY

The first author of this chapter has had the good fortune of working with a Kansas school district interested in empirically validating their district-wide curriculum efforts. As a part of this working relationship, it was deemed politically important for the teachers to select the instrument by which to study the self. After much discussion, the teachers selected the Piers-Harris Self-Concept Scale with the proviso that it be given just once a year during the first week in December. While that eliminated within-grade contrasts, between-grade contrasts with an eye to elementary to middle to high-school transitions were possible. What follows is what we have learned to date about the self in terms of school transitions and more importantly about the CA-schooling-experience relationship.

The most important issue examined by the following analyses was the possible influence of age (within grade) on the reporting of self-esteem information. The central question concerned the hypothesis that students differing in age, but in the same grade, might view themselves differently as a function of the normative properties of age (Neugarten 1969; Wells & Stryker 1988). The following analyses, therefore, used age level and sex as quasi-independent variables. In addition to these variables, grade (which allows for an examination of the transition from fifth to sixth grade and eighth to ninth grade) and subscale scores were entered into the analyses of variance.

As previously noted the data that will be discussed here did not lend themselves to the complete type of design and analysis that we are advocating. However, the results of the analyses do strongly suggest that age level as a variable is crucial to understanding development and change in self-esteem. Future research undertaken by the authors of this chapter in this area will be designed to more fully address the design issues outlined here.

The participants involved in the present study came from a larger three-year longitudinal study which examined the self-esteem of school-aged students from kindergarten through the twelfth grade. Because the present study was primarily interested in the transition from elementary school to middle school and middle school to high school, only the fifth- and eight-graders were included (see table 3.1).

Table 3.1
Participant Characteristics Collapsed between Cohorts

	Grade 5		Grade 8	
	Age Level		Age Level	
Sex	Older	Younger	Older	Younger
Male	8	9	20	27
Female	8	18	10	19

In addition, two different cohorts were examined (fifth- and eighth-graders in 1986, and fifth- and eighth-graders in 1987). Both the fifth- and eighth-graders were initially assessed in the fifth and eighth grades and were then assessed after they had made the transition into the sixth or ninth grades, respectively.

To examine the possible influence of age level, each of the participants were assigned to an older or younger age level based on their age in rounded years. For example, a ten-year-old fifth grader would be considered to be younger while an eleven-year-old would be considered as older. That is, each half of the age dichotomy serves as the referent for the other half. Although this is a less than perfect method for assigning individuals to age levels, the nature of the data did not allow us to make finer discriminations.

The Piers-Harris Children's Self-Concept Scale (Piers 1985) was the instrument used to assess each student's self-esteem. It is a self-report questionnaire consisting of 80 items that assess how children and adolescents feel about themselves. According to Piers, the instrument "gets at" what is usually meant by self-esteem (Beane & Lipka 1980). This scale provides a total score and six subscale or cluster scores (that is, behavior, intellectual and school status, physical appearance and attributes, anxiety, popularity, and happiness and satisfaction). The students were administered the Piers-Harris with their classmates in their regular classes during the first week in December. The students again took the Piers-Harris one year later after they had made the transition into their next respective grade.

The purpose of the analyses was to determine if there were any changes in self-esteem after transition, the nature of the changes in self-esteem, if any, and whether age, sex, or grade was important to these changes. A preliminary analysis of variance (including subscale scores) was conducted on the transitional self-esteem data to examine the possibility of cohort effects. The analysis revealed that there were no differences between the two different cohorts (1986 versus 1987, $ps < .44$). The fifth-graders who responded in 1986 did not significantly differ in their self-esteem responses from those who were in fifth grade in 1987 and so on.

As a result, the data were collapsed across cohorts with the following caveat: It may be that the effect of cohort when examining cohorts that were born within relatively similar time periods is minimal. Equally plausible is that cohort effects are task-specific and require a more fine-tuned instrument than the Piers-Harris Self-Concept Scale. The latter viewpoint seems very plausible given that Piers in 1985 found no age differences in her standardization sample.

The self-esteem data were subjected to two grade x age level x sex of participant x subscale analyses of variance, with one for each transitional period (that is, fifth to sixth grade and eighth to ninth grade). The results of the analysis of variance for the participants who made the transition from fifth to sixth grade indicated that there was a significant interaction of grade and sex of participant, $F(1,195) = 9.9$, $p < .003$. Males' total self-esteem scores decreased while females' total self-esteem scores increased from the fifth to the sixth grade (see figure 3.2).

Although the grade x sex of participant x age level interaction only approached significance, $F(1,39) = 3.6$, $p < .065$, it suggests that the reason why the males' self-esteem scores decreased in the grade

Figure 3.2
Percentage of Self-esteem Scores on the Piers-Harris Children's Self-
Concept Scale by Grade and Sex for the Transition into Middle School.

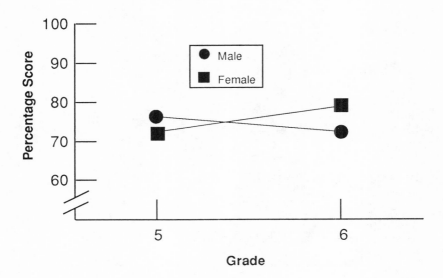

x sex of participant interaction was a result of older males' self-
esteem decreasing dramatically from the fifth to the sixth grade,
while the younger males' self-esteem scores remained unchanged
(see figure 3.3).

A more powerful test of this hypothesis (one that included
more participants, for example) would more than likely reveal a significant interaction of transition, sex of participant, and age level.
These interactions indicate quite strongly that it is very useful to
consider age as a factor when examining self-esteem even within the
same grade. The conclusion that would have been reached had age
level not been included in the analysis would be that males' self-
esteems are hurt by the transition into the middle schools. This is
patently not true. Younger males' self-esteems seem to be unaf-
fected by the transition, while older males' self-esteems are strongly
affected.

The grade x age level x subscore interaction did reach significance, $F(5,195) = 2.6$, $p < .03$. The older individuals had lower self-
esteem than did the younger individuals across the various
subscales, both before and after the transition was made. However,

Figure 3.3
Percentage of Self-esteem Scores on the Piers-Harris Children's
Self-Concept Scale by Grade, Sex, and Age Level for the Transition
into Middle School.

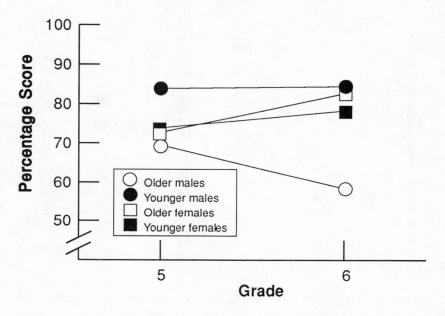

the older individuals increased their self-esteem scores on the sub-scales of intelligence and appearance while decreasing on the pop-ularity subscale as they moved into the middle school.

Interestingly, the self-esteem scores of the younger individuals remained fairly similar before and after they had made the transi-tion into the middle school. The younger students had higher scores on the anxiety subscale, indicating less anxiety, after they had made the transition into the middle school (see figure 3.4). No other main effects or interactions reached significance.

Interestingly, there was only one interaction—that of sex of participant and subscore, $F(5,360) = 6.0$, $p < .0001$—that reached significance for the individuals who made the transition from eighth to ninth grade. As can be seen in figure 3.5, and confirmed by post hoc analyses, the interaction was due to males and females dif-fering on the anxiety subscale. Females were significantly more anx-ious than were males $(p < .05)$. No other interactions or main effects reached significance.

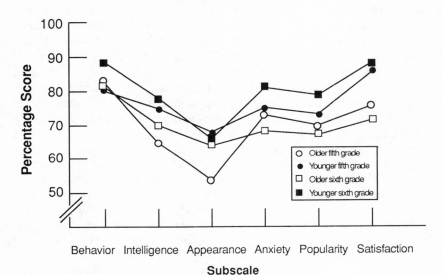

Figure 3.4
Percentage of Self-esteem Scores on the Piers-Harris Children's
Self-Concept Scale by Subscale, Grade, and Age Level for the Transition
into Middle School.

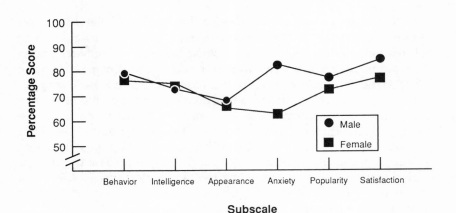

Figure 3.5
Percentage of Self-esteem Scores on the Piers-Harris Children's
Self-Concept Scale by Sex and Subscale.

The results of these analyses indicate that changes in self- esteem may be dependent on the sex of the student as well as the relative age of the student. At least as far as the transition from the elementary grades to the middle school grades is concerned, sex and age of the student seem to be *very* important. When discussing changes in self-esteem, it may be necessary to describe the participants in terms of their sex as well as their age level. It would be inappropriate to assume, for example, that the self-esteem of all males' decreases when they enter middle school when, in fact, younger males' self-esteem does not decrease. (See chapters 2 and 4 of this volume concerning subgroup differences in self-esteem.)

To examine more closely the issue of age and grade effects, the entire sample of kindergarten through twelfth grade was included for each time of measurement so that there were many more individuals at each grade level in this larger sample. There were also more fifth- and eighth-graders since data from those who did not make the transitions from fifth to sixth or eighth to ninth grade during the years of data collection were also included. The same approach was taken here as was previously used. That is, the students' total self-esteem scores were examined with regard to their age level within each grade.

When the age level of the participants is considered, an entirely different picture emerges regarding their self-esteem. This further refinement of the data strongly suggests that it is necessary to include age level as a possible contributor or source of variation when self-esteem scores are being examined. The self-esteem data from each of the grades were collapsed across cohort. Each grade, therefore, is composed of data from three different years of data collection (1986, 1987, and 1988).

The self-esteem data are presented in terms of difference scores between the two age levels. The difference score was calculated by taking the mean self-esteem score of the older-age-level participants in each grade, respectively, and subtracting the mean self-esteem score of the younger-age-level participants. In figure 3.6 the zero difference line represents the area in which the younger-and older-age-level participants do not differ in their self-esteem scores. Self-esteem scores that are above the zero difference line indicate that the older-age-level participants for this grade had higher self-esteem scores than did the younger-age-level participants. The opposite is true for the scores that are below the zero difference line. That is, the younger-age-level participants had higher self-esteem scores than did the older-age-level participants.

Figure 3.6
Difference of Self-esteem Scores on the Piers-Harris Children's
Self-Concept Scale by Grade and Age Level.

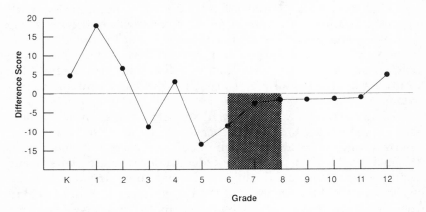

As can be seen in figure 3.6, except for the third grade, the older-age-level participants enjoy the highest self-esteem scores until the fifth grade. Interestingly, the largest difference between the older and younger age levels in any grade occurs in the first grade. Students may be becoming aware of some of the differences in physical size or school performance that might result from maturation that they did not notice in kindergarten. If this is true, less mature individuals' self-esteem may be especially vulnerable during this grade. This advantage, which was realized for the older-age-level participants, soon disappears. The self-esteem scores of the younger-age-level students exceeds the self-esteem scores of the older-age-level students. During the fifth grade, the difference in favor of the younger-age-level students is thirteen raw score points.

An examination of the overall data seems to indicate that the middle school provides some type of security as far as self-esteem is concerned. As already mentioned, fifth-grade younger-age-level students have considerably higher self-esteem scores. It should also be pointed out that, at this age, the participants should be able to provide very good estimates of their feelings regarding the questions that are asked on the questionnaire.

During the three years that the participants are in the middle school, the difference between younger- and older-age-level participants becomes increasingly smaller. By the last year in the middle school there is less than the standard error of mean of the Piers-Harris difference between the two age levels. This difference is whittled down even further during the next three years. For the seniors in high school, a small older-age-level advantage reappears.

The present data seem to support the structure of a school system that utilizes a middle school—a school configuration built upon the developmental characteristics and needs of the age group it serves. Large gains in self-esteem occurred for the older-age-level children during this time period. However, it would be necessary to collect self-esteem data from individuals in the fifth through the ninth grade in a school system that did not have a middle school system.

The present data, although supporting the middle-school structure, does not address whether the increases in self-esteem occur as a function of a supportive middle-school environment, or if the increased self-esteem of the older-age-level participants would occur anyway. It is equally as possible, and quite plausible, that individuals are becoming aware of their own potential skills and abilities as cognitive functioning increases. By the time these students are fourteen or fifteen years old, they may be able to balance their weaknesses and strengths so that their developing self-esteem more adequately reflects personal acceptance.

This is quite speculative, and definite answers must await further exploration. It is quite clear, however, that the raw scores of the older-age-level participants are considerably lower than those of the younger-age-level participants and that the difference becomes much less striking from the fifth to the eighth grades (see table 3.2).

Examination of table 3.2 will also reveal that the younger age level participants are surprisingly consistent in their self-esteem scores between the fifth and eighth grades. An interesting and necessary question concerning these data is whether the lower self-esteem scores of the older age level students would remain low if the students did not attend a middle school. A number of plausible explanations could be generated to account for these data with or without including a middle-school structure. As previously mentioned, further research will be required to more fully understand this phenomenon.

Several criticisms are also apparent with the present data set. The most obvious concerns the age level variable. There is surely some contamination of this variable due to a lack of control of participant inclusion into the age level groups. Some of the participants in the younger age level who are at the older end may be very close in age to those participants in the older age level who are at the younger end. This muddling of the age level groups can easily be

Table 3.2
Total Scores on the Piers-Harris Children's Self-Concept
Scale for the Fifth through the Eighth Grades

	Grade			
Age Level	5	6	7	8
Younger	34.4 (73)	33.4 (56)	32.5 (85)	33.7 (81)
Older	21.1 (48)	24.0 (56)	29.6 (72)	31.8 (67)

Note: The *n* for each group is in parentheses.
The larger sample sizes for these groups are due to the inclusion of some
participants with only one time of measurement.

dealt with by the use of age cutoffs. In addition, the type of design
that was discussed earlier examines age in a way that decreases the
necessity to closely control for age overlap.

In either case, some attention needs to be paid to the quality of
the age variable since many students will have birthdays very close
to other students across the school year. Recording the age variable
in months would also help tease apart this confound. Unfortunately,
age was recorded in years for the present data.

There might also be some debate regarding the terminology
used in this chapter. Traditionally, age, cohort, and time of measurement in the developmental literature is defined as chronological
age, generation, and the specific time or time interval in which data
collection occurred. As far as applying the terms to a school environment, age might be defined as chronological age or grade, and
has been so defined by a number of researchers. Cohort could be defined with birth dates or the student's grade level. It is our opinion
that grade level is more akin to a cohort than it is to age. Most individuals will be of one or two ages within a grade, but grade is more
aligned with a cohort than it is with age. Cohort implies that the
specific group of individuals share some common environmental
history.

A particular grade shares many of the same classes and teachers, and some research has suggested that intelligence levels are
more strongly correlated within a single classroom rather than between classrooms. This is especially true for the elementary grades.

Grade as a cohort may not be as identifiable at the secondary
level, but some emphasis is put on class standing so that grade level
may, in fact, still be a powerful variable for analysis. As a result,
grade level seems to represent more of the intention of cohort than
does age.

Chronological age is a much better indicator of the age variable than is grade level. To be sure, grade level and age are very tightly related for many students. Prediction of grade level by age would be fairly accurate. However, the younger individuals of one grade may be the same age as the older individuals of the adjacent lower grade. The only variable that poses no confusion, of course, is that of time of measurement. It is suggested, therefore, that age be defined by *chronological age* and what is usually considered as cohort be defined by *grade*.

An interesting aspect of examining age and cohort or grade-level effects in elementary, middle, and secondary schools is that, unlike the literature on aging, there is the possibility of examining age within grades. This possibility presents itself mainly as a function of the density of the cohorts and the fact that grades are not completely determined by age. That is, there will typically be several grade levels examined in a single study that differ by only small amounts. In this case, the age variable can be examined by looking at the difference between ages within a single grade or by examining the same age level between two or more grades.

In aging research, cohort is completely determined by age. The typical study in the aging literature would examine two or more cohorts separated by a great many years. Where, in the aging literature, twenty to forty years of separation between cohorts is not uncommon, in school settings, only one year separates the cohorts. It would not make much sense for aging researchers to examine age within cohorts (79.5 versus 80 versus 80.5, or 59.5 versus 60 versus 60.5, and so on). In these cases, the variability of age within cohort would be considerably less than the students' variability of age within cohort.

With the greater relative variability of the students' age within cohort comes a better chance to examine and tease apart the effects of age, grade level and age within grades. As the results of the previous study indicate, age within grades may prove to be a very fruitful area of investigation. It seems that, with adjacent grades, it may be possible to tease apart grade and age effects. The researcher's success in accomplishing this depends entirely on the types of questions which he or she is asking and the range of grades that is being examined.

A caveat seems to be in order regarding the use of the Piers-Harris Self Concept Scale. It is necessary to point out that this assessment device was not the choice of the authors of this chapter. We are not arguing that the Piers-Harris is the definitive device to use when addressing age, grade and time of measurement issues. The data did lend themselves to an examination of the issue of age and age within grades, but it is the data and not so much the instrument of data collection that are relevant in this chapter.

SUMMARY

It may be well that the age grading that typifies the American school (that is, starting school at age five, and the earliest legal departure age of sixteen) promotes the sense of life cycle that Neugarten (1969) thought was reserved for adult development. Our "olders-youngers" data pattern suggests that students may well be aware that every society is age-graded and has a set of expectations regarding age and appropriate behavior.

The experiences accumulated both within and outside of the school originate in an age-status system whereby a society allocates the rights, duties, and privileges to individuals differentially on the basis of age. In fact, the strong normative properties of the age-status system tend to act as "brakes" or "prods" in the movement into or out of social roles (Neugarten, Moore & Lowe 1968). The individual may begin to use age to deny a role and role self-perception. For example, an eleven-year-old may indicate, "I am a sixth grader," while another sixth-grader, fifteen years of age, may state, "I am too old to be a sixth-grader."

The age-norming process may also manifest itself in the way in which a person is viewed by other people in terms of age expectations. Does a teacher view a fifteen-year-old sixth-grader in the same manner that he or she views an eleven-year-old sixth-grader? Or what if the fifteen-year-old was a second semester senior about to graduate from high school?

We are suggesting that the normative properties of our age-status system permeate the self-perception process of young people as well as adults. And to perceive oneself as *on* or *off* time with regard to one's life span causes the individual to examine and reevaluate the generalized sense of self that he or she has established. To view oneself as *on* and *off* time makes for a sense of a predictable life cycle and positive self-esteem.

Unfortunately, some individuals come to believe that they are *off* time and have fallen short of their goals, aspirations, or the expectations held by significant others in their lives with a resultant decay of self-esteem. Individuals in this instance may misperceive, distort, or avoid any new situations or experiences that accentuate the perception which they hold of being *off* time. This may perhaps be a key ingredient in understanding dropouts from the school environment.

To us, it seems fair and reasonable to state that an individual creates a sense of self very early in life. It also seems reasonable and fair to us that young people, not just adults, can create a sense of the life cycle and begin to anticipate the sequence of events that will occur as they mature. Additional support for this view can be found in Harter's work in 1982 and 1988 in which the number of domains important to self-esteem increases from five in middle to late childhood to eight in adolescence. The additions are job competence, romantic appeal, and close friendships—domains clearly supportive of a "sense of the life cycle." This anticipation will most likely include the realization that their own lives will be similar to others in their society. The predictable life cycle or present-relative-to-the-future viewed as *on* or *off* time will be instrumental in a healthy or unhealthy sense of self.

While the focus of our present efforts has been upon the issues of age and school effects, there is no reason for other researchers to wear only these blinders. For example, in young adulthood, the transition issues include entering the world of work, marriage, parenthood, and investing oneself into the lives of a few significant others, such as spouse, or children. What does it do to your sense of self if you perceive yourself as *on* or *off* time?

REFERENCES

Adam, J. 1977. Statistical bias in cross-sequential studies of aging. *Experimental Aging Research* 3:325–333.

————. 1978. Sequential strategies and the separation of age, cohort, and time of measurement contributions to developmental data. *Psychological Bulletin* 85:1309–1316.

Baltes, P. B. 1968. Longitudinal and cross-sectional sequences in the study of age and generation effects. *Human Development* 11:145–171.

Beane, J. A., and Lipka, R. P. 1980. Self-concept and self-esteem: A construct differentiation. *Child Study Journal* 10:1–6.

————. 1986. *Self-concept, self-esteem, and the curriculum.* New York: Teachers College Press.

Blyth, D. A.; Simmons, R. G.; and Carlton-Ford, S. 1983. The adjustment of early adolescents to school transitions. *Journal of Early Adolescence* 3:105–120.

Botwinick, J. 1973. *Aging and behavior.* 1st ed. New York: Springer.

Buss, A. R. 1973. An extension of developmental model that separates ontogenetic changes and cohort differences. *Psychological Bulletin* 80:466–479.

Dusek, J. B., and Flaherty, J. F. 1981. The development of self-concept during the adolescent years. *Monographs of the Society for Research in Child Development* 46(4). Whole No. 191.

Eccles (Parsons), J.; Midgley, G.; and Adler, T. F. 1984. Grade-related changes in the school environment: Effects on achievement motivation. In *The development of achievement motivation,* edited by J. G. Nicholls. Greenwich, Conn.: JAI Press.

Eccles, J.; Wigfield, A.; Reuman, K.; and MacIver, D. 1987. Changes in self-perceptions and values at early adolescence. Paper presented at the annual meeting of American Educational Research Association. Washington, D.C.

Goulet, L. R. 1975. Longitudinal and time-lag designs in educational research: An alternative sampling model. *Review of Educational Research* 45:505–523.

Harter, S. 1982. The perceived competence scale for children. *Child Development* 53:27–97.

———. 1988. Developmental and dynamic changes in the nature of the self-concept. In *Cognitive development and child psychotherapy,* edited by S. Shirk. New York: Plenum. 119–160.

Horn, J. L., and Donaldson, G. 1976. On the myth of intellectual decline in adulthood. *American Psychologist* 31:701–719.

———. 1977. Faith is not enough: A response to the Baltes-Schaie claim that intelligence does not wane. *American Psychologist* 32:369–373.

Juhasz, A. 1992. Significant others in self-esteem development: Methods and problems in measurement. In *The self: Definitional and methodological issues,* edited by T. M. Brinthaupt and R. P. Lipka. Albany: State University of New York Press.

Kelley, E. C. 1962. The fully functioning self. In *Perceiving, behaving, becoming: A new focus for education,* edited by A. W. Combs. Washington, D.C.: Association for Supervision and Curriculum Development.

Kessen, W. 1960. Research design in the study of developmental problems. In *Handbook of research methods in child development,* edited by P. H. Mussen. New York: Wiley.

Kohr, R. L. 1974. A longitudinal study of self-concept from grade 5 to grade 9. Paper presented at the annual meeting of the National Council on Measurement in Education. Chicago, Ill.

Kuhlen, R. G. 1940. Social change: A neglected factor in psychological studies of the life span. *School and Society* 52:14–16.

Mead, G. H. 1934. *Mind, self, and society.* Chicago, Ill.: University of Chicago Press.

Nesselroade, J. R., and Baltes, P. B. 1974. Adolescent personality development and historical change: 1970–72. *Monographs of the Society for Research in Child Development* 39(1). Whole No. 154.

Neugarten, B. L. (1969) Continuities and discontinuities of psychological issues into adult life. *Human Development* 12:121–130.

Neugarten, B. L.; Moore, J. W.; and Lowe, J. C. 1968. Age norms, age constraints, and adult socialization. In *Middle age and aging,* edited by B. L. Neugarten. Chicago, Ill.: The University of Chicago Press.

Piers, E. V. 1985. *Piers-Harris children's self-concept scale.* Los Angeles, Calif.: Western Psychological Services.

Reuman, D. A. 1984. Consequences of the transition into junior high school in social comparisons of abilities and achievement motivation. Paper presented at the annual meeting of the American Educational Research Association. New Orleans, La.

Reuman, D.; MacIver, D.; Eccles, J.; and Wigfield, A. 1987. Change in students' motivation and behavior at the transition to junior high school. Paper presented at the annual meeting of the American Educational Research Association. Washington, D.C.

Rosenberg, M. 1965. *Society and the adolescent self-image.* Princeton, N.J.: Princeton University Press.

Schaie, K. W. 1965. A general model for the study of developmental problems. *Psychological Bulletin* 64:92–107.

Simmons, R. G., and Blyth, D. A. 1986. Effects of transition on adolescent adjustment: A review of findings from the Milwaukee Longitudinal Study. *Transescence* 14:9–17.

———. 1987. *Moving into adolescence: The impact of pubertal change and school context.* New York: Aldine De Gruyter.

Simmons, R. G.; Carlton-Ford, S. L.; and Blyth, D. A. 1987. Predicting how a child will cope with the transition to junior high school. In *Biological-psychological interactions in early adolescence,* edited by R. M. Lerner and T. T. Foch. Hillsdale, N.J.: Lawrence Erlbaum.

Wells, L. E. and Stryker, S. 1988. Stability and change in self over the life course. In *Life-span development and behavior,* Vol. 8, edited by P. B. Battes, D. L. Featherman, and R. M. Lerner. Hillsdale, N.J.: Lawrence Erlbaum Associates. 191–229.

Wigfield, A.; Eccles, J.; Flanagan, C.; Miller, C.; Reuman, D.; Yee, D.; and Lange, L. 1987. Self-concept change in early adolescents. Paper presented at the annual meeting of the American Educational Research Association. Washington, D.C.

Willower, D. J.; Eidell, T. L.; and Hoy, W. F. 1967. *The school and pupil control ideology.* The Pennsylvania State University Studies No. 24. University Park: The Pennsylvania State University.

Wohlwill, F. F. 1970. Methodology and research in the study of developmental change. In *Life-span developmental psychology: Research and theory,* edited by L. R. Goulet and P. B. Baltes. New York: Academic Press.

Wylie, R.C. 1979. *The Self-Concept.* Lincoln, NE: University of Nebraska Press.

DAVID H. DEMO
RITCH C. SAVIN-WILLIAMS

4

Self-concept Stability and Change during Adolescence

What we are trying to tackle in this one hour is what I think is the root of all the problems in the world—lack of self-esteem is what causes war because people who really love themselves don't go out and try to fight other people. . . . It's the root of all the problems. (Oprah Winfrey, cited in Harrison 1989)

INTRODUCTION

Similar to Ms. Winfrey, many sociologists, psychologists, clinicians, and educators consider self-esteem to be one of the most critical factors in understanding human behavior. As an independent or dependent variable, it has been related to behaviors ranging from academic performance, happiness, mate selection, and positive mental health to teenage pregnancy, alcohol and drug use, juvenile delinquency, and suicide. The prevailing assumption is that self-esteem—the motive to see oneself as a good person and one who is worthy of others' respect—"is universally and characteristically . . . a dominant motive in the individual's motivational system" (Kaplan 1975, 10). Thus, it is not surprising that talk show hosts, politicians, and the California Task Force to Promote Self-esteem recognize the necessity of positive self-esteem for personal well-being and social order!

At the same time, researchers and laypeople alike recognize the importance of adolescence as a critical time in the life course when issues of identity become central and a sense of self-worth must be established. It is common to portray adolescence as a period of "storm and stress" (Freud 1958) during which individuals seeking to establish their autonomy are confronted with strong social pressures to conform, most notably to satisfy the expectations of parents and peers. Compounding these social and developmental challenges, adolescents experience physical and physiological changes associated with pubescence (accelerating hormonal production, growth spurts, voice changes, and acne), altering their appearance as well as their sexual interests, attitudes, and behavior.

Cognitively, the acquisition of formal operational thought and sophisticated deductive reasoning enables adolescents to test hypotheses about themselves at a time when they may be extremely introspective and self-conscious. The resolution of these developmental tasks and the development of an integrated ego-identity are seen as critical for the individual's successful progression to adulthood and its challenges (Erikson 1950). Taken together, these concerns have stimulated countless studies designed to examine dimensions of adolescent self-concept.

Unfortunately, numerous problems plague this research literature, precluding a definitive assessment of stability and change in adolescent self-concept. First, the vast majority of studies have examined correlates of a single dimension of self-concept, namely global self-esteem, to the near exclusion of other dimensions (for example, self-confidence or self-efficacy). Self-esteem, as we use the term here, refers to an overall judgment of personal worth.

As important as self-esteem is, self-concept is much broader, referring to all self-referent thoughts and attitudes. Clearly, self-esteem and self-concept influence one another, but unfortunately, we know very little about the structure and processes of self-concept—about how adolescents feel and think about themselves—other than factors associated with self-esteem.

A second major limitation is overreliance on cross-sectional studies that are not well-suited to capture self-process, particularly processes of stability and change. Third, the relatively small number of studies designed to examine change and stability have focused on the transition into early adolescence or the transition from adolescence to early adulthood, with very few studies examining long-term processes through adolescence.

The objective of this chapter is to demonstrate that, for most adolescents and contrary to popular and clinical impressions, self-concept is characterized by growth and stability. Although early adolescence (ages twelve and thirteen) is unusually stressful and disorienting for many individuals, only a small percentage of older adolescents experience the turmoil and dramatic mood swings depicted in the mass media. For most adolescents, once the initial uncertainty of pubescence passes, the remaining years of this developmental stage are years of maturation, growth, development, self-understanding, and increasing self-acceptance.

In the next section, we discuss some of the social, psychological, and developmental processes related to adolescent self-concept, concentrating on factors that serve to stabilize notions of self-worth. In the second section, we examine the social context of adolescence in more detail, focusing on the two most influential socialization contexts for adolescents: family and peer relations. Finally, we explore developmental patterns of growth, change, and stability in self-esteem as individuals move through the adolescent years.

SELF-PROCESSES DURING ADOLESCENCE

During early adolescence, the self-concept is dominated by a psychological interior of self-reflective thoughts, feelings, attitudes, desires, beliefs, fears, and expectations (Damon & Hart 1982; Montemayor & Eisen 1977; Rosenberg 1979, 1986). Self-consciousness and introspection are the norm.

At the same time, early adolescents are confronted with a series of physical, social, psychological, and developmental challenges. Accustomed to thinking of themselves as children and having most decisions (important ones, at least) made for them, twelve- and thirteen-year-olds are now thrust into situations in which they must choose between parents and peers, or between the advice of teachers and older siblings. And they must live with the consequences. Their bodies remind them that they are not children any more.

Socially, the transition to middle school or junior high school necessitates adjustments associated with having several teachers, making new friends, and learning a foreign language (Hirsch & Rapkin 1987; Rosenberg 1979; Simmons, Blyth, Van Cleave & Bush 1979). Early adolescents seek to further individuate themselves from parents, one consequence of which is increased conflict with parents (Montemayor 1983). Peer influence intensifies as close friendships are sought, dating becomes a paramount concern, and sexual/romantic activities are initiated (Savin-Williams & Berndt 1990). Viewed in this context, it is understandable that early adolescents are unsure of themselves and that there are greater disturbances to the self-concept at ages twelve and thirteen than at any other point in the life course (Demo in press; Rosenberg 1979).

But as adolescents mature and adjust to new social roles, they redefine their self-theories. Many of the changes, such as physical growth and maturation, are culturally valued and thus personally satisfying. Routines are established for studying, classwork, dating, and leisure activities. Thoughts about the self are reorganized and reintegrated, a certain continuity of the self is achieved, self-consciousness wanes, and levels of self-esteem rise steadily as individuals move through this developmental period (Bachman, O'Malley & Johnston 1978; Demo & Savin-Williams 1983; McCarthy & Hoge 1982; O'Malley & Bachman 1983; Savin-Williams & Demo 1984). (See also Harter 1990, for an excellent overview of the literature on self-development.)

These trends reflect maturational growth, development, and self-understanding through the adolescent years. Of course, psychological maturation occurs within social contexts, experiences, and relationships, and progression through adolescence is measured against socially prescribed timetables for the acquisition of specific skills, attributes, and statuses. But further evidence of the important role played by maturational processes in shaping self-concept is provided in a recent study of a large national probability sample of adults (Gove, Ortega & Style 1989).

These authors demonstrate that psychological maturation is more important than are processes of role acquisition and change in accounting for steady improvement in self-evaluation through the adult years. They conclude that, with age, self-concept becomes somewhat better integrated and that "as persons age they become increasingly comfortable with themselves and their social environment" (Gove et al. 1989, 1138).

The evidence at hand would suggest that these processes are operating throughout adolescence, reshaping the self-concept and the sense of identity that at ages twelve and thirteen tend to be so disorganized and impressionable. Stated in Eriksonian terms, maturation facilitates a more stable and secure identity that replaces the sense of role confusion (see Chapter 2 of this volume). In the next section we discuss some of the specific mechanisms bolstering self-concept stability.

Maturational and Environmental Forces for Stability

From the adolescent's perspective—and given that numerous personal, physical, and environmental factors are related to feelings of self-worth—how is it that adolescent self-concept can be stable? A large part of the answer is that adolescents perceive slight and gradual changes in their growth, mood, physical appearance, personal responsibilities, and social relationships from one day to the next. Further, not all changes are negative. Many are positive and represent desired growth, maturation, and development. To be sure, individuals entering adolescence vary physically, psychologically, sexually, and socially from the individuals who exit adolescence as young adults. But change and discontinuity are not synonymous with instability.

Unfortunately, the personal, maturational, and environmental forces contributing to growth, development, and stability are often ignored in empirical research on adolescence. The literature on adolescent self-concept is heavily dependent on cross-sectional studies of global self-esteem, thus excluding possibilities for assessing change (or its correlates) from one situation to the next or one year to the next.

But even recognizing the limitations of the literature, the popular and clinical notion of adolescence as a period of storm and stress is not supported by empirical research (Dornbusch 1989). At least in contemporary American society, adolescents report that their identity as son or daughter is very important to them (Hoelter 1986), and that harmony rather than conflict is the norm in family life. About three-fourths report close relationships with parents (Dornbusch 1989), perhaps indicating closer relationships than in earlier times (Acock & Bengston 1980; Elder 1980). Otto asserted that it "is a myth, a widely held half-truth, that young people don't listen to their parents" (1988, 390), and cited as evidence the strong convergence between parents' and adolescents' values and beliefs on major issues such as education, religion, and life aspirations.

Drawing on observations both in the United States and the United Kingdom, Rutter concluded that, despite minor day-to-day altercations:

> . . . parent-adolescent relationships remain generally harmonious, communication between the generations continues and

young people tend both to share their parents' values on the major issues of life and also to turn to them for guidance on most major concerns. The concept of parent-child alienation as a usual feature of adolescence is a myth (Rutter 1980, 31).

Because family relations are an important context for adolescent self-esteem (Demo, Small & Savin-Williams 1987; Felson & Zielinski 1989; Gecas & Schwalbe 1986), it is reasonable to posit that family harmony and stability are major environmental forces promoting adolescent self-concept stability and self-esteem growth. But what of the increasing percentage of adolescents who experience discontinuity in their family environment as a consequence of parents' divorce?

Research indicates that adolescents benefit from their maturity in that, compared with younger children, they are generally better able to cope with such changes and transitions. One explanation for this is that teenagers have more frequent opportunities to discuss the situation with friends (many of whom have had similar experiences), to understand that they are not personally responsible for their parents' divorce, and to recognize beneficial consequences such as the end of parental fighting and improved relations with parents (Demo & Acock 1988; Kurdek & Siesky 1980). By not blaming themselves and not feeling responsible for their parents' divorce, self-evaluation (self-esteem) is protected and the core self-concept remains essentially intact.

A context of even greater significance for adolescent self-evaluation is the peer group (Harter 1990; Juhasz 1992). Adolescents spend more time with friends than with parents or other adults (Csikszentmihalyi & Larson 1984). They are very much aware of and sensitive to the influence of their friends, and they think of themselves as belonging to a specific group (Crockett, Losoff & Petersen 1984; O'Brien & Bierman 1988). But to what degree are peer relations characterized by stability? How are peer influences reconciled with those of parents, and with what consequences for self-concept stability?

Two dimensions of peer relations are strongly related to adolescent self-esteem: close friendships and acceptance by a peer group. Adolescents who have a number of close friendships and are accepted by their peers generally have high self-esteem, while adolescents without intimate friendships or who are rejected by their peers typically have low self-esteem (Savin-Williams & Berndt 1990).

Although very little attention has been devoted to assessing in longitudinal studies the stability of peer relations, there are a number of reasons for expecting interpersonal relationships with friends to provide a stabilizing effect on adolescent self-concept and sense of self-worth. First, close friendships provide a sense of attachment and a foundation of social support that moderate the impact of stressful life events (Dornbusch 1989).

Second, and perhaps more important for day-to-day interactions, adolescents are actively involved in choosing their friends and in deciding how much time to spend with particular friends. Adolescents most often choose friends who are similar in social background (such as race, social class, gender, and age) and personality characteristics (Savin-Williams & Berndt 1990). Friendships with similar others (homophily) reinforces personal values and behavior and confirms self-concept. Further, it is typically the case that peer expectations and values coincide with and reinforce those of parents (Bandura 1964), providing consistency across two powerfully influential socialization contexts.

As with adults, adolescents monitor feedback from others (Snyder & Gangestad 1982) and use this feedback to increase and decrease interaction with particular friends, or to pursue new friends. This principle, termed *selective interaction* by Rosenberg, illustrates the active, efficacious nature of the self as a force in social behavior, systematically regulating its own stability, and biased toward generating positive reflected appraisals.

> Friendship is the purest illustration of picking one's propaganda, for it is characteristic of a friend that not only do we like him but he likes us. To some extent, at least, it is probably that we like him because he likes us. Indeed, it is well-nigh impossible to be friends with someone who dislikes us, not only because we would have no taste for such a friendship but also because he would not allow the friendship to exist. (Rosenberg 1979, 261)

These processes are important because, as we will later discuss, adolescents routinely tease and ridicule each other. But our point is that these experiences do not inevitably result in self-domination, stress, and turmoil. Instead, we are suggesting that, when adolescents feel threatened or receive discrepant feedback from a friend, they have several options available. They can reinterpret, devalue, or dismiss the feedback (Kulik, Sledge & Mahler 1986;

Rosenberg 1979; Swann 1983; Tesser & Campbell 1983). They can also decrease interaction with the source of the information, or even terminate the relationship. Thus, even in the face of unkind or untimely remarks made by peers, adolescents have numerous self-protective options and strategies for minimizing damage to self-esteem and restoring stability of self-concept.

In summary, adolescents tend to be resilient in their quest for autonomy and self-definition. Although a small minority of adolescents may experience dramatic and multiple changes in family and peer relationships, generating uncertainty both in interpersonal relationships and self-concept, for most adolescents, there is substantial stability to family and peer relations. The next section is devoted to a discussion of these two socialization contexts as they relate to adolescents' overall sense of self-worth.

THE SOCIAL CONTEXT OF ADOLESCENT SELF-ESTEEM

A number of studies have demonstrated that sociodemographic variables—such as social class, race, gender, and family structure—do not impact strongly on adolescent self-esteem (Demo & Acock 1988; Rosenberg 1979; Savin-Williams & Demo 1983). Although other elements of self-concept (such as role-identities, personal efficacy, and self-confidence) are profoundly influenced by social structural arrangements, such as race or gender, adolescents do not seem to derive their overall sense of self-worth on the basis of these ascribed characteristics. Adolescents are more directly affected by immediate contextual variables, such as school setting, academic performance, peer relations, parent-adolescent relations (including communication, conflict, and participation in shared activities), and parent marital discord. In discussing family processes, friendships, and peer relations as they relate to adolescent self-esteem, it is particularly important to recognize reciprocal or bidirectional influences. We turn our attention now to the dynamics and intricacies of these reciprocal processes.

The Family and Parent-Adolescent Relations

Across family forms, parent-adolescent relations are critical to youthful well-being. Research demonstrates that adolescent self-esteem is correlated with parental support and control, parent-adolescent communication, and participation in shared activities (Demo et al. 1987; Felson & Zielinski 1989; Gecas & Schwalbe

1986). The self-esteem of parents is also influenced by the nature of parent-adolescent relations, as seen in support and affection expressed by adolescents for their parents (Demo et al. 1987).

Collectively, these findings support life-span developmental and symbolic interactionist perspectives emphasizing the bidirectional and reciprocal influence of parent-adolescent relations in shaping the self-concepts of children and parents alike. The ongoing private, personal, and emotionally charged nature of parent-adolescent dynamics is critical in that both adolescents and parents serve as significant others who routinely and openly evaluate each other, exchanging reflected appraisals that are consequential for each others' self-esteem. (See also Juhasz 1992, on the role of significant others in self-esteem development.)

Consistently, we find that adolescents' reports and parents' reports of family relations are quite different and that it is the adolescent's perceptions of the relationships that matter for his or her self-esteem (Demo et al. 1987; Felson & Zielinski 1989; Gecas & Schwalbe 1986). Similarly, parents' judgments of family relations matter more for their self-esteem than do children's accounts of the same relationships (Demo et al. 1987). This is important both theoretically and methodologically.

Theoretically, it substantiates symbolic interactionist and phenomenological principles that posit the psychological importance of subjective reality, or perceived rather than actual behavior. Methodologically, it suggests that greater attention needs to be devoted to measuring family dynamics and self-esteem from both the parents' and adolescents' perspectives, rather than relying on one family member's accounts to understand other member's self-esteem or other outcomes.

In sum, the cultural importance attached to parent-child relationships, combined with the frequency and emotional intensity of the interaction, creates an important context in which parent and adolescent self-evaluations are generated.

Peer Relations and Peer Influences

Peer relations and self-concept may be intimately interconnected during adolescence, especially for youths who are attentive and responsive to the attitudes and views of others. Developmentalists traditionally have been interested in the psychosocial consequences of peer relations, but only recently have empirical investigations begun in earnest (Hartup 1983; Parker & Asher 1987;

Serafica & Blyth 1985). The theoretical importance of this topic can be traced to the writings of Mead (1934) who argued that, through the process of social communication, an individual comes to understand and evaluate the self from the vantage point of significant others; and the writings of Sullivan (1953) who based his theory of psychic development on the nature and consequences of interpersonal relationships. Few theorists have reversed the causal direction to argue that self-esteem is relatively stable and that its positive or negative affect influences the types of relationships which one develops with peers.

Recent formulations emphasize that, during the adolescent years, the most important sources of validation are friendships, other interpersonal relationships with peers, and one's status among same-age peers. Peer relations, especially friendships, are viewed as enhancing psychosocial resiliency through their effects on one's sense of interpersonal competence and feelings of belonging (Rutter 1987). Adolescents who report that they are satisfied with their peer friendships also typically report high levels of self-esteem (Savin-Williams & Berndt 1990).

Among black American youths it is the supportive nature of peer relationships that accounts for the high correlation between friendships and a positive sense of self (Cauce 1986). Other studies demonstrate that interpersonal relations with friends and family are more important sources of self-esteem for blacks than for whites, providing a partial explanation for blacks having higher self-esteem than do whites (Hoelter 1982; Hughes & Demo 1989).

However, most empirical research on youths has focused on those who do not have a positive experience with age mates, thus suffering developmental deficits in conceptions of the self. The very same peers who can enhance one's self-esteem can also create and reinforce self-doubt, thus serving as a stressful context in which development is handicapped (Mechanic 1983).

Researchers have documented the everyday concern that many adolescents have with peer relationships (Coddington 1972; Greene 1988; Lewis, Siegel & Lewis 1984; Newcombe, Huba & Bentler 1981). In addition, clinicians and health-care providers frequently base their intervention programs for youth-at-risk on this principle (Bierman & Furman 1984; Bierman & McCauley 1987; Bierman, Miller & Stabb 1987). Here, we focus attention on the link between one's relations with peers and self-concept, and on the mechanisms by which peer-regard is conveyed to youths through, for example, teasing and ridicule. Following the literature, our primary concern is with youths who are perceived by their peers as being aversive, unattractive, friendless, and unwanted. We are also concerned with the consequences of this rejection for the individual's sense of self-worth.

Peer Rejection. There is a substantial body of evidence that links poor child and adolescent peer relationships with negative psychological outcomes. Parker and Asher concluded from their extensive review of the literature in 1987 that there are "striking individual differences in the extent to which children are accepted by their peers. In the extreme, some children are well regarded by all and enjoy many friendships, whereas others are nearly universally disliked and have no friends" (1987, 357). Furthermore, "poorly accepted children stand a greater chance than others of developing later life difficulties and, therefore, should be considered a group of children at risk" (1987, 357).

There is nearly universal agreement among researchers that many adolescents who are rejected by their peers face severe adjustment problems, which are manifested in various contexts and across a number of dimensions, such as poor scholastic performance and social interactions (Coie & Dodge 1983; East, Hess & Lerner 1987). Various investigations—using peer assessments, teacher ratings, and psychological measures—have reported that rejected youths are likely to be hyperactive, aggressive, obsessive-compulsive, delinquent, and friendless (Coie & Dodge 1983; East et al. 1987; Feltham, Doyle, Schwartzman, Serbin & Ledingham 1985; French & Waas 1985; Hartup 1983; King & Young 1981; Ladd 1983). Their self-conception suffers because they feel embarrassed and angry due to their rejection, leading them to further hostility toward and withdrawal from peers.

Some youths are rejected because of their aggressive, antagonistic manner; others, because of their manifest anxiety and social withdrawal (Parker & Asher 1987). The latter may reflect conditions of low self-esteem, loneliness, depression, and introspectiveness that interfere with developing peer relationships. In regard to the former, indiscriminant, impulsive, and hostile aggression directed at peers is likely to provoke a cycle of rejection and poor self-image.

For example, Olweus (1978, 1987) studied bullying and whipping boys, both of whom have low status among their peers. Bulliers frequently cause others to feel socially isolated and excluded through verbal, nonverbal, and physical harassment. Whipping boys are of two types: provocative and passive victims. The former are often bulliers as well. Perry, Kusel, and Perry (1988) characterized these youths as aggressive, hot-tempered, and impulsive. They picked fights, ridiculed others, and profoundly irritated their peers. Passive whipping boys seldom fought back or defended themselves, but withdrew into social isolation, frequently crying and acting humiliated. They were insecure, anxious, lonely, and sensitive individuals who seemed to invite attacks. Both the aggressors and the victims were disliked, ostracized by peers, and appeared to have poor self-esteem.

Many of the relationships noted above are, however, ambiguous in terms of directionality. For example, peers may be more likely to reject adolescents who appear to have poor self-image or, perhaps, youths who are rejected by peers develop low self-esteem as a consequence. Most likely, the influences are reciprocal. Eder (1987) proposed two options: Those without significant peer relations may not have the opportunity to learn the proper interpretation of the subtleties of interactions or, alternatively, perhaps such youths are rejected by peers because of their misinterpretations and poor self-presentation. Parker and Asher (1987) argued that the weight of current evidence favors the first explanation: deprivation of interactions with peers hinders development of the self. They labeled this the *necessity-not-luxury* model.

> Here the assumption seems to be that because they are excluded from normal patterns of peer interaction, low-accepted children are also systematically excluded from normal socialization experiences and deprived of important sources of support. As a result, these children become more extreme and more idiosyncratic in their modes of thought and behavior over time and are made more vulnerable to stress and breakdown. (Parker & Asher 1987, 378).

The shortcoming here is that factors that antedate poor peer relationships are frequently ignored. Rejected children appear biased to interpret ambiguous or relatively neutral behavioral stimuli as a personal statement against them. Thus, certain youths with preexisting poor self-concepts may be prime for rejection by their peers.

The second or incidental model does not attempt to causally link peer relations with conceptions of the self. "Accordingly, in this view it is the early forms of disorder that are responsible for both the early disturbances in peer group adjustment and the ultimate maladaptive outcomes" (Parker & Asher 1987, 378). Thus, a third factor (such as sensitivity or introspectiveness) may lead to both peer rejection and low self-esteem. Peer relationships could, therefore, serve as useful screening devices or lead indicators to designate at-risk individuals. This model unduly minimizes, according to Parker and Asher, the impact of prolonged peer rejection, which might lead a youth to view the self and the world in negative terms, affecting subsequent adjustment.

Thus, for reasons that are currently unknown, relations with peers may predict self-esteem for some individuals but not for others. Differentiating among the various reasons why a youth is rejected by peers would greatly increase our ability to predict those most at-risk for self-related problems during adolescence (French & Waas 1985). However, these reasons may be quite difficult for researchers to disentangle because the feedback loops among temperamental dispositions, peer status, and conceptions of the self are quite intricate and individually constructed.

One consideration that has not been adequately addressed is assessing the degree to which a particular youth is sensitive to his or her peer status. Those who are quite concerned and feel rejected may be most likely to have difficulties in self-image. On the other hand, some adolescents, such as those who do not feel vulnerable in solitude, may be relatively immune to peer recognition.

In sum, peer rejection and low self-esteem are strongly related, but the causal linkages are unclear. The following section elaborates on mechanisms that intervene in the relationship between peer status and adolescent self-evaluation.

Mechanisms of Influence

The processes by which peer status is translated into negative or positive outcomes during adolescence are little understood and thus are usually left unspecified. Researchers usually examine the degree of predictability between the two and ignore the mechanism through which peer acceptance or rejection brings about its hypothesized effects (Dornbusch 1989; Parker & Asher 1987). One possible mechanism, often anecdotally identified as verbal teasing, is frequently perceived by those who observe youth in naturalistic settings to be potentially consequential for their well-being (Eder 1987; Hollingshead 1949; Savin-Williams 1987; Sherif & Sherif 1964). Nevertheless, there have been few systematic studies of teasing as a process by which peers influence conceptions of the self.

An almost universal experience of American adolescents is to be teased by peers. This is documented in the field notes of anthropologists and sociologists (Eder 1987; Eder & Sanford 1986; Scho-field 1982; Sherif & Sherif 1964) and by empirical research findings from various disciplines (Kanner, Feldman, Weinberger & Ford 1987; Olweus 1978, 1987; Perry et al. 1988; Savin-Williams 1987; Savin-Williams & Fuligni in preparation). Few researchers, however, have separated teasing from its negative form of ridicule (Eder 1987; Savin-Williams & Fuligni, in preparation).

In terms of content, it is probable that teasing and ridicule are quite similar. However, of more importance, according to Eder (1987), is their meaning for adolescents. Teasing is playful, humor-ous verbal interactions among peers that expresses interpersonal at-traction, group solidarity, familiarity, and positive feelings. It is an indication of peer acceptance (Eder 1987). Ridicule, on the other hand, is a negative form of humor that communicates hostility, an-ger, embarrassment, and dislike—in a word, rejection. These two are frequently confused because the distinction between them can be quite subtle. For example, the content might appear to be posi-tive, but the tone is angry.

Eder (1987) noted that youths with advanced interpersonal skills—such as properly interpreting subtle cues, being sensitive to the intent of the initiator, and having a range of responses avail-able—can frequently turn ambiguous verbalizations from potential ridicule to teasing. Adolescents who already feel a strong sense of self-mastery, control, and esteem are most likely to pull this off. It also may be true that youths who have these skills are protected from feeling insulted or hurt and having their self-concept damaged by peers because ridicule is kept to the level of teasing.

Through these verbal interactions, peers convey their views, some of which express positive regard (teasing), while others com-municate dislike (ridicule). The latter may increase the tendency of an adolescent to scrutinize the self and this self-introspection may become a detriment to a positive self-conception (Mechanic 1983). Teasing, on the other hand, reinforces fun activities and experiences that pull the adolescent away from self-absorption.

The positive impact of peer teasing is difficult to document, primarily because of definitional convergence of teasing with ridi-cule in many research projects. A notable exception is Kanner's and colleagues' study of "hassles and uplifts" among early adolescents in 1987. Uplifts (fun and joking with kids) were experienced by 83 percent of the sample during the past month. These uplifts signifi-cantly predicted low levels of depression, anxiety, and distress, and high levels of perceived social competence and self-worth. To the extent that teasing reflects positive feelings and popularity among peers, one would expect teasing, for both the initiator and the recipient, to be associated with positive self-esteem (Hartup 1983; Savin-Williams & Berndt 1990).

In contrast, ridicule conveys rejection and dislike, distancing youths from the types of peer-group socialization that are considered by many to be essential for positive self-esteem. If such individuals develop friendships, then they are frequently with those who lack effective social skills (Eder 1987). In the extreme form, ridicule can become so abusive that the recipients become victimized and suffer greatly at the hands of their peers (Olweus 1978; Perry et al. 1988). Hassles (or ridicule, fights, and arguments) were significantly related in one study to emotional distress, anxiety, depression, low perceived social competence, and low self-worth (Kanner et al. 1987).

Clearly, there is ambiguity in the causal pathway among peer status (acceptance versus rejection), verbal interactions (ridicule versus teasing), and outcomes (positive versus negative self-esteem). In regard to negative self-esteem, one view is that adolescents are rejected by their peers for reasons that include personal (such as social anxiety) and/or social (such as minority status) characteristics. This rejection is expressed and reinforced by ridicule, which then contributes to low self-regard. Ridicule and teasing may also be independent of the rejection or acceptance that contributes to self-conceptions. Ridicule and teasing offer to investigators possible mechanisms by which relations with peers are conveyed and notions of self-concept are reinforced.

Given the intense social pressures confronting adolescents, it is reasonable to hypothesize that, as their relationships change (as in acceptance versus rejection), their self-images change. Self-esteem during this stage of the life course would thus be characterized by exuberant highs (following acceptance, achievement, and popularity) and abysmal lows (following setbacks, rejection, and defeat). In fact, this is the popular and clinical impression of adolescence alluded to earlier. In the next section we address the thorny issue of developmental change and stability in self-esteem.

DEVELOPMENTAL GROWTH, CHANGE, AND STABILITY

Although a number of studies have examined the short-term consequences of the transition into early adolescence on self-reported self-esteem, few studies have examined long-term trends throughout adolescence or assessed stability and change in other dimensions of self-concept. Because previous studies have demonstrated the multidimensionality of self-concept (Demo 1985; Gecas 1982; Marsh, Byrne & Shavelson 1992; Mortimer, Finch & Kumka 1982; Rosenberg 1979), we distinguish between three dimensions: experienced self-esteem, presented self-esteem, and self-feelings.

Experienced self-esteem refers to the widely studied dimension of self-regard that is measured by self-report, whereas presented self-esteem is a rarely studied dimension of self-regard that requires ratings-by-others. One assumption underlying most self-concept research is that the individual being studied is the only appropriate source of information regarding his or her private, self-reflective thoughts and feelings. However, we are interested in the relationship between this subjectively experienced, self-reported level of self-esteem, and presented self-esteem, the self-regard that one communicates to others in social interactions.

Given that adolescence is a period of intense social influence, it is reasonable to expect differences in levels of self-esteem that individuals experience and those which they present to others. However, because measures of the presented dimension have not been developed, few studies have examined the relationship between these dimensions, nor have they examined their stability and change through adolescence.

The third dimension we examine is self-feelings. This component refers to a diverse set of feelings about oneself, independent of self-esteem. Adolescents frequently feel tense, nervous, proud, or happy, quite apart from any evaluations of themselves as respectable individuals, and separate from judgments as to whether they like themselves. Here, we are interested in the experience of positive and negative self-feelings and the degree to which these feelings change over time.

Constancy and Change in Dimensions of Self-Concept

In an earlier study (Savin-Williams & Demo 1984), we employed a panel design to study the course of development for a group of adolescents as they moved from seventh to tenth grade. Multiple measures were used to assess, over the three-year period, constancy and change in three components of self-concept: experienced self-esteem, presented self-esteem, and self-feelings.

Experienced self-esteem was measured using two traditional self-report scales, the Rosenberg Self-Esteem Scale and the Coopersmith Self-Esteem Inventory.

Presented self-esteem was measured through two methods: adolescent peers assessed the target individual's self-esteem, and undergraduate college students assessed each adolescent's self-esteem on the basis of behavioral observations. Employing two sets of raters enabled us to determine the degree of correspondence between the two sets of ratings, providing insights regarding the stability of the self presented to various others in social interactions.

Finally, self-feelings were reported by having respondents describe how they felt in various naturalistic settings. Participants carried paging devices or beepers for a one-week period during which they were signalled randomly an average of seven times per day. Each time they were signalled, they completed a short questionnaire that contained forty self-feelings, such as confident, tense, and anxious.

The results indicated that the three dimensions are independent—that is, their intercorrelations reflect different self-processes. All three dimensions are also quite stable over the three-year period, and two of the dimensions (experienced and presented self-esteem) show gradual increases over the period. Significant increases in all three components occurred from ninth to tenth grade.

In Table 4.1 we present additional data on four measures of self-esteem for the period from ninth through twelfth grade. In addition to the Rosenberg and Coopersmith scales, personal interviews with the respondents were used to measure experienced self-esteem. (See Demo 1985 for further information on these measures

Table 4.1
Mean Self-esteem Levels by Four Measures,
Ninth Grade through Twelfth Grade

	9th	10th	11th	12th
Experienced				
Rosenberg	17.67	17.97	20.06	20.33
(N)	(41)	(35)	(34)	(36)
Coopersmith	29.24	32.43	34.09	34.34
(N)	(42)	(35)	(35)	(35)
Interview	NA	49.82	52.37	52.86
(N)		(34)	(35)	(35)
Presented				
Peer Rating	3.43	3.45	3.41	3.46
(N)	(54)	(38)	(37)	(41)

and their validity.) Peer ratings were used to measure presented self-esteem over the three-year period.

The data indicate that stability and gradual growth in self-esteem continue through twelfth grade. There is consistent (and statistically significant) growth in the experienced dimension from ninth through eleventh grade, with nonsignificant increases from eleventh to twelfth grade. These findings corroborate those of other investigators who have documented developmental increases in self-esteem during adolescence (Bachman et al. 1978; Demo & Savin-Williams 1983; McCarthy & Hoge 1982; O'Malley & Bachman 1983). (See a review in Harter 1990.) Considering the consistency of this finding and the diversity of samples on which it has been replicated, there is strong evidence of developmental growth and maturation enhancing self-evaluation during the adolescent years.

Presented self-esteem exhibits a somewhat different pattern. It is stable rather than escalating from ninth through twelfth grade, although there is a modest increase from eleventh to twelfth grade. Perhaps because attributions by others tend to be very stable and resistant to change, peer ratings do not suggest improvements in adolescent self-esteem during this period. Another possible explanation is that feelings of self-worth improve over this period, but adolescents do not manifest this in their behavior nor do they adequately communicate this to others in their interactions. This is clearly an area in which considerably more research is necessary if we are to understand the intricacies and complexities of self-conception and self-presentation.

In sum, contrary to popular and clinical impressions of adolescence, the research evidence indicates that both experienced self-esteem (measured by traditional self-report scales) and presented self-esteem (measured by peers and participant observers) are stable components of the self-concept during the supposedly turbulent adolescent years. Neither component of self-esteem rises dramatically nor falls sharply during the teenage years.

There is, however, intraindividual variation from one social context to the next. Most people view themselves in a fairly consistent manner over extended periods of time but occasionally feel better or worse about themselves than is typically the case. This suggests that, for most adolescents, self-feelings can be represented by a baseline or standard self-picture from which situational variations emanate. An adolescent who, on most occasions, has high self-regard may experience temporary self-doubts following a rejection, a poor grade on a test, or a lackluster athletic performance. The situational fluctuations appear greatest during early adolescence, generating higher highs and lower lows, after which personality solidifies and becomes less susceptible to social influence. Individual differences also exist, both in level and stability of self-evaluation.

PATTERNS OF STABILITY

In the preceding section, we examined self-esteem stability from a nomothetic or interindividual approach. Because individuals maintained their relative position from one year to the next, we concluded that self-esteem during adolescence is essentially a stable phenomenon, with some growth or change in the experienced dimension. But a nomothetic approach blurs or, some might assert, obscures individual variations. That is, although as a group adolescents appear to be stable in self-esteem, not all individual youths necessarily or equally share in this characterization. To address this issue, we submitted one set of data to an idiographic research methodology, examining stability of the self within individuals across time. We rescue these data from becoming merely case studies in research design by using statistical procedures that enable us to ascertain if study participants were similar in particular ways that indicated the presence of unique patterns of self-esteem stability across time.

Methods

Twenty-eight of the tenth-grade youths (nineteen females and nine males) agreed to participate in an additional data collection procedure after completion of the primary study described above and in Savin-Williams and Demo (1983, 1984). The youths carried a beeper for one more week, but this time, the Rosenberg Self-Esteem Scale (RSE) rather than the forty words was placed on the back side of the beep sheet. In all other respects, the procedures were identical to the earlier data collection. To minimize response set, the RSE questions were inverted one-half of the time. The youths responded to 84 percent of the beeps by completing the RSE.

Within Subject Variation in Self-esteem

Applying the Rasch simple logistic model to the youths' RSE scores, estimates of self-esteem and standard error measurement were obtained. (See Schilling & Savin-Williams 1985 for details of the modeling assumptions and procedures.) Each youth's RSE scores were examined to test if she or he exhibited trait stability relative to the measurement error.

Rather than answering the commonly tested question "Is self-esteem stable for a particular youth?", this procedure allows us to address the far more significant question of "Does the individual exhibit a degree of self-esteem instability which can be measured?" If the variance in the estimates of self-esteem can be accounted for by the unreliability of the RSE, then we can state with confidence that a youth demonstrates a stable level of self-esteem over time. If, on the other hand, the amount of variance is large relative to the mean square error, then self-esteem is unstable for the youth. Previous analyses have shown the RSE to be an extremely reliable measure structurally (Schilling & Savin-Williams 1985).

Of the twenty-eight adolescents, nearly one-half (41 percent) were classified as stable based on the criteria just described. Thirty percent were very unstable in that their self-esteem scores span two or more statistically distinct strata. The remaining youths were characterized as moderately unstable (22 percent), with stratas between one and two, or as exhibiting relatively little instability (7 percent), with stratas below one in their self-esteem scores. Thus, over the course of one week, one-half of the youths were stable in self-esteem and the rest displayed varying levels of instability, from extreme to relatively moderate amounts.

Patterns of Self-Esteem Stability

The findings reported here are, in a sense, difficult to reconcile. We have documented both stability and change in dimensions of self-esteem. In the previous section we reported considerable stability in self-esteem level from one year to the next, even for those who experienced moment-to-moment instability in self-feelings. We interpret this to mean that there are strong maturational and environmental forces bolstering stability of core self-concept and overall self-esteem, despite situational fluctuations in self-images. As adolescents (and adults) move across social contexts, relationships, and role-identities, different self-images or working self-concepts (Burke 1980) are evoked. But over extended periods of time, there is remarkable consistency and stability to self-concept and overall judgments of self-regard. This conclusion, that self-concept is at once both stable and malleable, is consistent with Rosenberg's

(1986) and Markus's and Kunda's (1986) interpretations of the empirical evidence.

We further propose that, even as individuals are characterized by the same degree of self-esteem stability or instability over time, they may also share their pattern of stability with others. Thus, it is not unreasonable to combine the nomothetic and idiographic approaches to examine intraindividual variations in self-esteem stability from the perspective of grouping individuals who display similar stability patterns. Furthermore, these subgroups may differ in terms of the degree to which their self-esteem is truly trait-like and not susceptible to external influences, such as those from family and peers.

We leave this option open, not necessarily because we have sufficient evidence that family members and friends causally influence self-esteem, at least beyond a small amount of variance, but with the knowledge that definitive studies have yet to be conducted. Our previous attempts (Savin-Williams & Demo 1983; Schilling & Savin-Williams 1985) failed to find influences based on settings, activities, or associates. But other researchers, most notably Harter (1990), are inclined to believe that self-esteem is impressionistic. We remain unimpressed with the data currently available. Whether the trait-like quality of individual self-esteem patterns precede or extend beyond adolescence is open to data gathering as well.

We are neither the first nor the last to propose differential patterns of individual lifestyles, although the ones with which we are familiar tend to emphasize the affective dimension. For example, Offer's and Offer's eight-year longitudinal study published in 1975 reported three pathways toward psychological growth that were characteristic of their sample from early adolescence to young manhood. These developmental routes were based on factors such as childrearing practices, genetic heritage, personal experiences, and defense or coping mechanisms.

Continuous-growth young men (23 percent of the total sample) progressed toward maturity smoothly, with self-assurance, order, and social success. Surgent-growth youths (35 percent) experienced developmental spurts of energy in a pattern of progression and regression toward maturity. The 21 percent who were characterized by tumultuous growth manifested patterns of internal turmoil, behavioral problems, self-doubts, conflicts, and discordance.

Block (1971) described five personality types based on ego strength, adaptation style, success, and happiness that remained relatively stable from early adolescence to adulthood. Two clusters were particularly noteworthy: changers and nonchangers. In previous analyses of our self-esteem data, we described three groups of youths who experienced different patterns of oscillating self-feelings or moods during a one-week period of time: stable self-feelings from one moment to the next; oscillating self-feelings (usually less than 10 percent of the sample) with significant fluctuations in positive/ negative affect over time; and unpredictable self-feelings (one-half to three-quarters of the group) with a stable baseline level and mild fluctuations from one moment to the next (Savin-Williams & Demo 1983).

Building on these studies, Bence (1989) reported multiple patterns of affect during the years of adolescence that did not appear to be influenced by external activities. Based on a diary measure of mood during one week, she assessed both rate and mood change and intensity of mood experienced. Two of her eight patterns resembled the oscillators in our study (Savin-Williams & Demo 1983), and Offer's and Offer's (1975) surgent growth group. This 25 percent of the sample experienced fluctuating, quickly changing, and intensely felt moods, but appeared fairly well-adapted with self-esteem and depression scores within normal ranges. Another pattern, representing 17 percent of the sample, was similar to the continuous growth and stable self-feelings adolescents: slow mood swings, small mood fluctuations, positive moods, and normal levels of self-esteem and depression. A fourth pattern was also stable in mood variability but experienced a preponderance of negative affect. Other patterns resembled Offer's and Offer's tumultuous youths. They experienced high depression, low self-esteem, intense negative moods, and slow mood changes.

Delineating patterns of affect or self-attitudes appears to be an acceptable compromise between the usual nomothetic approach of assessing group mean level of a characteristic and the more clinical approach of focusing on intraindividual variations in a characteristic.

Many research questions remain unanswered, including (1) the stability of patterns throughout the life course; (2) psychological (such as happiness) and social (as in career success) outcomes of the patterns; (3) the degree to which these patterns are trait- or state-like; and (4) assuming state-like, if different patterns are affected by different external influences. Nonetheless, this approach may be the best way to address the perplexing issue of self-esteem stability during the life course.

We believe that the proper answer to Hall's characterization in 1904 of adolescence as turbulent is, "Yes, for some—but this turbulence is not confined to the time of adolescence." The extent to which these patterns of self-esteem stability remain immune to typical life-course events (such as leaving home) and processes (as in puberty) or are affected by them offers to future researchers on extensive array of extremely significant and challenging studies.

CONCLUSIONS AND RESEARCH AGENDA

Early adolescence is unquestionably a period characterized by persistent challenges and disturbances to self-concept. But as individuals move through adolescence, they mature. Their developing cognitive abilities enable broader self-understanding. Their thoughts and feelings about the self become more resistant to social influence, and self-acceptance increases. At least this is the case for the majority of youths.

For a small percentage of youths the stress and turmoil persist throughout the adolescent years. What factors might be responsible for continually shifting self-conceptions and poor self-esteem? We propose, as one important direction for future research, that a combination of maturational and environmental factors undermine self-concept stability for these youths.

Although family structure per se is unrelated to children's self-esteem (Demo & Acock 1988), this is not to say that *repeated* changes in family living arrangements during the teenage years have no effects on adolescent self-esteem or other self-attitudes. Although stability of the familial environment is rarely studied (Dornbusch 1989), recent evidence suggests a strong relationship between multiple changes in family living arrangements and the incidence of personal and social problems in adolescence (Pulkkinnen 1982; Simmons, Burgeson, Carlton-Ford & Blyth 1987).

Typically, children in single-parent, divorced families lose contact with noncustodial parents (Furstenberg, Nord, Peterson & Zill 1983), while children in reconstituted families face other problems (Clingempeel, Brand & Ievoli 1984; Kellam, Ensminger & Turner 1977). The process of reconstitution may involve new siblings, new relatives, new expectations and sanction systems, a new school, new home, and new friends. For adolescents who have been playing a confidant and coparental role, the addition of a stepfather may be a serious threat. These changes and transitions undoubtedly influence the ways in which adolescents view themselves, but a thorough understanding of the short-term and long-term influences of family structure on adolescent self-concept requires investigation of the timing and sequencing of family formation, disruption, and reconstitution.

Another important issue for research on self-concept stability is the possibility of gender differences. Are male or female adolescents more susceptible to situational and environmental fluctuations? Two recent studies suggest that family relations (such as parental support, affection, and parent-adolescent communication) are more important for the self-esteem of boys than girls (Demo et al. 1987; Gecas & Schwalbe 1986). There is also evidence that among gay and lesbian youths, males' self-evaluations are more strongly influenced by family relations than are those of females (Savin-Williams 1990). However, these cross-sectional studies address the issue of stability indirectly (if at all), and the only longitudinal study of which we are aware (Felson & Zielinski 1989) reports that girls are more strongly influenced by parental behavior.

Studying Milwaukee public school students, Simmons and her associates found that white females suffer losses to self-esteem upon entering junior high school, but white males and blacks of both sexes experience increased self-esteem during this transition (Simmons & Blyth 1987; Simmons et al. 1979; Simmons, Brown, Bush & Blyth 1978). Girls who attend seventh grade in schools with kindergarten through eight grade also report increases in self-esteem. Further, early pubertal development is associated with higher self-esteem for boys, but it negatively impacts on girls' self-esteem, especially for girls who date early. The authors suggest that, at least in terms of early adolescent self-esteem, boys respond positively to physiological changes (most of which represent growth and symbolize masculinity), while girls respond negatively to environmental discontinuities. (Also see chapter 3 of this volume, on differences in self-esteem due to school transitions and school organizational patterns.) Rosenberg (1986) argued that, although long-term stability in self-concept over the course of adolescence is similar for boys and girls, girls' self-images exhibit greater moment-to-moment volatility largely due to concern with their changing physical characteristics.

In another recent study, Hirsch and Rapkin (1987) conducted a longitudinal investigation of the transition to junior high school and its impact on the psychological well-being of black and white students. They found that perceived quality of school life plunged regardless of academic competence and that somatic symptoms increased from sixth to seventh grade, suggesting that the transition to a new school organizational structure and the discontinuity in peer groups are indeed stressful. No change in global self-esteem was reported from sixth grade to the middle of seventh grade, with a slight increase by the end of seventh grade. Although there were no sex differences in self-esteem, girls were move vulnerable to depressive and other symptoms over the transition relative to boys.

More important, the consequences of environmental discontinuity and setbacks to self-esteem may be longlasting. In follow-up analyses of the Milwaukee students, Simmons and Blyth (1987) found that, although self-esteem levels rose for the total sample between grades six and ten, the girls who experienced negative changes in self-esteem upon entering junior high school for grade seven were least likely to recover their sense of self-worth by grades nine and ten. There is also evidence that gender differences in depression begin in early adolescence (Sroufe & Rutter 1984).

We are suggesting new avenues of investigation for studying and measuring the changing properties of self-concept over the life course. It is important for researchers to move beyond cross-sectional examinations of differences in global self-esteem by race, gender, family structure, and social class, all of which tend to produce at most very modest differences. We are not the first to call for this redirection in research on self-concept. Rosenberg reached the same conclusion in 1979.

Unfortunately, continued overreliance on classroom administrations of paper-and-pencil measures of global self-esteem among convenience samples has provided little insight into self-stability and inadequate information with which to judge whether other dimensions of self-concept are more or less stable than self-esteem. It is plausible, for example, that survey methods overestimate true stability due to response sets and self-attribution processes. More qualitative methods (perhaps autobiographies or case studies), more dynamic, and more naturalistic measures must be developed to capture self-process and understand the contextual determinants of self-concept.

Specifically, more follow-up, longitudinal studies with extensive nonclinical populations are needed, rather than follow-back investigations with clinical samples that already manifest a negative outcome (such as low self-esteem) primarily because there are more false negative than false positive errors reported in the findings. Follow-back studies reveal that many adults with low self-esteem had poor peer relationships during their adolescence but one cannot thus conclude that all or most youths who have poor peer relations will have low self-regard as adults (Parker & Asher 1987).

Greater attention also needs to be given to developmental considerations. Relations with peers may have differential predictive validity for self-esteem depending, in part, on the age of the individual. For example, the importance of same-sex peers for issues of self-validation during early adolescence indicates that peer status at that point in time has great impact on self-esteem (Savin-Williams & Berndt 1990). But during late adolescence—when one or two friends are likely to be sufficient for fulfilling developmental needs for affiliation, recognition, and intimacy—peer status may become relatively unimportant in predicting self-esteem (Parker & Asher 1987).

In addition, there are important differences among individuals and across subgroups. Improvements in self-esteem are more gradual for some adolescents than for others, and the core of self-concept is more stable across social contexts for some individuals than for others. Sociologists and social psychologists need to devote more attention to understanding and conceptualizing individual differences, while developmental psychologists need to devote more attention to understanding and conceptualizing social structural influences. The task for self-concept researchers—and it is an ambitious but necessary task—is to disentangle the influences of biological processes, social relationships, experiences, events, and accomplishments on particular dimensions of self-concept for different subgroups of adolescents.

REFERENCES

Acock, A. C., and Bengston, V. L. 1980. Socialization and attribution processes: Actual versus perceived similarity among parents and youth. *Journal of Marriage and the Family* 42: 501–515.

Bachman, J. G.; O'Malley, P. M., and Johnston, J. J. 1978. *Youth in transition, Vol. 6. Adolescence to adulthood: A study of change and stability in the lives of young men.* Ann Arbor, Mich.: Institute for Social Research.

Bandura, A. 1964. The stormy decade: Fact or fiction. *Psychology in the Schools* 1: 224–231.

Bence, P. J. 1989. The experience of mood during adolescence. Doctoral dissertation. Ithaca, N.Y.: Cornell University.

Bierman, K. L., and Furman, W. F. 1984. The effects of social skills training and peer involvement on the social adjustment of preadolescents. *Child Development* 55: 151–162.

Bierman, K. L., and McCauley, E. 1987. Children's descriptions of their peer interactions: Useful information for clinical child assessment. *Journal of Clinical Child Psychology* 16:9–18.

Bierman, K. L.; Miller, C. M; and Stabb, S. 1987. Improving the social behavior and peer acceptance of rejected boys: Effects of social skill training with instructions and prohibitions. *Journal of Consulting and Clinical Psychology* 55:194–200.

Block, J. 1971. *Lives through time.* Berkeley, Calif.: Bancroft.

Burke, P. J. 1980. The self: Measurement requirements from an interactionist perspective. *Social Psychology Quarterly* 43: 18–29.

Cauce, A. M. 1986. Social networks and social competence: Exploring the effects of early adolescent friendships. *American Journal of Community Psychology* 14:607–628.

Clingempeel, W. S.; Brand, E.; and Ievoli, R. 1984. Stepparent-stepchild relationships in stepmother and stepfather families: A multimethod study. *Family Relations* 33: 465–473.

Coddington, R. D. 1972. The significance of life events as etiologic factors in the diseases of children: II. A study of a normal population. *Journal of Psychosomatic Research* 16: 205–213.

Coie, J. D., and Dodge, K. A. 1983. Continuities and changes in children's social status: A five-year longitudinal study. *Merrill Palmer Quarterly 29: 261–282.*

Crockett, L.; Losoff, M.; and Petersen, A. C. 1984. Perceptions of the peer group and friendship in early adolescence. *Journal of Early Adolescence* 4:115–118.

Csikszentmihalyi, M., and Larson, R. 1984. *Being adolescent.* New York: Basic Books.

Damon, W., and Hart, D. 1982. The development of self-understanding from infancy through adolescence. *Child Development* 53:841–864.

Demo, D. H. In press. The self-concept over time: Research issues and directions. *Annual Review of Sociology* 18.

―――― . 1985. The measurement of self-esteem: Refining our methods. *Journal of Personality and Social Psychology* 48: 1490–1502.

Demo, D. H., and Acock, A. C. 1988. The impact of divorce on children. *Journal of Marriage and the Family* 50:619–648.

Demo, D. H., and Savin-Williams, R. C. 1983. Early adolescent self-esteem as a function of social class: Rosenberg and Pearlin revisited. *American Journal of Sociology* 88:763–774.

Demo, D. H.; Small, S. A.; and Savin-Williams, R. C. 1987. Family relations and the self-esteem of adolescents and their parents. *Journal of Marriage and the Family* 49:705–715.

Dornbusch, S. M. 1989. The sociology of adolescence. *Annual Review of Sociology* 15:233–259.

East, P. L.; Hess, L. E.; and Lerner, R. M. 1987. Peer social support and adjustment of early adolescent peer groups. *Journal of Early Adolescence* 7:153–163.

Eder, D. 1987. The role of teasing in adolescent peer group culture. Paper presented at the Conference on Ethnographic Approaches to Children's Worlds and Peer Cultures. Trondheim, Norway.

Eder, D., and Sanford, S. 1986. The development and maintenance of interactional norms among early adolescents. In *Sociological studies of child development*, Vol. 1, edited by P. Adler. Greenwich, Conn.: JAI. 283–300.

Elder, G. H., Jr. 1980. Adolescence in historical perspective. In *Handbook of adolescent psychology*, edited by J. Adelson. New York: Wiley. 3–48.

Erikson, E. H. 1950. *Childhood and society*. New York: Norton.

Felson, R. B., and Zielinski, M. A. 1989. Children's self-esteem and parental support. *Journal of Marriage and the Family* 51:727–735.

Feltham, R. F.; Doyle, A. B.; Schwartzman, A. E.; Serbin, L. A.; and Ledingham, J. E. 1985. Friendship in normal and socially deviant children. *Journal of Early Adolescence* 5:371–382.

French, D. C., and Waas, G. A. 1985. Behavior problems of peer-neglected and peer-rejected elementary-age children: Parent and teacher perspectives. *Child Development* 56:246–252.

Freud, A. 1958. Adolescence. *Psychoanalytic Study of the Child* 13:255–278.

Furstenberg, F. F., Jr.; Nord, C. W.; Peterson, J. L.; and Zill, N. 1983. The life course of children of divorce: Marital disruption and parental contact. *American Sociological Review* 48:656–668.

Gecas, V. 1982. The self-concept. *Annual Review of Sociology* 8:1–33.

Gecas, V., and Schwalbe, M. L. 1986. Parental behavior and dimensions of adolescent self-evaluation. *Journal of Marriage and the Family* 48:37–46.

Gove, W. R.; Ortega, S. T; and Style, C. B. 1989. The maturational and role perspectives on aging and self through the adult years: An empirical evaluation. *American Journal of Sociology* 94:1117–1145.

Greene, A. L. 1988. Early adolescents' perceptions of stress. *Journal of Early Adolescence* 8:391–403.

Hall, G. S. 1904. *Adolescence.* New York: Appleton.

Harrison, B. G. 1989. The importance of being Oprah. *The New York Times Magazine.* June 11. 28–30, 46, 48, 54, 130, 134, 136.

Harter, S. 1990. Adolescent self and identity development. In *At the threshold: The developing adolescent,* edited by S. Feldman and G. Elliot. Cambridge, Mass.: Harvard University.

Hartup, W. W. 1983. Peer relations. In *Handbook of child psychology.* Vol. 4. Edited by E. M. Hetherington. New York: Wiley. 103–196.

Hirsch, B. J., and Rapkin, B. D. 1987. The transition to junior high school: A longitudinal study of self-esteem, psychological symptomatology, school life, and social support. *Child Development* 58:1235–1243.

Hoelter, J. 1982. Race differences in selective credulity and self-esteem. *Sociological Quarterly* 23:527–537.

———. 1986. The relationship between specific and global evaluations of self: A comparison of several models. *Social Psychology Quarterly* 49:129–141.

Hollingshead, A. B. 1949. *Elmstown's youth.* New York: Wiley.

Hughes, M., and Demo, D. H. 1989. Self-perceptions of black Americans: Self-esteem and personal efficacy. *American Journal of Sociology* 95:132–1959.

Juhasz, A. 1992. Significant others in self-esteem development: Methods and problems in measurement. In *The self: Definitional and methodological issues,* edited by T. M. Brinthaupt and R. P. Lipka. Albany: State University of New York Press.

Kanner, A. D.; Feldman, S. S.; Weinberger, D. A.; and Ford, M. E. 1987. Uplifts, hassles, and adaptational outcomes in early adolescents. *Journal of Early Adolescence* 7:371–394.

Kaplan, H. B. 1975. *Self-attitudes and deviant behavior.* Pacific Palisades, Calif.: Goodyear.

Kellam, S. G.; Ensminger, M. E.; and Turner, R. J. 1977. Family structure and the mental health of children: Concurrent and longitudinal community-wide studies. *Archives of General Psychiatry* 34:1012–1022.

King, C. A., and Young, R. D. 1981. Peer popularity and peer communication patterns: Hyperactive versus active but normal boys. *Journal of Abnormal Child Psychology* 9:465–482.

Kulik, J. A.; Sledge, P.; and Mahler, H. I. M. 1986. Self-confirmatory attribution, egocentrism, and the perpetuations of self-beliefs. *Journal of Personality and Social Psychology* 37:499–514.

Kurdek, L. A., and Siesky, A. E., Jr. 1980. Effects of divorce on children: The relationship between parent and child perspectives. *Journal of Divorce* 4:85–99.

Ladd, G. W. 1983. Social networks of popular, average, and rejected children in school settings. *Merrill-Palmer Quarterly* 29:282–307.

Lewis, C. E.; Siegel, J. M.; and Lewis, M. A. 1984. Feeling bad: Exploring sources of distress among preadolescent children. *American Journal of Public Health* 74:117–122.

Markus, H., and Kunda, Z. 1986. Stability and malleability of the self-concept. *Journal of Personality and Social Psychology* 51:858–866.

Marsh, H.; Byrne, B.; and Shavelson, R. 1992. A multidimensional, hierarchical self-concept. In *The self: Definitional and methodological issues,* edited by T. M. Brinthaupt and R. P. Lipka. Albany: State University of New York Press.

McCarthy, J. D., and Hoge, D. R. 1982. Analysis of age effects in longitudinal studies of adolescent self-esteem. *Developmental Psychology* 18:372–379.

Mead, G. H. 1934. *Mind, self, and society.* Chicago, Ill.: University of Chicago Press.

Mechanic, D. 1983. Adolescent health and illness behavior: Review of the literature and a new hypothesis for the study of stress. *Journal of Human Stress* 9:4–13.

Montemayor, R. 1983. Parents and adolescents in conflict: All families some of the time and some families most of the time. *Journal of Early Adolescence* 3:83–103.

Montemayor, R., and Eisen, M. 1977. The development of self-conceptions from childhood to adolescence. *Developmental Psychology* 13:314–319.

Mortimer, J. T.; Finch, M. D.; and Kumka, D. 1982. Persistence and change in development: The multidimensional self-concept. In *Life-span development and behavior.* Vol. 4. Edited by P. Baltes and O. G. Brim, Jr. New York: Academic Press. 263–313.

Newcombe, M. D.; Huba, G. J.; and Bentler, P. M. 1981. A multidimensional assessment of stressful life events among adolescents: Derivation and correlates. *Journal of Health and Social Behavior* 22:400–415.

O'Brien, S. F., and Bierman, K. L. 1988. Conceptions and perceived influence of peer groups: Interviews with preadolescents and adolescents. *Child Development* 59:1360–1365.

Offer, D., and Offer, J. B. 1975. *From teenage to young manhood.* New York: Basic.

Olweus, D. 1978. *Aggression in the schools: Bullies and whipping boys.* Washington, D.C.: Hemisphere.

———. 1987. Bully/victim problems among school children in Scandanavia. In *Psykologprofesjonen mot ar 2000,* edited by J. P. Myklebust & R. Ommundsen. Oslo: Universitetsforlaget. 345–413.

O'Malley, P. M., and Bachman, J. G. 1983. Self-esteem: Change and stability between ages 13 and 23. *Developmental Psychology* 19:256–268.

Otto, L. B. 1988. America's youth: A changing profile. *Family Relations* 37:385–391.

Parker, J. G., and Asher, S. R. 1987. Peer relations and later personal adjustment: Are low-accepted children at risk? *Psychological Bulletin* 102:357–389.

Perry, D. G.; Kusel, S. J.; and Perry, L. C. 1988. Victims of peer aggression. *Developmental Psychology* 24:807–814.

Pulkkinen, L. 1982. Self-control and continuity from childhood to late adolescence. In *Life span development and behavior,* edited by P. B. Baltes and O. G. Brim, Jr. New York: Academic Press.

Rosenberg, M. 1979. *Conceiving the self.* New York: Basic Books.

———. 1986. Self-concept from middle childhood through adolescence. In *Psychological perspectives on the self,* Vol. 3, edited by J. Suls and A. G. Greenwald. Hillsdale, N.J.: Lawrence Erlbaum Associates. 107–136.

Rutter, M. 1980. *Changing youth in a changing society.* Cambridge, Mass.: Harvard University Press.

Rutter, M. 1987. Psychosocial resilience and protective mechanisms. *American Journal of Orthopsychiatry* 57:316-331.

Savin-Williams, R. C. 1987. *Adolescence: An ethological perspective.* New York: Springer-Verlag.

──────. 1990. *Gay and lesbian youth: Expressions of identity.* Washington, D.C.: Hemisphere.

Savin-Williams, R. C., and Berndt, T. J. 1990. Friendships and peer relations during adolescence. In *At the threshold: The developing adolescent,* edited by S. S. Feldman and G. R. Elliot. Cambridge, Mass.: Harvard University Press.

Savin-Williams, R. C., and Demo, D. H. 1983. Situational and transitational determinants of adolescent self-feelings. *Journal of Personality and Social Psychology* 44:824–833.

──────. 1984. Developmental change and stability in adolescent self-concept. *Developmental Psychology* 20:1100–1110.

Savin-Williams, R. C., and Fuligni, A. J. In preparation. The stress of teasing—or is it ridicule?—during adolescence. Unpublished manuscript. Department of Human Development and Family Studies. Ithaca, N.Y.: Cornell University.

Schilling, S., and Savin-Williams, R. C. 1985. The assessment of adolescent self-esteem stability: A new application of the beeper technology and the Rasch measurement model. Paper presented at the biennial meetings of the Society for Research in Child Development. Toronto, Canada.

Schofield, J. W. 1982. *Black and white in school: Trust, tension, or tolerance?* New York: Praeger.

Serafica, F. C., and Blyth, D. A. 1985. Continuities and changes in the study of friendship and peer groups during early adolescence. *Journal of Early Adolescence* 5:267–283.

Sherif, M., and Sherif, C. W. 1964. *Exploration into conformity and deviation of adolescents.* New York: Harper and Row.

Simmons, R. G., and Blyth, D. A. 1987. *Moving into adolescence: The impact of pubertal change and school context.* New York: Aldine de Gruyter.

Simmons, R. G.; Blyth, D. A.; Van Cleave, E. F.; and Bush, D. M. 1979. Entry into early adolescence: The impact of school structure, puberty, and early dating on self-esteem. *American Sociological Review* 38:553–568.

Simmons, R. G.; Brown, L.; Bush, D. M.; and Blyth, D. 1978. Self-esteem and achievement of black and white adolescents. *Social Problems* 26:86–96.

Simmons, R. G.; Burgeson, R.; Carlton-Ford, S.; and Blyth, D. A. 1987. The impact of cumulative change in early adolescence. *Child Development* 58:1220–1234.

Snyder, M., and Gangestad, S. 1982. Choosing social situations: Two investigations of self-monitoring processes. *Journal of Personality and Social Psychology* 43:123–135.

Sroufe, L. A., and Rutter, M. 1984. The domain of developmental psychopathology. *Child Development* 55:17–29.

Sullivan, H. S. 1953. *The interpersonal theory of psychiatry.* New York: Norton.

Swann, W. B., Jr. 1983. Self-verification: Bringing social reality into harmony with the self. In *Psychological perspectives on the self.* Vol. 2. Edited by J. Suls and A. G. Greenwald. Hillsdale, N.J.: Lawrence Erlbaum Associates. 33–66.

Tesser, A., and Campbell, J. 1983. Self-definition and self-evaluation maintenance. In *Psychological perspectives on the self.* Vol. 2. Edited by J. Suls and A. G. Greenwald. Hillsdale, N.J.: Lawrence Erlbaum Associates. 1–31.

PART III: ADULTHOOD AND OLD AGE

5

Variations in Self-esteem in Daily Life: Methodological and Developmental Issues

The purpose of this chapter will be to report several recent research findings about fluctuations in the current ongoing self-esteem of a group of women as they went about their daily lives. Such findings have implications for both methodological and developmental issues. Three major points will be discussed: (1) that current ongoing self-esteem was shown to fluctuate significantly over the daily lives of a group of American women; (2) that these fluctuations were seen over a number of different types of contexts and over different aspects or characteristics of contexts; and (3) that current ongoing self-esteem must be seen as different from other types of self-esteem, such as overall generalized self-esteem.

Previously, self-esteem has been conceptualized as an overall stable and evaluative disposition toward self, that is believed to affect behavior over time and contexts (Wylie 1979). Wylie concluded that research on self-esteem was disappointing and measurement of self-esteem had not been convincingly demonstrated. She thought that self-esteem had been approached too simplistically and suggested revising theories and improving measurements. In the following study, self-esteem was conceptualized as something other than *overall self-esteem* and measured with a relatively new methodological procedure.

In terms of developmental research, conceptualizing self-esteem as an overall stable and evaluative disposition toward self made it difficult to conceptualize or measure change in self-esteem either as people developed or in response to particular life events. In terms of methodology, researchers found that different measures of overall generalized self-esteem correlated only moderately with each other (Fiske 1971), raising two questions. Were we adequately measuring self-esteem? Was there something wrong with the idea that there were stable underlying traits or dimensions that affected behavior over time and contexts (D'Andrade 1965; Fiske 1971, 1978; Mischel 1968; Shweder 1975, 1982; Shweder & D'Andrade 1979, 1980)?

Some authors have proposed that self-concept, self-evaluation, and self-esteem are neither overall dimensions nor stable over time or situations. Self-esteem has been looked at in different roles, such as school self-esteem (Wylie 1979) and parental competence (Gibaud-Wallston & Wandersman 1978) and studied in different contexts such as in class, with family, friends, the opposite sex, and adults (Gecas 1971, 1972; Jaquish & Savin-Williams 1981; Savin-Williams & Demo 1983).

Researchers have thought of self-esteem as multidimensional and looked for different types or aspects of self-esteem, such as self-power and self-worth (Gecas 1971, 1972, 1982); experienced and presented self-esteem (Demo 1985. Also see chapter 4 of this volume.); inner and outer self-esteem (Franks & Marolla 1976; Van Tuinen & Ramanaiah 1979); general and academic self-esteem (Marsh, Byrne & Shavelson 1992; Shavelson & Bolus 1982); and self-regard and confidence in social, school, and physical ability (Fleming & Courtney 1984).

There have also been indications of significant fluctuations in (1) self-esteem measured in experimental settings (Fierro 1986; Gergen 1968, 1971, 1977; Morse & Gergen 1970); (2) adolescent self-esteem in daily life (Jaquish & Savin-Williams 1981; Savin-Williams & Demo 1983); and (3) maternal self-esteem during and after pregnancy (Leifer 1980). The efforts to conceptualize and measure self-esteem in more limited roles and contexts and to demonstrate that self-esteem is multidimensional have shown that self-esteem is different in different contexts and may fluctuate over contexts. Thus, self-evaluation may be a complex ongoing process.

In terms of development, the view that self-evaluation may be a complex ongoing process and that self-esteem may fluctuate allows us to conceptualize development of self-esteem over time, in different areas at different points in the life cycle, and in response to different life experiences. For example, it allows us to conceptualize the possible formation of a core sense of self-esteem early in life that is added to as we mature in areas such as school, work, marriage, and parenthood. It also allows us to understand that self-esteem may be affected by our ongoing experiences and to search for specific factors that may be related to changes in self-esteem.

In terms of methodology, it means that researchers are faced with much more complex questions. What is the relationship between different aspects of types of self-esteem and what factors affect the different types of self-esteem? The relationship between self-esteem in different contexts or different aspects of self-esteem remains to be seen (Briggs & Cheek 1986).

The purpose of the following study was to determine if self-esteem does fluctuate over daily life. Working mothers were chosen for two reasons. First, Patterson (1980) had found, when studying behavioral reinforcement in interactions between mothers and normal children and mothers and aggressive children with behavior problems, that even mothers of normal children were subject to high rates of aversive events when interacting with their children (such as whining, crying, hitting, and so on).

He suggested that high rates of aversive events and lack of positive affirmation as a person or mother could lead to dissatisfaction, stress, and lower self-esteem. His thoughts lead to the question of whether self-esteem was less when mothers were with their children than when they were not. (See Wells 1988a for further discussion of this question.)

Second, selecting working mothers made it possible to look for fluctuations in self-esteem beyond different contexts because these women had both work and family responsibilities. Thus, the primary focus of the study was to see if there were fluctuations in self-esteem during daily life, and then to illuminate the contexts in working mothers' lives in which these fluctuations occur.

DESCRIPTION OF THE STUDY

Respondents

Using a relatively new procedure to assess self-esteem, the Experience Sampling Method (ESM) (Csikszentmihalyi & Larson 1987; Hormuth 1986; Larson & Csikszentmihalyi 1983), a study was done to look for significant variations in self-esteem as a group of American working mothers went about their daily lives. A relatively homogeneous group was sought since self-esteem has been asserted to be related to race, socioeconomic status (SES), intact versus broken homes, and normal versus disadvantaged children (Cummings, Bayley & Rie 1966; Wylie 1979). Wylie, however, reported contradictory findings for race and SES.

Thus, participants were forty-nine middle-class Caucasian women who worked at least part-time and who came from intact families with at least two normal children between the ages of two and fourteen. Experienced mothers—those who had already learned to be mothers—and mothers whose children were between two and fourteen were selected to reduce the possibility that women would be dealing with changing self-views due to life-cycle changes, such as having a new baby or children leaving home.

Women lived in stable communities in a large midwestern American city and came from a variety of religious backgrounds. Ages ranged from twenty-five to forty-five with a mean of thirty-five years. This was an educated group: 10 percent had Ph.D. or M.D. degrees, 33 percent had done graduate work, 47 percent had either graduated college or done college work, and 10 percent were high school graduates. Hollingshead's index of social position (1957) was used to rate socioeconomic status (SES) for both women and their husbands. These were averaged to produce family SES ratings that ranged from lower-middle- to upper-middle-class. Average family income the previous year had been $35,000.

Women's occupations varied from being doctors, lawyers, artists, and teachers to babysitting and typing in their homes. Thirty-five percent worked full time, 40 percent half-time, and 25 percent part-time. Most expressed a desire to work. Thus, the findings describe women who choose to work and have children, and therefore have both work and family responsibility (Wells 1986, 1988a, 1988b; Wells & Csikszentmihalyi 1989).

The ESM

The ESM (Csikszentmihalyi & Larson 1987; Csikszentmihalyi, Larson, & Prescott 1977; Hormuth 1986; Larson & Csikszentmihalyi 1983) was used to collect samples of women's experiences as they went about their daily lives. Women carried pagers and booklets of seventy one-page questionnaires (ESM forms). In response to randomly scheduled signals between 8:00 a.m. and 10:00 p.m, women filled out one form approximately four or five times a day for two weeks. (The ESM was modified when a pilot study showed that working mothers' schedules could not tolerate being signalled seven to eight times a day.)

Women were told that this was a study of usual experience, and the researcher stressed the importance of responding immediately and accurately to the signal. Of the 3,136 total signals sent, 71 percent were responded to within five minutes and 73 percent (2,287) within thirty minutes. Since current experience was being studied, only data from forms answered within thirty minutes were included in data analysis (n = 2,287). The number of forms filled out per woman ranged from twenty-five to sixty with a mean of forty-seven.

In the debriefing portion of the second home visit, most women reported that they enjoyed participation in the study. They stated that they became accustomed to the pager very quickly, and filling out the forms took only a few minutes. They confirmed that being paged four to five times a day had been manageable. Women also reported being interested in seeing that their moods fluctuated. Many women had enthusiastically discussed their lives and what helped them to feel better about themselves. They reported the experience of talking about themselves and carrying the pager was a positive one.

The Current Ongoing Self-esteem Score

To form a basis for measuring self-esteem on the ESM, each time women were signalled they were asked about two core aspects of experience: (1) how good they felt about themselves, and (2) how satisfied they were with how they were doing. In addition, questions were asked about factors (from self-esteem theory and research) thought to be related to self-esteem (such as, anxiety, control of the situation, living up to expectations of self and other important people). The study also explored other factors such as moods (such as happy), activation levels (for example, alert), motivations (such as, wish to be doing the task), and estimations of skill.

To determine which aspects of experience were related to the two core aspects, women's average levels of each aspect of experience queried were then correlated. A cluster of five interrelated aspects appeared, which comprised women's self-esteem on a moment-to-moment basis: (1) how good they felt about themselves; (2) how satisfied they were with how they were doing; (3) how much in control of the situation they felt; (4) how much they were living up to their expectations of themselves; and (5) how well they were fulfilling the expectations of important others.

The latter three aspects were highly correlated, with the two core aspects initially designed to measure self-esteem (average

$r(49) = .77, p < .0001$. In addition, the next highest correlation of any other item with this cluster was .68 or less.

Adding women's scores on the five correlated items provided a measure of current ongoing self-esteem each time women were signalled. An estimate of overall average current ongoing self-esteem was found by averaging the current ongoing self-esteem scores over all of each woman's forms over the two-week period of data collection.

The average correlation between items that made up this score was .77, $p < .0001$, Cronbach's alpha = .94. As an estimate of test-retest reliability, the correlation between women's average current ongoing self-esteem scores for the first half of the data collection period with their average scores for the second half of the data collection period was .86, $p < .0001$.

Women's responses to this ESM measure of current ongoing self-esteem were compared to their responses to two one-time overall generalized measures of self-esteem: Rosenberg's ten item Self-Esteem Scale (SES) (1965, 1979); and Bills, Vance and McLean's forty-nine item Index of Adjustment and Values (IAV) (1951).

The IAV produces two scores—IAV-self and IAV-accept—which describe how much a person likes who he or she is. Their responses were also compared to one one-time generalized measure of self-esteem limited to a more specific role, that of being a parent, under Gibaud-Wallston's and Wandersman's seventeen item Parent Competence Scale (PCS) (1978).

The PCS has two subscales describing parents' reports of their skills as parents (PCS-skill), and their value of parenthood and comfort in the role (PCS-value).

FINDINGS

Relationship of Current ongoing Self-Esteem to Other Self-esteem Measures

According to Fiske's ideas in 1971, the one-time generalized measures of self-esteem and the ESM measure of current ongoing self-esteem are different types of procedures and should produce different information. Results suggest that, although both types of procedures did give a view of self-esteem, the views differed and cannot be considered to be interchangeable (Wells 1988a). Results (see table 5.1) showed that women's overall average levels of current ongoing self-esteem on the ESM (ESM-SE(average)) were moderately related

Table 5.1

Correlations of ESM Self-esteem scores with generalized self-esteem measures

Measure	ESM-SE (average)	ESM-RBS (average)	SES	PCS	PCS-skill	PCS-value	IAV-self	IAV-accept
ESM-SE (average)	—	.72***	.42***	.34*	.13	.49***	.50***	.30*
ESM-RBS (average)		—	.62***	.26	.14	.35*	.55***	.30*
SES			—	.28*	.21	.40**	.55***	.30*
PCS				—	.86***	.83***	.22	.32*
PCS-skill					—	.50***	.22	.27
PCS-value						—	.25	.30*
IAV-self							—	.50***
IAV-accept								

Note: $N = 49$. ESM = Experience sampling method. SE = self-esteem. SES = the Rosenberg Self-Esteem Scale. PCS = parent competence. IAV = index of adjustment and values. RBS = self-esteem score derived from items from the SES placed on the ESM forms. *From:* Wells, A. J. 1988. Variations in mothers' self-esteem in daily life. *Journal of Personality and Social Psychology* 55:661–668. (Copyright 1988 by the American Psychological Association. Used by permission of the publisher.)

*p < .05
**p < .01
***p < .0005.

to their scores on the SES, IAV, and the PCS. The correlations ranged from a nonsignificant .13 to a significant .55 ($p < .0001$) with a mean of .36, and were within the range of those usually found between tests of similar constructs (.35 to .50, see Fiske 1971). This suggested that the ESM procedure did yield overlapping but somewhat different information than did the generalized procedures.

Nine of the Rosenberg SES items had appeared on both the ESM forms and on the Rosenberg SES generalized rating procedure. If the two types of procedures were measuring the same information, we would expect the correlation between the total scores and the correlations between the same items on the two procedures to be consistently high and near the level allowed by the reliability of the scales. However, this was not the case.

Reliability using Cronbach's alpha for the Rosenberg items on the ESM was .95, and, for the SES, it was .77 with a mean of .86. Correlations between SES items 2 to 10 on the two procedures ($n = 49$) were, respectively: (2) .42 , $p < .01$; (3) .44, $p < .01$; (4) .34, $p < .05$; (5) .30 , $p < .05$; (6) .24, n.s.; (7) .38, $p < .05$; (8) .74, $p < .0001$; (9) .64, $p < .0005$; and (10) .29, n.s. The mean was .42.

The correlation between women's total SES scores and their total scores on the Rosenberg items on the ESM (ESM-RBS(average)) was .62, $p < .001$. Given the .62 correlation, one procedure accounted for only 38 percent of the variance of the other. This indicated that, although the two procedures tapped similar information, they yielded considerably different information and cannot be considered interchangeable. These data suggest that current ongoing self-esteem needs to be considered different from generalized self-esteem.

Fluctuations in Current Ongoing Self-esteem

Current ongoing self-esteem did fluctuate significantly as the women went about their daily lives. Fluctuations in self-esteem were first looked at over two types of contexts: what women were doing when signalled, and whom they were with. Women's primary activities were divided into five categories: primarily involved in work, home maintenance, self-care, child care, and leisure interactions. Whom women were with was divided into four categories: alone, with adults only, with both children and adults, and with children only.

Using multivariate analysis of covariance for repeated measures, results showed that women had significantly higher self-esteem when they reported they were primarily engaged in work and leisure-interactions and significantly lower self-esteem when engaged in home maintenance and child care (Wells 1986). In terms of whom they were with, women had significantly higher self-esteem when with adults only than with children and adults or with children only (Wells 1988a). However, these results do not prove that it is home maintenance, child care, or children that causes the drops in self-esteem. They only point to the contexts in which this happens.

It is possible that, as Patterson (1980) suggested, the drops in self-esteem are related to negative reinforcement from children. However, the drops could also be related to women feeling more stress during these times, experiencing more responsibility, or feeling that they are not utilizing their skill level. (See the following section on competence.) Much more work needs to be done to show what specifically it is within these contexts that causes the drops in self-esteem.

Stability in Current Ongoing Self-esteem

Results also showed stability in current ongoing self-esteem. Although women's ongoing self-esteem fluctuated over contexts, their overall average levels of current ongoing self-esteem remained relatively stable over the two-week period of data collection. As noted earlier, test-retest reliability of the current ongoing self-esteem scores over the two week period of data collection was $r = .86$ (Wells 1988a).

Such results suggest that overall average levels of current ongoing self-esteem may be relatively stable, even though it may be necessary to measure self-esteem repeatedly to find the stability. Such stability could be interpreted as a measure of general or core self-esteem or a "trait-like" phenomenon (Buss 1986, 1989; Shavelson & Bolus 1982). However, only further research can show whether this stability holds over the longer periods of time which would be necessary to suggest a trait or core self-esteem interpretation.

Current Ongoing Self-esteem and Aspects
of the Interpersonal Context

In the next set of analyses, self-esteem was predicted by different aspects in different contexts. Self-esteem has long been thought to be related to interpersonal experience (Cooley 1902; Mead 1934).

However, several authors have suggested that different dimensions may be used to evaluate self in different contexts. (Breckler & Greenwald 1986; Brinthaupt 1986; Gecas 1971, 1972; Higgins, Strauman & Klein 1986; Markus & Nurius 1986; McGuire & Padawer-Singer 1976).

Using the contexts of "with children" and "with adults," the question was asked whether four aspects of the interpersonal context were more strongly predictive of women's current ongoing self-esteem in one context than in another. The aspects explored were, was this a time when: (1) you did not feel tension and conflict between you and others present; (2) you were likely to take the initiative; (3) your goals were compatible with others present; and (4) feelings and emotions of others were more important than getting the task done. Findings that different aspects of context were more strongly predictive of self-esteem in one context than in another would support a view of self-evaluation as a complex, ongoing process.

Using multiple regression analysis, results showed that, when women were with children only, all four of the interpersonal variables tested were important to feeling positive about themselves (see Table 5.2). But, when women were with adults only, only three of the interpersonal variables tested were important to feeling positive about the self. Emotions as being more important than the task was unimportant. Also, feeling that emotions were more important than getting the task done, was more important to a positive self-evaluation when with children (difference in beta weights F $(1,88) = 4.12$, $p < .04$), whereas perceiving one's goals as compatible with others was more important to a positive self-evaluation when with adults (difference in beta weights F $(1,88) = 5.82$, $p<.01$).

In addition, a similar analysis was done with the five items that make up the ESM current ongoing self-esteem score. Results showed that one item—living up to expectations of others—was a significantly more important predictor of self-esteem when with children than with adults (difference in beta weights F $(1,94) = 5.06$, $p<.02$).

Thus, two of the interpersonal variables and one variable that makes up the current ongoing self-esteem score were not related to self-esteem in the same way within the two contexts. Not only do we acquire a clearer view of what factors within the two contexts are likely to be important to self-esteem, but also we acquire a clearer view of what the self-evaluative process may be like. These findings support a view of self-evaluation as a complex process in

Table 5.2

Multiple Regression Analysis of Relationship between Self-esteem and Interpersonal Aspects of Situation within Contexts of Adults Only and Children Only

Interpersonal variables[a]	Equation 1 With adults only[b]		Equation 2 With children only[b]		Difference in beta weights[c]	
	t ratio	p	t ratio	p	F ratio	p
Feelings and emotions important.	0.63	.53	2.60	.01	4.12	.04
Goals compatible.	5.41	.0001	2.37	.02	5.82	.01
Likely to take initiative.	3.99	.0002	3.99	.0002	0.16	.68
Did not feel tension and conflict with others.	2.48	.02	2.48	.02	0.03	.85

Note: Correlation across models = .58; R^2 for system = .53, df = 90. *From:* Wells, A. J. 1988. Variations in mothers' self-esteem in daily life. *Journal of Personality and Social Psychology* 55:661–668. (Copyright 1988 by the American Psychological Association. Used by permission of the publisher.)

[a]Presented in the direction responses were scored.

[b]df = 90.

[c]df = 1,88.

which certain aspects of experience may become more important to self-evaluation in one context than in another (Wells 1988a).

Current ongoing Self-esteem and Competence

Results also suggest that current ongoing self-esteem is likely to be related to competence. Two aspects of contexts were evaluated which were thought to be related to "flow experiences," how challenging women felt their activities were, and how much skill they thought they were using. Csikszentmihalyi and associates (Csikszentmihalyi 1975, 1982; Csikszentmihalyi & Csikszentmihalyi, 1988) have identified a configuration of experience called *flow* or *optimal experience* characterized by involvement and concentration, which appears to be sought out and intensely enjoyed. These *optimal* or *flow* experiences were described as times when (1) people thought their skills were equal to the challenges of the activity; (2) they were intensely involved in the activity; (3) goals of the activity and means to reach them were clear; (4) feedback was immediate and unambiguous; (5) attention was focused on the activity; (6) there was loss of self-consciousness; and (7) action and awareness seemed to merge.

Csikszentmihalyi and Graef (1980) suggested that self-esteem could be related to flow experiences. To explore this idea, women's experiences were placed into four different contexts defined by the relation of how challenging they reported their present activity to be and how much skill they thought they were using.[1] The four contexts were: (1) when the challenge of the activity in which the women were involved was higher than the skills they were using (C/S category 1); (2) when the challenge of their activity and the skills they were using were approximately equal, and both were above a woman's average challenge and skill level (the expected flow context) (C/S category 2); (3) when the skills they were using were higher than the challenge of their activity (C/S category 3); and (4) when the challenge of the activity and the skills they were using were about equal but both were below a woman's average challenge and skill level (C/S category 4) (Wells 1988b; Wells & Csikszentmihalyi 1989).

Results using multivariate analysis of covariance for repeated measures (see figure 5.1) showed that self-esteem was highest when challenges were approximately equal to skills being used and both were above a woman's average (the flow context, C/S category 2). Self-esteem was the lowest when challenges were about equal to

Figure 5.1
Multivariate Analysis of Covariance for Repeated Measures: Self-esteem
Scores of Women within Challenge/Skill Categories by Occupation

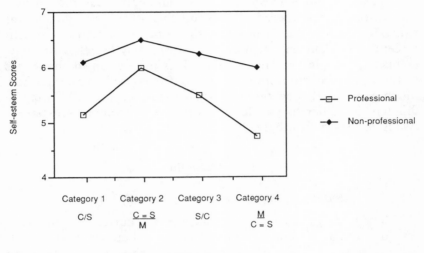

Challenge/Skill Category

skills being used but both were below a woman's average (C/S category 4) (Wells 1988b).

Analysis also showed that women who worked full-time and women who had professional jobs had significantly lower average current ongoing self-esteem than did women who worked part-time and women with non-professional jobs.[2] See figure 5.1 for information on professional level.

Specifically, the self-esteem of full-time working women and professional women was significantly lower than was the self-esteem of part-time working women and nonprofessional women in all of the challenge/skill contexts except flow (C/S category 2). It was only in the flow context (that is, the context in which challenge and skill were about equal and both were above average) that the self-esteem of full-time working women and professional women went up to levels that part-time working women and nonprofessional women were already experiencing. One clue as to why this might have been the case was that full-time working women and professional women reported they were using significantly less skills than did part-time working women and nonprofessional women in all of the challenge/skill contexts except in flow. It was only in the flow condition that full-time working women and professional women felt that they were using as much of their skills as did the part-time working women and nonprofessional women.

These results showed that how challenging was the activity that a woman experienced and how much skill she thought she was using were important aspects of the context in relation to self-esteem. Thus, current ongoing self-esteem may be related to how competent people experience themselves in relation to challenges in their everyday environments. Also, it may be the case that how much people feel they are using their capacities (or skills) may be different for different people and that this may affect self-esteem (Wells & Csikszentmihalyi 1989).

DISCUSSION

Understanding Current Ongoing Self-esteem

The findings described here suggest that current ongoing self-esteem must be considered differently from overall generalized self-esteem. How can we understand what current ongoing self-esteem may be measuring? And how might it differ from overall generalized self-esteem? In order to deal with these questions, we may need to ask not only how measures of self-esteem relate to each other, but also how they relate to self-concept. In order to deal with these questions I had to first find a working definition of self-concept.

Developing a View of Self-concept. Philosophers, theoreticians, and researchers have struggled with a definition of self and self-concept for centuries (Baumeister 1987; Schlenker 1985). From the time of William James (1890–1950) people have struggled with how to think about the self. James suggested we must deal with both the self as known (the content of self-concept) and the self as knower (the process of how self-concept is developed and altered, and how it functions to affect a person's perception, cognition, memory, emotional reactions, and behavior). Recent work in social cognition (Schlenker 1985) has suggested that we think of self-concept as a schema that contains both knowledge about the self (the content) and the rules for activating and processing that knowledge. In the words of Greenwald and Partkanis (1984), we can think of the self-concept as both the data that is handled by a computer program, and as the program that loads, codes, organizes, stores, and manipulates the data, and then produces the output or knowledge about the self that people use in various other aspects of their functioning. When studying self-concept, one can focus upon either the content or the rules governing the content. However, for a complete picture researchers will have to learn about both.

There have been numerous proposals of ways in which to categorize the content of self-concept. I will present one view in order to provide a background for thinking about self-esteem. The present view has been taken largely from the ideas of Higgins and associates (Higgins 1987; Higgins, Klein & Strauman 1985; Higgins, Strauman & Klein 1986) and expanded to include ideas about core aspects of self-concept and working versions of self-concept (Markus & Nurius 1986).

First, it seems necessary to keep in mind that people do vary in how much they focus upon self and how much they elaborate a conscious self-concept (Buss 1989). With this qualification in mind and using ideas from social cognition (Schlenker 1985), I began by thinking of the *self-concept* as a series of interrelated schemata about self, some conscious and some not so conscious, that are learned throughout life. One would also hypothesize as Markus and associates have proposed that not all of these schemata may be active at any one point in time (Cantor, Markus, Niedenthal & Nurius 1986; Markus & Nurius 1986, 1987; Markus & Wurf 1987). It seems likely that combinations of these schemata, or parts of them, may be called into service at particular moments to form a working view of self. This working view of self would likely depend upon a person's context and that person's construction or interpretation of the context—including what the person believes and feels may be expected of him or her at that particular moment—as well as the person's internal state and motivation.

Overall, these self-schemata can be hypothesized to have both core and role aspects. Core aspects can be thought of as the more or less generalized beliefs and conclusions about self. These generalized beliefs and conclusions about self may contain both affective and cognitive information and be more or less independent of contextural cues that might activate them (such as, "I'm a failure," "I'm good with people," or "When I'm with women, I'm nervous and can't do anything right.")

Role aspects can be thought of as the more social categories and characteristics by which people classify self (such as, gender, race, family positions, or occupation) as well as the categories and characteristics of social scripts that people might think of themselves as performing (for example, patron at an opera, or person going out to dinner). It is likely that both core and role aspects, learned throughout life, are used both to define self and to evaluate self.

Among the theorists who have focused upon what one might characterize as core aspects of self are psychoanalytic, psychodynamic, cognitive, and personality theorists. For example, theorists such as Basch (1988) and Stern (1985) have pointed out that the affective basis for beliefs and conclusions about self may get laid down before the child has the capacity to conceptualize self as an entity or to think about self in words. Stern (1985) suggested that affective appraisals ("Does it feel good or bad, calming or upsetting?") made in relation to self may be more primitive than are cognitive appraisals—that is, these may be potentially independent of and developmentally prior to the cognitive appraising process. Basch (1988) suggested that early affective experience gets preserved in affective memory and this forms the basis for what will become character or personality.

Early affective memories related to self may later be put into words after children acquire the capacity for verbal communication. One example of this may be when a client tells a therapist, "I feel as if I can't take care of myself. Yes, I know I hold a job, but I'm always afraid I'll fail at looking after me and my family."

Cognitive theorists such as Beck and associates, have focused upon the overgeneralizations about self and self in relation to the world, that can be learned through early experience, and that continue to affect functioning throughout life (Beck 1967, 1976; Beck, Rush, Shaw & Emery 1979). Personality theorists have suggested that self-concept and self-esteem be looked at as underlying, stable, and relatively enduring traits or tendencies that are laid down by early experience and continue to shape people's experience and behavior throughout life (Wylie 1979).

Among the theorists who have focused upon the role aspects of self-concept are the symbolic interactionists and the self-presentation theorists. Symbolic interactionists, such as Cooley (1902) and Mead (1934), analyzed the more social aspects of self-concept. The symbolic interactionists have pointed out that both the self and the world are ambiguous until defined by participants who actively construct reality by using socially organized systems of knowledge. These socially organized systems of knowledge define the contexts, participants, participants' roles, and scripts of expected behavior. Self is seen as an internal cognitive representation of a set of public characteristics and roles which are used in interaction with others. These roles are viewed as having been learned from years of socialization, and it is assumed that they are constantly defined, constructed, and negotiated in interactions with others (Schlenker 1985).

Theorists such as Jones (1964) and Goffman (1959) have focused upon aspects of self that are presented to others. Jones and associates (Jones 1964; Jones & Pittman 1982) have hypothesized that people develop strategic presentations of self which are activated by various motives such as, ingratiation, power, intimidation, or gaining help (Schlenker 1985). The view of self that is presented to another should therefore be determined in part by whatever motive is operative at a particular moment in time, for example, whether a person wishes to be helped versus wishing to intimidate another. Thus, theorists such as Jones have suggested that the role or script that may be activated (or the view of self that is presented) may be different given a person's motivation.

In discussing their socioanalytic theory, Hogan, Jones, and Cheek (1985) have suggested that we should think of self-concept in terms of both core and role aspects. They propose that there is a stable core of personality made up of stable structures that are both biological and social in origin. They suggest that humans are motivated by two basic needs—the need for acceptance and approval, and the need for power, status, and control. They believe that self-concept is the result of the process of identity negotiations that begin at birth and result in a relatively stable internal structure by adulthood. For these authors, role playing is the arena in which the process of identity negotiations are carried out. The authors do not believe that roles determine the self-concept but that a person has some negotiating room as to what roles he or she identifies with.

In discussing their self-discrepancy theory Higgins and associates suggest that self-concept be divided into three domains: the actual, the ideal, and the ought self-concepts. (Higgins 1987; Higgins et al. 1985, 1986). The actual self is thought to be the representations of attributes that people think they actually possess. The ideal self is thought to be the representations of attributes that people would like to possess—that is, their aspirations, hopes, and goals. The ought self is thought to be the representations of attributes that people think they should or ought to possess—that is, the rules they should follow, and the prescribed duties and obligations they should attend to which carry a sense of duty or moral obligation.

These authors also propose that there are different self-concepts related to different viewpoints of the self. Individuals can have a self-concept related to either their own point of view or to the viewpoint of another person (usually a significant other) or a group in their lives. Thus, one can have self-concepts related to how one views one's actual, ideal, and ought self, as well as how one believes others view one's actual, ideal, or ought self. Further, discrepancy between any two self-concepts induces various states of discomfort.

Markus and associates have focused upon the likelihood that not all self knowledge will be available for use at any one point in time. (Cantor et al. 1986; Markus & Nurius 1986, 1987; Markus & Wurf 1987). They propose that there is a working self-concept which is the set of self-concepts that are presently active in thought and memory. These can be thought of as being a shifting array that changes with variation in internal states and social circumstances. This collection of self-conceptions and self-images can include good, bad, hoped for, feared, not-me, ideal, ought, past, and future selves. They can vary in their degree of affective, cognitive, and behavioral elaboration and can evoke different affective and evaluative responses. Some concepts of self may be accessible most of the time, and others may be influenced by a person's prevailing affective or motivational state or by present social circumstances (Markus & Nurius 1986).

Now to summarize, I began to think of *self concept* as a series of interrelated schemata about self—some conscious and some not so conscious—that could be categorized according to a scheme such as Higgins and associates have proposed actual, ideal and ought self-concepts (Higgins 1987; Higgins et al. 1985, 1986). Further, I thought it is possible that discrepancies between any two of these self-concepts might induce not only states of discomfort as Higgins and associates have shown, but also might lower self-esteem. Also, as Markus and associates proposed, it seems likely that only some of a person's self schemata would be operative at any point in time (the working self-concept), and that what is operative may depend upon present affective and/or motivational states and actual and/or constructed contexts (Cantor et al. 1986; Markus & Nurius 1986, 1987; Markus & Wurf 1987).

We can also think of the different self-concepts, as well as the working self-concepts, as made up of both core and role aspects. Some core or role aspects may be operative much of the time (such as, "I'm a capable man"), coloring whatever roles or scripts are operative at a particular time (as in "I'm a capable banker and husband dining out with my wife and friends"). Other core and role aspects may be operative only in certain contexts (for example, "when I'm with my mother-in-law, I begin to feel as if I don't belong and that she thinks I'm not capable of looking after her son"). (See figure 5.2.)

Relating Self-concept and Self-esteem. The theories already presented suggest that the self-concept may be a complicated and perhaps varying set of schemata containing a variety of core and role aspects. It seems likely that there may be a subset of self-knowledge available and operative at any one point in time and that this subset may depend on a person's internal state, motivation, context, and interpretation of the context. If this is the case, this would make measurement of self-esteem very complicated indeed. If we add to this Fiske's ideas published in 1971 that people provide different information in response to different measurement tasks, the situation becomes even more complicated.

One way to deal with the resulting confusion may be to step back and make two assumptions. First, as with the old fable of the blind men trying to describe an elephant, those, including this author, who are describing self-concept today, may be able to see and describe only a portion of what we will eventually learn about the self-concept. This would mean that we still await an overall theory that would include the development, maintenance, and change of self-concept, the functioning of self-concept, and the content of self-concept.

Second, researchers trying to measure self-esteem may need to step back, as our physics colleagues have had to do, and add to our definitions of self-esteem the context or method by which such self-esteem was measured. As physicists must say "light (photons) measured in this way behaves like a wave," we may have to say "self-esteem measured by a particular method gives us a particular view of the self-evaluation process." At present, none of the views may give us a complete picture of the process of evaluating the self.

Categories of Self-esteem Measures and Possible Relationships to Self-concept. For now, we can categorize self-esteem measures into five categories according to the task given to respondents—that is, what respondents are asked to do (Fiske 1971; Wells, 1988a). Each of these categories may be providing us with a view of the evaluation of different aspects of the self-concept. (See also Brinthaupt & Erwin 1992.)

First, overall generalized and experienced self-esteem asks respondents what they are generally like (Rosenberg's Self-esteem

Figure 5.2
Self-Schemata

	Core Aspects	Role Aspects	Working Self-concepts
Actual [1] Self-concepts	Attributes that people think they actually possess. Examples Capable, active cute, controlled	Gender, race, family position, occupation	The working self may consist of a varying combination of actual, ideal, and ought selves. These may contain a varying array of core and role aspects. Example A man who is out to dinner with his wife may be experiencing actual selves of husband and father. When his wife complains about his tie he may compare his wife's view of him with one of his ideal selves derived from his fantasy of his very competent older brother. He may conclude he is not the capable husband he wishes he were, and he may feel that he has not lived up to either his own or his wife's expectations of him. He may then experience a drop in self-esteem.
Ideal Self-concepts	Attributes that people would like to possess their aspirations, hopes and goals. These may include wished-for selves and may be done to gain approval. Examples Friendly, successful, organized	Fantastic doctor, the organizer in the family, good mother with well-behaved children	
Ought Self-concepts	Attributes that people think they should or ought to possess the rules they should follow, the prescribed duties and obligations that carry a sense of duty or moral obligation. These can include feared and not-me selves and carry the threat of disapproval and loss of security. Examples Trustworthy, reliable, strong	Honest banker, the "sick one" in family, bag lady	

[1] Higgins and associates (Higgins, Klein & Strauman 1985) further divide self-concepts into self-views and other views of self which result in six types of self views: (a) actual-self, (b) actual-other, (c) ideal-self, (d) ideal-other, (e) ought-self, and (f) ought-other.

Scale 1965). These procedures are thought to give a view of an over-all evaluation of the self. This view could be thought of as tapping into the evaluation of all core and role aspects, covering all self-concepts, and self-concept discrepancies, as well as all of a person's experience.

Second, generalized experienced self-esteem limited to particular contexts or roles asks respondents what they are like in particular roles such as students or parents (Gibaud-Wallston & Wandersman's Parent Competence Scale 1978). This view is likely to be tapping into both core and role aspects of self-concept, but limited to a particular role or a particular subset of self-concepts and self-concept discrepancies, and to a subset of experience.

Third, generalized presented self-esteem asks respondents "What is your friend's or acquaintance's self-esteem generally like?" (Demo 1985. See also chapter 4 of this volume.) When people describe another's self-esteem, what is likely to be tapped is the presented view of self which may contain both core and role aspects, different self-concepts, and different self-concept discrepancies. Results may also be affected by motivation and social circumstances.

Fourth, preconscious or unconscious self-esteem is an analyst's impression of a respondent's self-esteem, and is formed by observing transference reactions in therapeutic situations with the use of the empathic method (Cohler 1980; Kohut 1980). This view is likely to tap into the evaluation of unconscious or preconscious core aspects of self that have been learned early in life.

Fifth, current ongoing experienced self-esteem (measured with the ESM) asks respondents what they are like at a particular moment in time. This procedure is likely to be giving us a view of the evaluation of the working self-concept, which is likely to vary over time and be affected by a person's interpretation of the context as well as by affective and motivational factors. This view could involve any number of self-concept discrepancies, and the self-concept discrepancies are likely to affect current ongoing self-esteem, just as Higgins and associates have shown that self-concept discrepancies affect peoples' affective states (Higgins et al. 1985).

Current ongoing self-esteem can be thought of as the phenomenological experience that is the result of the evaluation of self when using the current working concept of self. Self-esteem, then, is peoples' conscious evaluation of themselves throughout fluctuating senses of self—that is, during varying roles and sets of expectations of themselves and through varying motivational and affective states. Current ongoing self-esteem may be hypothesized to have both an overall setpoint and perhaps even within-context or within-role set-point levels from which fluctuations occur. (See chapter 4 of this volume for a similar view of self-esteem.) Use of the idea of set-point levels implies not only that self-esteem may fluctuate from average levels but also that these average levels may change over time depending upon experience.

To give an example of possible relationships between working self-concepts, self-concept discrepancies, and self-esteem, a woman who is with her children may have a working self-concept made up of a number of possible views of self. These can include, to name just a few aspects, her view of herself as a mother, her beliefs about what an ideal mother should be like, memories of what her own mother was like, her own evaluation of how her mother handled her, and some knowledge of how various members of her family think she should be as a mother.

If at this particular time she should compare her view of herself as a full-time working mother with her memory of her own mother as a nonworking mother, she may experience some discrepancy between her actual self and one of her ideal selves, and worry that she is not available enough to her children. It may also be the case that, when she is with her children, the emotional reactions of others are important to her—that is, she might be particularly sensitive to the reflected appraisals of her children. If she then interacts with her children, and they express displeasure with her, she may indeed experience a drop in her current ongoing self-esteem.

That same woman, when she is with coworkers who are displeased with her may not experience such a drop in self-esteem because, now, her working self-concept may consist of being a capable lawyer who is actively trying to get a job done. Here, the emotional reactions of others may not be as important to her self-evaluation as getting the job done. So the reflected appraisals of others may not count as heavily as when she is with her family. If the task is also challenging, and she feels she is using her skills, she may even experience an increase in her current ongoing self-esteem.

Methodological Issues

In terms of methodology, one can see that it is unlikely that one measure of self-esteem will be able to cover the total self-evaluation process. This means we need to be careful about what aspects of self-esteem we are measuring and how the different aspects are related to each other. As I have pointed out elsewhere, which of these types of measures of self-esteem or which of these views of the self-evaluation process will help us predict behavior is a research question (Wells 1988a). The question may become what view of the self-evaluation process or evaluation of which part of the self-concept will help us predict whether a child or young adult will do well in school, whether a parent will abuse a child, or whether an adult will succeed in a particular job. And, in terms of treatment, if we discover that a person makes unrealistic generalizations about himself or herself (such as, "I'm a failure") and then acts on these impressions, what part of the self-evaluation process or self-concept needs to be changed and how do we go about helping a person accomplish this? These are research questions.

Findings have confirmed both fluctuations and stability in current ongoing self-esteem. How can we understand the stability found in the average levels of current ongoing self-esteem? Such stability could result from a number of sources, and sorting these out are research questions. First, the stability could be the result of stable core self-esteem that was developed earlier in life and that now exerts an influence on the average set-point levels from which fluctuations occur. In order to come to such a conclusion, one would have to show that these average levels do remain relatively stable over a longer period of time and over a variety of changing circumstances, and that the stability is not due to methodological artifacts like response sets.

Second, the stability could have resulted from the fact that these women may have been in similar contexts over the period of data collection. Third, women could have constructed their contexts and opportunities to be similar. And fourth, women might experience their contexts to be similar, and, as a result of this, their working self-concepts might have consistently included certain core and role aspects, or they might have encountered certain consistent self-concept discrepancies. (See Swann 1985 for a description of a number of ways in which people can construct and end up in similar environmental circumstances, such as selecting particular people to interact with or giving others clues as to what reaction we expect from them).

The findings that women's self-esteem fluctuates over several aspects of context—such as activity, or whom they are with—and over varying aspects of the interpersonal context and varying degrees of challenge and skill-using level show that a number of aspects of context can possibly be related to current ongoing self-esteem. Two methodological issues are raised by such findings—

how to define *context,* and how to look at more than one aspect of context at a time.

In terms of defining context, the data show that there are a number of aspects of context that can be used as contextual variables. Deciding which aspects of the context are to be examined becomes a research challenge. Certainly we must be guided by theory as to what aspects might be important. However, researchers should become more specific about defining what aspects of the context they think might be affecting behavior as well as how to go about measuring these aspects.

One problem encountered is that contextual variables can vary by how much the definition of context can be validated by an outside observer. One can see that whom someone is with can be validated by an outside observer. But how challenging a woman finds her present activity to be is defined by the woman herself and cannot be validated by an outside observer. Although the difficulty of her activity could be rated by another, how the woman herself experiences her world may well be the more important information in predicting her self-esteem.

Recent discussions in the area of personality theory and research have focused upon not just whether behavior is determined by stable internal factors or by external circumstances or some statistical interaction of these, but has begun to focus more clearly on how behavior may be determined by a combination of external and internal factors. For example, researchers such as Emmons, Diener and Larsen (1986) have suggested that internal factors may affect the circumstances that people choose to enter, and, in turn, their circumstances may affect their moods. These data raise the possibility that the definition of some contextual variables (such as, challenge of the activity) may well be affected by internal factors which will vary with people. How a women construes the challenge of her activity may well be affected by internal factors such as her own self-concepts. This would mean that the variable "challenge of the activity" is defined by a combination of internal and external factors.

In addition, we may need to think of much more complicated processes than linear ones to explain and predict both internal states and behavior. Fierro suggested in 1986 that we take a look at recursive processes such as how a person's internal experience and/or behavior contributes to determining the situation which the person is in, and which, in turn, affects the person's internal experience and/or behavior. It is likely that the variable of skill-using is measured in relation to self-concepts that have previously been developed.

Thus, current self-esteem can be affected not only by the present evaluation of skill-using in relation to challenge, but by the premise that the evaluative scale being used is likely to be affected by internal factors that preceded the current evaluation of self. We can also ask whether previous evaluative experiences have had an effect on women's self-concepts and evaluative standards that may be used to determine present self-esteem. One of our methodological challenges is to expand our understanding and measurement of such processes in our attempt to predict behavior. As Emmons, Diener, and Larsen (1986) suggested, we must take into account that a person's internal state may affect his or her experience, behavior, or choice of situations, and we must look to see how that, in turn, affects a person's internal experience.

The second methodological issue that must be addressed is how to look at more than one aspect of the context at a time. Presently, it is difficult to examine the relationship between current ongoing self-esteem and any other aspect at one time. We must find ways in which to test interactions of various aspects of context to determine which of these is more important to the self-evaluative process in specific contexts at specific points in time and with specific groups of people. Questions must include which aspects of context are always important to current ongoing self-esteem, and which are important only some of the time and only with some people. We must be careful not to assume that one aspect of the context (such as reflected appraisals of others) will be important in all contexts.

One can also see that more than one set of theoretical ideas can be used to generate aspects of the context to examine. Finding ways to examine more than one aspect of context would make it possible to build hypotheses that would allow investigation into how well one set of theoretical ideas explains the findings versus another.

Developmental Issues

When discussing developmental issues we must keep in mind whether we are discussing development of self-concept or self-esteem. When studying development of self-concept, researchers should take into account a number of factors, such as the development of children's conceptual abilities or their capacity to form and relate self-schemata, and how these are stored in and retrieved from memory (Edler 1989); the development of children's ability to communicate their experiences; and researcher's ability to design study methods that allow children to communicate their experiences to us (Brinthaupt & Lipka 1985).

Several other factors that must be taken into account have to do with the fact that children grow up in a variety of contexts and have a variety of life experiences which affect the development of self-concepts. Children's experiences will vary because families, groups, and cultures vary as to the world views they hold, the roles that are available, and the rules and values that are supported. Children will have varying experiences as a result of having different specific life experiences (e.g., traumas), and as a result of having different long-term experiences, such as the result of being male or the oldest child in a family. They will also have varying experiences as the result of having different life sequences, such as learning to read early versus late, puberty occurring earlier than in other members of one's group, a woman having a child at age nineteen while in college versus one who has a child at thirty after becoming a lawyer. Such varying life experiences must affect the self-schemata that develop including the criteria and standards by which the self is evaluated.

If we use Higgins and associates' ideas, we can see that development of actual, ideal, and ought self-concepts are likely to be dependent upon the surrounding context and might vary within families, between families and groups, and over cultures (Higgins 1987; Higgins et al. 1985, 1986). For example, within a family, a son who is the oldest and named for his father might well develop different self-concepts than does a second son who was born shortly before his mother became depressed and is described by his family as "like his mother." Children from a family which values independence and educational achievement will likely have different self-concepts than do children from a family which values family cohesion to the point that no one is allowed to leave the family.

So when we begin to think of the development of self-esteem we must assume that people will be working with different self-concepts which will include different evaluative rules and standards. Also, when we look at the development of self-esteem we must keep in mind that there is a difference between the self-evaluative process and the result of this evaluative process which we call self-esteem. The self-evaluative process is how we go about evaluating self. (See Higgins et al. 1986 for one description of the process.) Self-esteem is the result of this process—that is, the resulting evaluative thoughts, feelings, and conclusions about self that we are presently experiencing or have stored in memory.

One might hypothesize that the development of a core sense of self-esteem early in life is then added to as a person moves through the life space, such as the development of gender related self-esteem, school related self-esteem, job and parental related self-esteem and more. (See Stern's proposals in 1985 of basic senses of self that could generate hypotheses about possible core evaluative experiences of self.) I would also hypothesize—as Stern and Basch have suggested in 1985 and 1988—that our earliest evaluations of self are affective reactions to the self (both of self and others) that are stored in memory. It would be my guess that, as the child begins to be able to understand and label entities, self-schemata are built that include these early affective memories.

In terms of factors and criteria that are involved in the self-evaluation process, certain abilities are probably so innate to being human that we all evaluate the self on these factors, such as the abilities to engage others in interaction, organize information, learn about the world, use our capacities, accomplish tasks, and fulfill some of our needs. Others are more likely to be socially determined and assimilated as children grow up. These may vary over groups of people, such as families or cultures. For example, how independent should we be from our families, what roles are available, and what are the standards by which we are considered to be successful in particular roles?

I would speculate that, as various self-concepts develop, fluctuations in self-esteem occur as children struggle to evaluate themselves. Children must struggle with two types of evaluations—their own evaluations of self in relation to the world, and the evaluations of others. One would hypothesize that children could come to different evaluative conclusions about themselves in terms of various abilities and in various roles and contexts. One might hypothesize that both overall set-point levels of self-esteem might develop and change in relation to particular life events—such as school, traumas, psychotherapy, and marriage—and that the criteria for evaluating the self might also develop and change at different times.

One could certainly use the ESM to look at the development of self-esteem as children grow up. Larson and Lampman-Petraitis (1989) used the ESM with children as young as nine to look for variability in moods. It would be illuminating to use the ESM to measure current ongoing self-esteem in various roles and contexts in conjunction with methods designed to measure the development of self-concept.

The study findings also make us question whether everyone may follow a single developmental sequence. We need to ask what effect do particular life events or sequences of life events have on the development of different types of self-esteem—having a depressed parent when one is a toddler, experiencing puberty earlier or later than one's own group, choosing a professional career versus a nonprofessional career, getting married and having children at different times in the life cycle.

Several issues are raised in relation to context. First, are there aspects of context that are always likely to be important to self-esteem both in terms of its development and maintenance, such as the feeling that one can or is using one's capacity? Which aspects will be important only in certain contexts? Do aspects of the context that are important to self-esteem change as a person develops? One could certainly hypothesize that feeling capable or that one could operate as an independent entity would be an important task that one would evaluate self on at every point in the life span. However, how one might evaluate the use of one's capacity might change as one developed and changed.

We might step back for a moment and ask the question of what are some of the functions of self-esteem? We can begin by assuming that, in order to meet goals and life's requirements, a person must learn to operate with at least some competence in the world. We might hypothesize that information about surrounding context and a person's functioning in that context must be processed and used to guide and alter behavior to accomplish the goals. We can think of a person as processing information in a feedback cycle such that the result of behaviors is fed back into the system to guide and alter behavior to reach goals. (See Basch 1988 for a discussion of feedback cycles, affect, competence, and self-esteem.)

We tend to think in terms of two types of internal information that is used in the feedback cycle: cognitive or thoughts and affective or feelings. Self-esteem contains both cognitive conclusions and affective information related to self. I would hypothesize that self-esteem functions as part of the feedback cycle which a person uses to alter behavior to try to reach goals. In other words, I am suggesting that self-esteem may be a major piece of information that people use in their feedback cycles that guide behavior.

In addition, we can see that building a model of self in relation to the world (or self-concepts) would help a person to guide behavior to achieve goals. Self-concepts could be seen as a person's past record of self in relation to the world from which predictions of future experience could be built. I would hypothesize that one's evaluative experience of self is used to build and alter self-concepts. It is likely that the person whom one believes he or she to be, and the evaluative standards which that person finally accepts as relevant to his or her self are somehow affected by a person's ongoing evaluative experiences.

In summary, we must be mindful, when we study self-esteem, that we are measuring a particular subset of information about self-esteem for particular groups of people at particular points in their life cycles, and that we are looking at a particular subset of contextual aspects that could affect the self-evaluation process.

NOTES

1. This variable is different from "how much skill do you have" which has previously been used to study flow (Csikszentmihalyi 1975, 1982; Csikszentmihalyi & Csikszentmihalyi 1988). In this study, the question "How much skill are you using?" correlated .55, $p < .001$, with "How much skill do you have?" For further discussion see Wells and Csikszentmihalyi (1989).

2. Although worktime and occupation were significantly correlated (r (49) = .58, $p < .0001$) so that one accounted for 34 percent of the variance of the other, this left considerable variability unaccounted for. Further study is needed to sort out what combined and separate effects worktime and occupation may have on challenge, skill using, and self-esteem.

REFERENCES

Basch, M. F. 1988. *Understanding Psychotherapy* New York: Basic Books.

Baumeister, R. F. 1987. How the self became a problem: A psychological review of historical research. *Journal of Personality and Social Psychology* 52:163–176.

Beck, A. T. 1967. *Depression: Clinical, experimental, and theoretical aspects* New York: Harper & Row.

―――. 1976. *Cognitive therapy and the emotional disorders* New York: International Universities Press.

Beck, A. T.; Rush, A. J., Shaw, B. F., and Emery, G. 1979. *Cognitive therapy of depression*. New York: Guilford.

Bills, R. E.; Vance, E. L.; and McLean, O. S. 1951. An index of adjustment and values. *Journal of Consulting Psychology* 15:257–261.

Breckler, S. J., and Greenwald, A. G. 1986. Motivational facets of the self. In *Handbook of motivation and cognition,* edited by R. M. Sorrentino and E. T. Higgins. New York: Guilford Press. 145–164.

Briggs, S. R., and Cheek, J. M. 1986. The role of factor analysis in the development and evaluation of personality scales. *Journal of Personality* 54:106–148.

Brinthaupt, T. M. 1986. The social elements of self-concept/self-esteem: Developmental issues. Paper presented at Midwestern Educational Research Association Meeting, Chicago, Ill.

Brinthaupt, T. M. and Erwin, L. J. 1992. Reporting about the self: Issues and implications. In *The self: Definitional and methodological issues*, edited by T. M. Brinthaupt and R. P. Lipka. Albany: State University of New York Press.

Brinthaupt, T. M., and Lipka, R. P. 1985. Developmental differences in self-concept and self-esteem among kindergarten through twelfth-grade students. *Child Study Journal* 15:207–221.

Buss, A. H. 1986. *Social behavior and personality.* Hillsdale, N.J.: Lawrence Erlbaum Associates.

——— . 1989. Personality as traits. *American Psychologist.* 44:1378–1388.

Cantor, N., Markus, H., Niedenthal, P.; and Nurius, P. 1986. On motivation and the self concept. In *Handbook of motivation and cognition* edited by R. M. Sorrentino and E. T. Higgins. New York: Guilford Press. 23–63.

Cohler, B. J. 1980. Developmental perspectives on the psychology of the self in early childhood. In *Advances in self-psychology* edited by A. Golberg. New York: International Universities Press. 69–115.

Cooley, C. H. 1902. *Human nature and the social order.* New York: Scribner's.

Csikszentmihalyi, M. 1975. *Beyond boredom and anxiety.* San Francisco: Jossey-Bass Publishers.

——— . 1982. Toward a psychology of optimal experience. In *Review of personality and social psychology.* Vol. 2. Edited by L. Wheeler. Beverly Hills, Calif.: Sage Publications. 13–36.

Csikszentmihalyi, M., and Csikszentmihalyi, I. 1988. Eds. *Optimal experience: Psychological studies of flow in consciousness.* New York: Cambridge University Press.

Csikszentmihalyi, M., and Graef, R. 1980. The experience of freedom in daily life. *American Journal of Community Psychology* 8:401–414.

Csikszentmihalyi, M., and Larson, R. 1987. The experience sampling method: Toward a systematic phenomenology. *Journal of Nervous and Mental Disease* 175:526–536.

Csikszentmihalyi, M.; Larson, R.; and Prescott, S. 1977. The ecology of adolescent activity and experience. *Journal of Youth and Adolescence* 6:281–294.

Cummings, S. T.; Bayley, H. C.; and Rie, H. E. 1966. Effects of the child's deficiency on the mother: A study of mothers of mentally retarded, chronically ill and neurotic children. *American Journal of Orthopsychiatry* 36:595–608.

D'Andrade, R. G. 1965. Trait psychology and componential analysis. *American Anthropologist* 67:215–228.

Demo, D. H. 1985. The measurement of self-esteem: Refining our methods. *Journal of Personality and Social Psychology* 48:1490–1502.

Edler, R. A. 1989. The emergent personologist: The structure and content of 3½, 5½ and 7½ year-olds' concept of themselves and other persons. *Child Development* 60:1218–1228.

Emmons, R. A.; Diener, E.; and Larsen, R. J. 1986. Choice and avoidence of everyday situations and affect congruence: Two models of reciprocal interactionism. *Journal of Personality and Social Psychology* 51:815–826.

Fierro, A. 1986. Personality theorems and research programs focusing on self-evaluation and self-esteem. In *Progress in experimental personality research*. Vol. 14. Edited by B. A. Maher. New York: Academic Press. 63–113.

Fiske, D. W. 1971 *Measuring the concepts of personality*. Chicago, Ill.: Aldine Publishing Co.

Fleming, J. S., and Courtney, B. E. 1984. The dimensionality of self-esteem: II. Hierarchial facet model for revised measurement scales. *Journal of Personality and Social Psychology* 46:404–421.

Franks, D. D., and Marolla, J. 1976. Efficacious action and social approval as interacting dimensions of self-esteem: A tentative formulation through construct validation. *Sociometry* 39:324–341.

Gecas, V. 1971. Parental behavior and dimensions of adolescent self-evaluation. *Sociometry* 34: 466–482.

———. 1972. Parental behavior and contextural variations in adolescent self-esteem. *Sociometry* 35:322–345.

———. 1982. The self-concept. *Annual Review of Sociology* 8:1–33.

Gergen, K. J. 1968. Personal consistency and the presentation of self. In *The self in social interaction*. Vol. 1. Edited by C. Gordon and K. J. Gergen. New York: John Wiley & Sons, Inc. 299–308.

Gergen, K. J. 1971. *The concept of self.* New York: Holt, Rinehart & Winston, Inc.

Gergen, K. J. 1977. The social construction of self-knowledge. In *The self: Psychological and philosophical issues,* edited by T. Mischel. Totowa, N.J.: Rowman & Littlefield. 115–167.

Gibaud-Wallston, J., and Wandersman, L. P. 1978. Development and utility of the parenting sense of competence scale. Paper presented at the American Psychological Association. Toronto, Canada.

Goffman, E. 1959. *The presentation of self in everyday life.* Garden City, N.Y.: Doubleday Anchor.

Greenwald, A. G., and Pratkanis, A. R. 1984. The self. In *Handbook of social cognition.* Vol. 3. Edited by R. S. Wyler and T. K. Srull. Hillsdale, N.J.: Lawrence Erlbaum Associates. 129–178.

Higgins, E. T. 1987. Self-discrepancy: A theory relating self and affect. *Psychological Review* 94:319–340.

Higgins, E. T.; Klein, R.; and Strauman, T. 1985. Self-concept discrepancy theory: A psychological model for distinguishing among different aspects of depression and anxiety. *Social Cognition* 3:51–76.

Higgins, E. T.; Strauman, T.; and Klein, R. 1986. Standards and the process of self-evaluation: Multiple effects from multiple stages. In *Handbook of motivation and cognition,* edited by R. M. Sorrentino and E. T. Higgins. New York: Guilford Press. 23–63.

Hogan, R.; Jones, W. H., and Cheek, J. M. 1985. Socioanalytic theory: An alternative to armadillo psychology. In *The self in social life,* edited by B. R. Schlenker, New York: McGraw Hill. 175–198.

Hollingshead, A. B. 1957. *Two factor index of social position.* New Haven, Conn.: Author published.

Hormuth, S. E. 1986. The sampling of experiences in situ. *Journal of Personality* 54:262–293.

James, W. [1890] (1950). *The principles of psychology.* Vol. 1, reprint. New York: Dover.

Jaquish, G. A., and Savin-Williams, R. C. 1981. Biological and ecological factors in the expression of adolescent self-esteem. *Journal of Youth and Adolescence* 10:473–485.

Jones, E. E. 1964. *Ingratiation: A social psychological analysis.* New York: Appleton Century-Crofts.

Jones, E. E., and Pittman, T. S. 1982. Toward a general theory of strategic self-presentation. In *Psychological perspectives on the self.* Vol. 1. Edited by J. Suls. Hillsdale, N.J.: Erlbaum. 231–262.

Kohut, H. 1980. Reflections on advances in self-psychology. In *Advances in self psychology*, edited by A. Goldberg. New York: International Universities Press, Inc. 473–554.

Larson, R., and Csikszentmihalyi, M. 1983. The experience sampling method. In *Naturalistic approaches to studying social interactions: New directions for methodology of social and behavioral science.* No. 15. Edited by H. T. Reis. San Francisco: Jossey-Bass. 41–56.

Larson, R. and Lampman-Petraitis, C. 1989. Daily emotional states as reported by children. *Child Development* 60:1250–1260.

Leifer, M. 1980. *Psychological effects of motherhood: A study of first pregnancy.* New York: Praeger Publishers.

Markus, H., and Nurius, P. 1986. Possible selves. *American Psycholgist* 41:954–969.

———. 1987. Possible selves: The interface between motivation and the self-concept. In *Self and identity: Psychological perspectives*, edited by K. Yardley and T. Hones. John Wiley & Sons.

Markus, H., and Wurf, E. 1987. The dynamic self-concept: A social psychological perspective. *Annual Review of Psychology* 38:299–337.

Marsh, H.; Byrne, B.; and Shavelson, R. 1992. A multi-dimensional, hierarchical self-concept. In *The self: Definitional and methodological issues*, edited by T. M. Brinthaupt and R. P. Lipka. Albany, N.Y.: State University of New York Press.

McGuire, W. J., and Padawer-Singer, A. 1976. Trait salience in the spontaneous self-concept. *Journal of Personality and Social Psychology* 33:743–754.

Mead, G. H. 1934. *Mind, self, and society.* Chicago: University of Chicago Press.

Mischel, W. 1968. *Personality and assessment.* New York: John Wiley and Sons.

Morse, S., and Gergen, K. J. 1970. Social comparison, self-consistency and the concept of self. *Journal of Personality and Social Psychology* 16:148–156.

Patterson, G. R. 1980. Mothers: The unacknowledged victims. *Monographs of the Society for Research in Child Development.* 45(5, Serial No. 186).

Rosenberg, M. 1965. *Society and the adolescent self-image.* Princeton: Princeton University Press.

──────. 1979. *Conceiving the self.* New York: Basic Books, Inc.

Savin-Williams, R. C., and Demo, D. H. 1983. Situational and transituational determinants of adolescents self-esteem. *Journal of Personality and Social Psychology* 44:824–835.

Schlenker, B. R. 1985. Introduction: Foundations of the self in social life. In *The self in social life,* edited by B. R. Schlenker. New York: McGraw Hill.

Shavelson, R. J., and Bolus, R. 1982. Self-concept: The interplay of theory and method. *Journal of Educational Psychology* 74:3–17.

Shweder, R. A. 1975. How relevant is an individual difference theory of personality? *Journal of Personality* 43:455–484.

──────. 1982. Fact and artifact in trait perception: The systematic distortion hypothesis. In *Progress in experimental personality research,* Vol. II, edited by B. A. Maher & W. B. Maher (Eds)., New York: Academic Press. 65–100.

Shweder, R. A., and D'Andrade, R. G. 1979. Accurate reflection or systematic distortion? A reply to Block, Weiss, and Thorne. *Journal of Personality and Social Psychology* 37b:1075–1084.

Shweder, R. A., and D'Andrade, R. G. 1980. The systematic distortion hypothesis. In *Fallible judgment in behavioral research: New directions for methodology of social and behavioral science.* No. 4. Edited by R. A. Shweder. San Francisco: Jossey Bass Publishers. 37–57.

Stern, D. N. 1985. *The interpersonal world of the infant.* New York: Basic Books.

Swann, W. B. 1985. The self as architect of social reality. In *The self in social life.* Edited by B. R. Schlenker. New York: McGraw Hill.

Van Tuinen, M., and Ramanaiah, N. V. 1979. A multimethod analysis of selected self-esteem measures. *Journal of Research in Personality* 13:16–24.

Wells, A. J. 1986. *Variazioni nell autostima delle madri nei diversi contesti quotidiani: Influenza della presenza dei figili.* [Variations in mothers' self-esteem in the different contexts of the daily life.]. In *L'esperienza quotidiana,* edited by F. Massimini and P. Inghilleri. Collana di psicologia diretta da M. Cesa-Bianchi, Franco Angeli: Milano, Italy. 369–389.

Wells, A. J. 1988a. Variations in mothers' self-esteem in daily life. *Journal of Personality and Social Psychology* 55:661–668.

————. 1988b. Self-esteem and optimal experience. In *Optimal experience: Psychological studies of flow in consciousness*, edited by M. Csikszentmihalyi and I. Csikszentmihalyi. New York: Cambridge University Press. 327–341.

Wells, A. J., and Csikszentmihalyi, M. 1989. Fluctuations in womens' self-esteem and optimal experiences (flow), Manuscript submitted for publication.

Wylie, R. C. 1979. *The self-concept: theory and research on selected topics.* Vol. 2, 2d ed. Lincoln: University of Nebraska Press.

DANIEL M. OGILVIE
MARGARET D. CLARK

6

The Best and Worst of It: Age and Sex Differences in Self-discrepancy Research[1]

INTRODUCTION

The primary purpose of this chapter is to present and discuss certain age and sex differences regarding individuals' self-assessments within the boundaries of their judgements of the *good* life and the *bad* life. To this end, the bulk of the chapter is devoted to reporting the results of several studies that, together, form an increasingly coherent package that may provide a framework for advancements in both theory and future empirical work.

Most readers will be unfamiliar with a concept that inspired the studies reviewed in this chapter. That concept is the *undesired-self*. The idea that there is a domain of selfhood that can be identified and described as undesirable is somewhat novel. The undesired-self is not a usual item on researchers' lists of potential variables for inclusion in generating and testing hypotheses pertaining to human thought, feelings, and behavior. Thus, given the newness of the concept, the first three sections of this chapter are devoted to describing the conditions of its "discovery" and early theoretical formulations regarding its place in self-concept research.

THE IDEAL-SELF

For a time during this century, attempts were made to remove the word *self* from the vocabulary of serious scientific researchers because of its inferential and unmeasurable status. If tender-minded psychologists needed the concept to further their poetry, so be it. For the tough-minded, however, it was observable behavior that really mattered. But the concept of *self* would not vanish, and it now appears—usually in hyphenated form with some other word such as *esteem, efficacy, regulation, regard*—in psychological literature with greater frequency than ever before.

Carl Rogers (1954) is among several theorists in various branches of both psychology and sociology who contributed to keeping the self alive amidst the behavioral period in academic psychology when the concept was held in low regard. Rogers is singled out here because he was one of the first to attempt to bridge the gap between theory and research. Based on his theory of self-incongruity, Rogers created a method for measuring the distance between the *real-self* and the *ideal-self*, constructs that also occupied the attention of Alfred Adler (see Ansbacher & Ansbacher 1956) and Karen Horney (1950).

Using a modified Q-sort method (Stephenson 1953), Rogers had a client sort two duplicate stacks of one-hundred cards into nine piles according to the requirements of normal, inverted U-shaped distributions. Each card contained a statement such as "I am shy with strangers," "I am attractive," and so on.

The first sort was performed for the real-self. The participant distributed the cards in such a way that cards with statements on them that were "least like me" were placed at or near one end of a row and cards containing statements "most like me" were positioned at or near the other end.

The second sort was done in a similar fashion except that, this time, the participant performed the task from the perspective of her ideal-self, sorting the cards according to "most like my ideal-self" and "least like my ideal-self." Both sets of cards were similarly numbered and coded according to their locations in the two sorts, permitting the computation of a correlation between the two rows of cards. This correlation became known as the *real-/ideal-self discrepancy score*. To add substance to the claim that this score meant something, Rogers (1954) showed that the scores became increasingly less discrepant—or more highly correlated—during and after successful therapy.

Rogers not only paved the way for quantitative analyses of self-related notions but he also gave researchers a "fix" on what was important to measure. Attention became riveted to real-/ideal-self discrepancies. A few researchers continued to compute these discrepancies using the Q-sort method (Berg 1974) but, soon, numerous other methods were devised by modifying existing measures in ways that made real- and ideal-self comparisons possible. For example, semantic differential scales (Clifford & Clifford 1967), adjective checklists/scales (Czaja 1975), Leary's Interpersonal Checklist (Beard & Pishkin 1970), self-esteem scales/inventories (Boshier 1972), and the Minnesota Multiphasic Personality Inventory (MMPI) (Parsons, Yourshaw & Borstelmann 1968) were all adapted for computing real-/ideal-self discrepancies.

Using these and other measurement strategies, researchers showed the relations between real-/ideal-self discrepancies and numerous aspects of self-perception and personality functioning, including anxiety (Gough, Fiorvanti & Lazzari 1983), depressive affect (Higgins, Bond, Klein & Strauman 1986), self-esteem (Eisenman 1970), academic adjustment and satisfaction (Bailey & Bailey 1971), effects of therapeutic treatment (Perlman 1972), adolescent development, (Jorgensen & Howell 1969), alcohol abuse (Carroll & Fuller 1969), drug abuse (Burke 1978), attitudes toward retarded persons (Gottlieb 1969), acceptance of disabilities (Lindowski & Dunn 1974), fear of death (Neimeyer & Chapman 1980–81), and dozens of other variables related to human functioning.

Nearly four-hundred studies have been published since 1967 that include real-/ideal-self discrepancies as primary or secondary variables. Hundreds more appeared prior to 1967, and there is no indication that researchers' reliance on discrepancies involving the ideal-self has abated. Indeed, it is probably the case that real-/ideal-self discrepancies rank among the top three or four personality variables used in modern research.

We view this extensive interest in the relation between the real-self and the ideal-self by researchers as an expression of our culturally nurtured investment in the future. As a future-oriented society, we are predisposed to constructing idealized images of ourselves and are taught (or find it natural) to assess our standing in life in terms of our present distance from fully enacting our dreams.

A point may have been reached, however, in which there is something like a compulsion to compute real-/ideal-self discrepancy scores. In many respects, it has become a standard practice that receives unquestioning nods of understanding. While the various methods of computation occasionally come under critical scrutiny (Hoge & McCarthy 1983), the idea that how individuals feel about themselves largely rests on their subjective assessments of where they are now (their real-selves) vis-à-vis where they would like to be (ideal-selves) seems not to be a matter of debate.

We concur with Adler (as cited in Ansbacher & Ansbacher 1956) that viable fictions are essential ingredients of well-being and some tension between *now* and *someday* is a mark of healthy engagement in life. "It's not what I am now, it's what I'm gonna be that counts" is a slogan announcing that an ideal-self is being developed. Ideal-selves contain goals giving direction to lives, offering hope, providing a purpose. Without images of *me* in the future, our lives would be characterized by random, unrelated movement toward nothing in particular.

On the other hand, we do not want to set such rigid and lofty standards that might place us under a "tyranny of shoulds" (Horney 1950). Rather, we seek to establish a balance between our current capabilities and imagined future talents. We wish not to peak too early lest we become complacent and bored. Nor do we want to cast our lines so far from sight that the game of catch-up would be too discouraging.

There is a type of folk wisdom behind these ideas. They fit individuals' experiences, and many researchers have correctly identified real-/ideal-self discrepancies as a meaningful domain of assessment. But, with our eyes focused by culturally shared lenses on the relationship between real- and ideal-selves, another domain of selfhood may have missed our attention.

THE UNDESIRED-SELF

The concept of an undesired-self was not originally formulated as a result of deep logical reasoning. Rather, it was spontaneously discovered from desperation on a dreary day when the first author was delivering a lecture to his class about the ideal-self as contained in the theories of Adler, Horney, and Rogers. Normally, this topic is a refreshing one for students because finally, after having sat through numerous lectures on concepts seemingly foreign to their experiences, the students are now faced with an idea that describes familiar mental operations. Relieved and enlivened, they are not hesitant to engage in open, good-natured, and often jovial public descriptions of their grand images of themselves in the future.

This time, however, most class members were singularly uninterested in participating. The instructor was of virtually no assistance because of his own distractions concerning the tattered condition of his umbrella, his broken-down car, materials that were to be handed out to the class today but had not been collated as promised, a recent letter from a distressed family member, and various administrative matters that were taking far too much time to resolve. He was in no shape to generate much class enthusiasm on the topic of the self made perfect. Resisting a strong desire to end class an hour early, he reflected for a moment and then placed his lecture notes aside.

"You know something?" he asked his students. "I couldn't care less about the ideal-self. Today, right now, the concept is meaningless to me. The very idea of it makes me sick. Not one of the authors we are discussing ever talks about the self we don't want to be, our miserable self, the me-at-my-worst self, the self that appears when nothing, I mean *nothing*, works. The ideal-self is too nice. It leaves out the nitty-gritty of life. It's too clean, and life is sometimes incredibly dirty."

Encouraged by responses from the audience like "Right on, professor!" and "Go for it, brother!," the instructor proceeded to question the field's preoccupation with real-/ideal-self discrepancies to the exclusion of real-/undesired-self discrepancies. The class continued well beyond its scheduled time limit and none of the 240 or so students noticed that a university policy had been violated.

This cathartic episode eventually led to a more subdued and systematic review of self-discrepancy literature. With very few exceptions—the only two being Sharma in 1970 and Van Dyne and Carskadan in 1978—unrelenting attention had been given to real-/ideal-self discrepancies in research.

In contrast with the research literature, the dark side of human personality had not been ignored by several theorists. Sullivan's work in 1953 on the personifications of the *bad-me* and the *not-me* is rich in its implications for the development of the undesired-self.

Freud's theory of the etiology of the superego and the concurrent repression of threatening impulses is another model for representing the formation of the undesired-self. Jung's concept of the shadow—that portion of the psyche that wants to do those things we will not allow ourselves to do—provides a different conceptual option (Fordham 1953). Similarly, Rank (1971) wrote of the inner enemy, the problematic double, that occasionally appears in dreams and literature as a self-mirroring target for destruction. And the recent work of Stern (1985) on the disavowel of affects in young children has provided a new framework for studying self-development, including that of the undesired-self, at its earliest stages.

INSIGHTS FROM THE LIFE OF JENNIFER

Interest in the role which the undesired-self might play in the conduct of life was serendipitously maintained as a result of the first author's investigation of the belief system of a twenty-two-year-old college senior named, in this report, Jennifer. This case study was conducted for the purpose of gaining familiarity with certain methods of investigating beliefs about the self that were beginning to take shape about that time (DeBoeck 1983).

Associated with the theoretical and empirical work of Rosenberg in 1977 and Gara and Rosenberg in 1979, DeBoeck created an algorithm for analyzing matrices in a manner that revealed patterns of both co—occurring and nonoverlapping ratings. A novel aspect of the algorithm was its ability to identify subset/superset relations in matrix data as well as contrasting categories.

DeBoeck's prototype-analysis method was the forerunner of the set-theoretical, hierarchical classes (HICLAS) model discussed by Ashmore and Ogilvie in a companion volume (1992). Especially since HICLAS has replaced the early version used in studying Jennifer, the present discussion would not be advanced if we were to describe the prototype analysis method in much detail here. Rather, we will concentrate primarily on the results of Jennifer's work.

Jennifer's first task was to name her various identities. As a sociology major, she was more comfortable thinking about herself as a bearer of roles and easily named ten present roles (such as lover and pet owner) and three past ones (such as college freshman). Her next task was to generate words and phrases that she or others might use to describe herself, either now or in the past. She named twenty traits (such as thoughtful, serious, and stubborn). Seventeen additional traits, qualities, and feelings were named as a result of her describing someone she liked and a second person whom she disliked. Henceforth, our shorthand for these thirty-seven descriptors will be *features*.[2]

A matrix of thirteen roles and thirty-seven features was formed from the information which Jennifer provided. Jennifer was then instructed to rate each role in terms of all features. This was done in the following manner: in an interview, she was asked to form an image of herself in a given role (such as, rescue squad member) and rate herself in that role using all thirty-seven features.

The format used was as follows. The interviewer asked "As a rescue squad member, to what degree are you thoughtful?"

(Thoughtful was the first feature on her list.) In this instance, Jennifer judged *thoughtful* to be very descriptive of her as a rescue squad member and gave it a score of 2. Had she considered herself to be somewhat thoughtful, she would have answered 1. If thoughtful was not judged to be a term relevant to the role, her response would have been 0.

After the first rating was made, the next feature, *shy*, replaced *thoughtful*, and Jennifer was asked "As a rescue squad member, to what degree are you shy?" As before, her answers were restricted to 0, 1, or 2 judgements. After rescue squad member was rated on all features, a new role was selected as the target of judgement.

Figure 6.1
Jennifer's Structure of Identities, Time 1

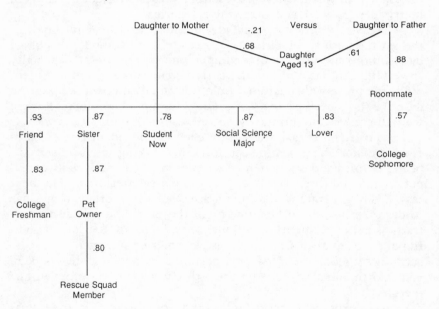

Jennifer's completed matrix was then analyzed using DeBoeck's prototype method. Output from the algorithm was structured in a manner that showed how Jennifer's roles were related to each other in terms of shared and unshared feature ratings. From this information, a top-down, tree-like structure was drawn showing the relationships among her roles. Figure 6.1 shows how this information was depicted. Not shown in the figure is the "glue" or the structure of feature ratings that holds the configuration together.

The daughter-to-mother role appears in the upper left portion of the figure. The location of that role makes it the prototype or superset of an elaborated cluster of interrelated roles that appears below it. A category becomes a superset when two or more other categories have more in common with it than it has with any of its subsets.

The subset roles—such as friend, sister, and so on—that appear beneath it arrive at their locations because Jennifer rated them somewhat (but not exactly) as she did daughter-to-mother. The degree of similarity is conveyed in the percentage figures above each role.

For example, Jennifer's ratings of the role of friend came close to duplicating her ratings of daughter-to-mother. The .93 above friend indicates that 93 percent of the time, Jennifer rated friend exactly as she rated daughter-to-mother. Prominent among the shared features describing herself in these two roles and the other roles connected to them in figure 6.1 were loyal, competent, generous, trustworthy, loving, honest, and understanding.

In contrast with the daughter-to-mother cluster is a smaller cluster headed by the prototype daughter-to-father. This cluster emerged primarily on the basis of shared ratings on features such as defensive, rejected, bitchy, anxious, unfriendly, worried, and cynical.

Jennifer was shown the diagram of her roles and, in regard to her relationship with her father, stated that things had not gone well between them for several years. She reported that she had dropped out of college her sophomore year, feeling defeated and worthless as a result of not passing an important pre-med course. Her father was extremely disappointed by this event. Jennifer's impression was that he actively avoided interacting with her, and was unable or unwilling to give her the support she needed at the time. Even prior to withdrawing from school, her relationship with her father had been, as she described it, "tense and uncomfortable"—a quality that also characterized her relationship with her then-current roommate, a person who had rejected her overtures to friendship. Indeed, it appears that experience of perceived rejection is the primary element that united daughter-to-father, roommate, and college sophomore.

Several weeks later, Jennifer was asked to make some new judgements about her roles. Each presently enacted role was paired with several other contemporary roles, that is, past roles were excluded from this exercise. Jennifer's task now was to assess the degree in which one would change if the other were to be taken away.

What stood out the most from these ratings was that positive roles were always judged to change a great deal if negative roles were removed, but negative roles would remain fixed and unchanged if positive roles were imagined as gone. It was assumed that these results reflected Jennifer's fantasy that positive roles would get even better if negative ones would go away. On the other hand, if a positive role or a "good" self were to vanish, the "bad" self would remain the same because things simply couldn't get any worse than they already were.

Jennifer graduated from college and a year later returned to pay a visit. She was most anxious to communicate the fact that she had been in therapy and the primary result of her sessions had been a vastly improved relationship with her father. At the investigator's suggestion, Jennifer enthusiastically agreed to redo her ratings. Most of her previous roles were kept except that lover had been replaced by single (she had broken up with her boyfriend), and she changed college freshman and college sophomore to worker, as she now held a post-graduate position in the personnel office of a manufacturing firm. The results of this second set of ratings appear in figure 6.2.

Figure 6.2
Jennifer's Structure of Identities, Time 2

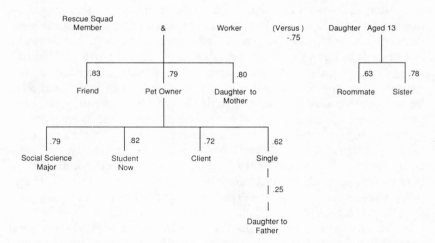

Similar to the first representation (figure 6.1), figure 6.2 contains a highly elaborated cluster of pleasurable roles countered by a smaller cluster of less desired roles. Of interest was the fact that daughter-to-mother was now a subset of rescue squad member and worker, suggesting that Jennifer had experienced some growth away from defining herself primarily as her mother's child. Also, daughter-to-father had, indeed, moved. While that role was not fully integrated into the positive cluster, it had moved in that direction.

On the contrasting side, daughter aged 13 (a past self which she variously remembered as having been endearing, rebellious, kind, and obnoxious in her first set of ratings) has become the prototype of bad roles. The location of the role of sister as a subset of the now repositioned role of daughter aged 13 was a surprise. Earlier, in figure 6.1, sister had been well-integrated into the positive cluster of roles. Jennifer's second set of ratings placed it in a clearly negative position in the structural space.

Asked about this change, Jennifer entered into an animated discussion of how she had begun to notice some things about her sister that she did not like. Some of these qualities included her style of avoidance, nit-picking, and occasional outright rejection of Jennifer. After giving numerous examples of these behaviors, Jennifer concluded, "She's been that way for a long time, but now, it's getting to me more than ever before. I haven't been taking well to these qualities of hers recently."

In an attempt to understand what might lie behind this role transformation, the investigator suggested the possibility that the role of sister had replaced daughter-to-father to make certain that the negative cluster remained occupied. Jennifer liked that interpretation. Indeed, her flush of excitement and immediate recognition of a fundamental insight temporarily made the investigator regret his decision many years earlier not to enter a field of psychology that might applaud such an accurate intuition.

As stated at the beginning of this section, this work with Jennifer fueled the investigator's interest in the so-called undesired-self. Here was a case of an individual who appeared to actively create new roles and maintain some old ones through which she could express qualities of herself that were clearly undesirable.

Freud (1959) addressed problems quite similar to this one in *Beyond the Pleasure Principle*. In that book, he acknowledged defeat in attempting to fit certain facts of mental life into his pleasure principle model. Despite heroic and ingenious efforts, he discovered that *all* mental activity simply *could not* be traced directly, or even indirectly, to the operation of sex instincts. In particular, the compulsion to repeat traumatic episodes (either in fantasy or through real-life "transferences") could not be squeezed into his pleasure-seeking paradigm. His solution—a landmark one that sparked years of psychoanalytic debate—was to propose the existence of a death instinct which he initially equated with the operation of ego instincts.

Following Freud's argument, are we to understand Jennifer's compulsion to create roles through which she could express dreaded aspects of herself as a manifestation of her death instinct? An alternative possibility is that Jennifer preserved her undesired-self (or negative roles) in order to keep her more positively construed selves in place. Without such an anchor, it might be difficult for Jennifer to assess how well she is doing in life. "Good-me" aspects might lose some of their robustness without some "bad-me" attributes acting as contrasts. At a metatheoretical level, then, one might differ from Freud and declare that compulsions to repeat unwanted experiences support life or survival instincts by providing needed contrast effect services.

At this point, it was recognized that further speculation about the operation of Jennifer's undesired-self could lead to the development of a grand theory to explain one life. However, we were more interested in formulating a general principle that could be tested nomothetically.

Ogilvie and Lutz (1984) argued that such a principle might be derived from evidence that Jennifer used her undesired-self as an anchor for assessing her overall sense of well-being. As noted earlier, most research had used the ideal-self as the preferred peg for self-evaluation. Our emergent theory was that the undesired-self is a more compelling reference point for self-esteem judgements because it is more grounded in the experiential history of the individual. By contrast, the ideal-self is a composite image of mostly unrealized future states of purified existence. That is, the ideal-self is a hoped-for self whereas the undesired-self is largely known because we've already been there. For these reasons, it was predicted that the undesired-self would be a more vital anchor than the ideal-self for making present-day self-evaluations.

THE UNDESIRED-SELF AND LIFE SATISFACTION

This section reviews the first study designed to test the prediction that real-/undesired-self discrepancy scores correlate more strongly with life satisfaction or self-esteem[3] ratings than do real-/ideal-self discrepancies (Ogilvie 1987a). Procedures followed in this study were largely based on the procedures worked out with Jennifer.

Forty-five undergraduate students (twenty-five females and twenty males) were asked to think about their lives in terms of their roles or identities. Specifically, they were instructed to label the "hats you wear in life." One male, for example, wrote down the following: son to mother, son to father, student, boyfriend in a rocky relationship, cafeteria worker, brother to Amy, magician at children's parties, former high-school wrestler, fraternity dropout, and future engineer.

Next, the students were instructed to begin a list of features by writing down the traits, characteristics, qualities, and feelings that they liked in themselves and other people. Following that, they completed the list by naming characteristics of themselves and others that they didn't like.

A matrix was then created for each respondent by placing their multiple selves in the rows and their features in the columns. All of the information contained in these selves-x-features matrices were participant-generated, except for three self categories placed at random in the rows by the researcher. These were the categories of *me mostly, how I hope to be*, and *how I never want to be*. Participants were told that *me mostly* referred to their real selves or "how I am most of the time these days." *How I hope to be* was defined as "images of myself at my best" or "my ideal-self," and *How I never want to be* referred to "images of myself at my worst" or "my undesired-self."

Participants followed the same set of instructions that had been given to Jennifer for rating each identity by all features. An example of a partially completed matrix is given in table 6.1. Finally, participants filled out a life-satisfaction questionnaire after they had completed their matrices.

DeBoeck's (1983) prototype analysis algorithm was again used for data reduction purposes. Instead of constructing self-structure diagrams for each subject as had been done with Jennifer, the focus was this time on a specific domain of the computer program's output. As previously mentioned, DeBoeck's method identifies both superset/subset relationships and contrasts among categories. It does so by computing the co–occurrences of each feature with all other features and, from these computations, deriving discrepancy scores between expected and observed co–frequencies of features.

The algorithm then locates a category (in this instance, a self, an identity, or a role) that is most typical of a given cluster of features. Any category that is most typical of one or more feature sets is labeled a *prototype*. Once prototypes are identified, belongingness

Table 6.1
Example of a Partially Completed Identity-x-Feature Matrix

Identities	Practical	Shy	Impatient	Thinker	Social	Jealous
			Features			
Friend	0	0	1	0	2	1
Daughter-to-mother	2	0	2	1	1	0
Hope never*	0	2	2	0	0	2
Future teacher	2	0	1	2	2	0
Employee	1	2	0	0	1	1
Me mostly**	1	1	1	1	2	1
Student	2	1	1	1	0	2
Would like to be***	2	1	1	2	2	0

*Refers to "undesired-self"
**Refers to "real-self"
***Refers to "ideal-self"
Note: 0s indicate never or rarely; 1s indicate sometimes, and 2s indicate frequently or always.

values are computed that show the degree of overlap or nonoverlap of every category to all prototypes. Table 6.2 shows the results of converting and recovering the ratings partially displayed in table 6.1 in terms of belongingness values.

The method used to calculate real-/ideal-self and real/undesired-self discrepancies in this study relied on the appearance of the ideal-self (how I hope to be) and the undesired-self (how I never want to be) as prototypes. In all cases, both categories were among participants' prototypes, permitting one to locate where the real-self (me mostly) is positioned, vis-à-vis each respondent's ideal-self and undesired-self.

That is, if a negative value (such as −.27) was at the intersection between the real-self and the ideal-self (or the undesired-self), it meant that the two selves being compared were rated quite differently and −.27 was treated as the score reflecting a large discrepancy. A high positive value (as with .72) meant that the real-self had been given a pattern of ratings that made it similar to, or less discrepant with, its paired prototype.

In the example contained in table 6.2, the real-/ideal-self discrepancy score is a relatively low .64, and the real-/undesired-self discrepancy score is a relatively high −.12. These two scores were extracted for all participants, and correlations were computed between real-/ideal-self discrepancies and life satisfaction and real/

Table 6.2
Belongingness Values of Nonprototype Identities to Prototype Identities

Nonprototype Identities	Prototype Identities			
	Daughter to mother	*How I hope to never be*	*Student*	*How I would like to be*
Friend	.47	−.61	.30	.37
Daughter-to-mother	1.00	−.42	.42	.69
Hope never	−.02	1.00	−.18	−.92
Future Teacher	.67	−.72	.76	.73
Employee	−.28	.31	.07	−.32
Me mostly	.37	<u>−.12</u>	.80	<u>.64</u>
Student	.55	−.24	1.00	.49
Would like to be	.62	−.89	.59	1.00

Note: The underlined figures would be the only values extracted from this table for the research participant which it represents. The first figure, −.12, is the (relatively large) discrepancy between this respondent's ratings of her real- and undesired-selves. The second figure, .64, is her (relatively small) real- versus ideal-self discrepancy score.

undesired-self discrepancies and life satisfaction. In the former case, $r = .37$ $(p < .01)$ and in the latter case $r = .72$ $(p < .0001)$. Supplementing these results, a multiple regression model showed that real-/undesired-self discrepancies explained more unshared variance $(p < .0001)$ in life satisfaction scores than did real-/ideal-self discrepancies $(p = .19)$.

The second part of this study tested the prediction that ideal-self descriptors are generally more abstract than are words applied to undesired-selves. This prediction paralleled the guiding theoretical view that the undesired-self is more experience-based than is the ideal-self and, thereby, is more likely to be described in more concrete terms. This prediction was tested in the following manner.

Fifty of the most frequently used features that participants generated to describe their ideal-selves were compared with fifty of the most frequently used undesired-self descriptors. These one-hundred features were randomly merged into one list, and each feature was rated by thirty-two judges on a seven-point concrete versus abstract scale. The results clearly showed that the majority of ideal-self descriptors were judged to be abstract, and that language used to depict features of the undesired-self was very concrete (Ogilvie 1987a, 383).

For example, a common feature of the ideal-self is *well-rounded* and an equally common feature of the undesired-self is *stupid*. Well-rounded was rated as highly abstract, whereas judges ranked stupid among the more concrete features. One interpretation of this result is that the ideal-self is largely ideational and, by comparison, the undesired-self is experiential.

That is, following from the examples of well-rounded and stupid, it is difficult to either experience or to describe experiences of well-roundedness. One research participant tried in this way. "Well-rounded? That's easy. I will feel well-rounded when I am not only this but I am also that and that and that. I'm sure your know what I mean. It will be something like being surrounded by a glow."

The same individual's description of being stupid was substantially more informative. Referring to a specific array of somatic reactions, she stated "When I realize I've done something stupid, I feel my head tightening. I get pulsating sensations in my temples. I get a weak feeling in my knees and ankles. I wonder if my legs will continue to allow me to stand. I get sweaty and embarrassed. If I've done something really stupid, I want very badly to disappear."

In summary, this study was the first to show that real-/undesired-self discrepancies co-vary more strongly with present-day self-evaluations than do real-/ideal-self discrepancy scores. Furthermore, evidence was gathered that supports the notion that undesired-selves are composed of words denoting mostly negative experiences, while ideal-selves consist of images of abstract possibilities.

A question raised as a result of this study was "Would the same pattern of results be found by using respondents much older than our college-age sample?" The next study was designed with this question in mind.

A SURVEY OF YOUNG AND OLDER ADULTS

Having shown the worth of including the undesired-self in self-discrepancy investigations, we wanted to know more about the overall contour of the land which we had entered. To do so—initially, at least—we set aside measurement devices and computer calculations from which discrepancy scores had been derived and focused instead on the following issue: We wondered if the notion of the undesired-self as experiential and the ideal-self as conceptual emerged only because the information being used had been gathered from a sample of college students. That is, were the results perhaps sample-driven?

Our hunch that a majority of college students judge themselves to have been at their worst or undesired-selves during adolescence or younger, and perceive their best or ideal-selves to be coming in the future was confirmed in a survey we will describe in this section.

But could the same argument be made for older adults? That is, do older adults show the same tendency to perceive their worst to have occurred in the past and the best as yet to come? Or rather does a reversal take place during the life span wherein some individuals in later life consider their best to be over and their worst to be now or coming in the future?

We addressed this question by replacing our earlier idiographic approach to data collection with a simple interview format that asked respondents to reflect on two domains of their lives (Ogilvie 1987c). First, we asked, "At what age were you or do you think you will be at your best?" That question was followed by "Please tell me what that was, is, or will be like."

The next question—one that often surprised respondents—was, "At what age were you or do you think you will be at your worst?" As with the first set of questions, respondents were asked to describe what being at their worst was, is, or will be like.

In collecting responses to these questions, we concentrated on two samples of convenience—college students and retirees, most of whom were interviewed at senior citizens' centers. Neither of these samples can be considered as truly representative of either age group and, as yet, we have paid only limited attention to individuals between the ages of twenty-five and fifty-nine—the ages between our two samples. Despite these limitations, our data offer some interesting leads.

First, group differences emerge when the age-at-best and age-at-worst data are collapsed. A respondent had the option of stating that the best was in the past, is now, or is anticipated to come in the future. The same three possibilities are available for answering the age-at-worst question. Nine categories are thus available for placing respondents. These categories are listed in the first column of table 6.3, which also contains the percentage of young adults and older adults, as well as male and female, in each category. These percentage figures are based on a sample of ninety-seven young adults and sixty-one senior citizens. The numbers of males and females in both samples are nearly equal.

Table 6.3
Past, Present, and Future "At Best" and "At Worst" Judgments

	Percentages of young adults (18–24 years old)		Percentages of older adults (60–85 years old)	
	Males	Females	Males	Females
1. Best to come/Worst over	55	59	0	3
2. Best to come/Worst to come	15	13	0	0
3. Best to come/Worst now	5	7	3	0
4. Best now/Worst over	7	3	14	24
5. Best now/Worst to come	4	0	20	20
6. Worst now/Best over	5	5	16	29
7. Worst over/Best over	2	7	20	12
8. Worst to come/Best over	5	5	27	12
9. Worst now/Best now	2	0	0	0

The most striking difference between young adults and older adults surfaces when the first three categories in table 6.3 are totaled. That done, 75 percent of the young adults state that the best is to come and only two older adults hold that belief. In addition, of the young adults who foresee the best to come, about three-fourths also believe that the worst is over. Most of the remainder of these individuals imagine themselves at their worst in old age.

So far, these results paint a bleak picture for elderly individuals. The picture brightens, however, when we look at the best-now categories located in rows 4 and 5. Here, 34 percent of the males and 44 percent of the females in the older group state that the best is now compared with a much smaller percentage of young adults (11 percent of the males and 3 percent of the females). But, it is also true that there is a higher percentage of older adults who judge their worst to be now and their best to have been in the past (row 6) than there are younger individuals in that category (approximately 20 percent versus 5 percent). Also of considerable interest is the fact that 63 percent of the older males indicate that their best is over (rows 6, 7, and 8). The comparable figures for the other groupings are 53 percent of older females, 17 percent for younger females, and 12 percent for younger males.

These data are rich in their potential for giving us quite useful life-span information that, in turn, can lead to the formulation of research to guide investigators in their efforts to interpret patterns of results. For example, it may be that the high proportion of older males (nearly two-thirds) who state that their best is over do so on the basis of our culture's emphasis on male physical prowess and ability to earn wages, both of which decline in later life. Indeed, our analyses of the words which people use to describe their best and worst conditions suggest that this may be the case.

In general, there is a strong tendency, regardless of sex or age, for respondents to first mention roles (such as, positions in a family, careers, ownerships, friendships, memberships, and the like) when they describe themselves at their best. For example, a twenty-two-year-old male stated, "I will be at my best when I am employed in a job that I like, own a nice home with a two-car garage with plenty of space left over for a workshop, and am married to an equally successful wife. Kids might be in the way, so I don't know whether or not we'll have any."

A seventy-three-year-old woman also made liberal use of roles when she reported, "I was at my best at around the age of fifty. My children were grown. My husband and I had a small farm we operated as a hobby. We were active in the Grange, in our church, and in a number of other social organizations."

However, when individuals describe themselves at their worst, most of them begin immediately by listing various negative features. Some examples are "I was at my worst during adolescence. I was confused, awkward, lonely, and felt pretty much worthless." "I am at my worst now. I am lost, really anxious, and things seem to be almost hopeless to me." "I'll be at my worst when I am old and dependent. I will have lost all of my hard-earned mental capacities."

This tendency toward role descriptions of the best and feature descriptions of the worst is consistent with earlier findings that the ideal-self is more abstract and conceptual while the undesired-self is more concrete. Again the undesired-self (or worst) may serve as an experiential anchoring point for judgements about the self. One can envision respondents deriving their answers by bringing to mind and cross-referencing two different mental lists.

One list contains roles, and the other contains self-referent features. The second list—the features list—is subdivided into a list of positive features and another list of negative ones. When addressing the "at-best" question, respondents first access their roles list and select one or more roles to convey their ideal-selves. When a role referred to is probed, the features list is cross-referenced and positive features of the self are named.

For example, one interviewer asked a subject, "Can you tell me what it will be like when you complete your internship?" The respondent stated, "I will be on my own, independent of all supervision. I will be relieved, happy, respected, productive, and able to make my own decisions."

The opposite happens in response to "at-worst" questions. Here, the features list is accessed first and negative features are called forth. When these features are probed—as in, "Can you tell me more about feeling lonely and confused?"—respondents cross over to their roles list and describe a time when a role to which they were, are, or plan to be committed (such as, an identity or valued self), was, is, or may be seriously challenged, disrupted, or rendered inoperative.

For adults, when such an event occurs or is imagined, our most-feared features of the self are laid bare, and we stand face-to-face with our undesired selves. For example, the least satisfied elderly males in this study were individuals who had lost major roles through retirement and had not been able to replace them with new roles that would have enabled them to express valued aspects or features of the self. This phenomenon is consistent with research showing that an important aspect of self-esteem in older adults is the amount of time these individuals spend in identities that are most central to their self-definitions (Ogilvie 1987b).

However, as the following example makes clear, it is not necessary to lose a role through retirement, death of a spouse, injury, or some other major event in order to give rise to negative features. Sometimes, the role itself is reevaluated and found wanting. A thirty-six-year-old housewife—one of the few middle-aged individuals we have interviewed—reports, "I've been at my worst for several years now. Previous to then, I had been satisfied being a wife and mother. I enjoyed having a nutritious meal prepared when everyone came home. I took pride in how clean I kept the house. Then I became a witch. Something went wrong. I got depressed. When I wasn't depressed, I was angry. I became a monster and hated it. When I functioned at all, I functioned like a robot doing all those things that my mother did, my grandmother did, and probably my grandmother's mother did. I am still a housewife, but I've gotten interested in some other things and I am taking some classes now. My condition is improving. I'm liking myself a lot better now, and I think my family is liking me more, too."

A PARADOX

It is convenient to think of the ideal-self and the undesired-self as terminal points at the opposite ends of a single dimension with the real-self moving back and forth along that dimension in accordance with present-day circumstances. Thus, an individual who is "close to my best" must, by definition, also be "far from my worst." However, our psychological worlds appear not to be that parsimonious. Rather, it seems that individuals' at-best and at-worst assessments are made in reference to two independent and interacting spheres of mental activity.

Consider the example of the individual appearing in row 9 of table 6.3 who stated that he was experiencing both his best *and* his worst at the present time. This person, a twenty-three-year-old male returning student, was participating in a drug rehabilitation program. He stated, "I am at my best right now because I am working hard on becoming a drug-free person, clean." Later, in reference to being at his worst, he said, "The worst is now. It's horrible. Every cell in my body is screaming out for cocaine. Streams and tributaries are opening up in my brain, and sometimes I can't stand it. I am anxious and terribly frightened. Even those words don't describe how awful it is."

Reference was made to an abstract versus concrete dimension in the first study already described in which it was found that features used to describe ideal-selves were rated to be more abstract than were the words selected to depict undesired-selves. The open-ended interview format used in our survey of college students and retirees permitted this phenomenon to reappear in a different form. That is, individuals tend to bring to mind roles (such as drug-free person) when describing their ideal-selves and features (usually those connoting negative affect such as alone, frightened, or anxious) when describing their undesired-selves. That result could not be obtained in the first study because research participants were restricted to rating their different selves in terms of features.

Although it is still quite likely that the undesired-self is more experiential than is the ideal-self for younger subjects, older subjects have taught us to broaden our conception and think in terms of two mental circuits—one being abstract and role-related, and the other being specific and affect-related—that are differentially brought into working memory in response to our "at-worst" and "at-best" questions. Thus, what initially appeared to be a violation of common sense falls into place when the image of a single at-best or at-worst evaluative dimension is discarded.

The degree of independence of mental operations activated by making at-best and at-worst judgements was among the next issues to be addressed. Before such assessments could be made, however, some additional work had to be done on the problem of measurement.

FROM COMPLEX TO SIMPLE: THE DEVELOPMENT OF A NEW SELF-DISCREPANCY MEASURE

It appeared unlikely that anyone would attempt to replicate Ogilvie's first study using the procedures he described (Ogilvie 1987a). That was virtually assured by the fact that the algorithm used in the study had been replaced by a new model (DeBoeck and Rosenberg 1988) that, despite its elegance, does not compute belongingness values. Even if that event had not taken place, there was a definite need for the development of more convenient and user-friendly measures of real-/ideal-self and real-/undesired-self discrepancies.

Several possibilities were considered and finally it was agreed to adopt a principle of "simpler is better." Following that guideline, two measures were created. One measure, named the *Best-Scale* asks respondents to rate how close or far they are from their ideal-selves using the following instructions and rating format:

In terms of the variety of ways I think and feel about myself in life, I would say that currently (during the past week or so) I am:
Close to being   Far from being
   at my best _ _ _ _ _ _ _ _ _ _ _ _ _ _ _at my best
            Place an "X" on the line that best represents
                           your answer.

The other scale—the worst-scale—is exactly the same except the ends of the scale are defined by "Close to being at my worst" at left and "Far from being at my worst" at right. Real-/ideal-self and real-/undesired-self discrepancy scores are calculated by counting the number of line segments that separate the X from the scale-end position at right.

SELF-DISCREPANCY AND DEPRESSIVE AFFECT

Paprota (1988) was the first investigator to use the best- and worst-scales. In a two-part study of *(a)* the statistical relationship between real-/ideal-self and real-/undesired-self discrepancies and *(b)* the degree to which both discrepancies covary with depressive affect, Paprota administered these scales along with the Center for Epidemiologic Studies Depression Scale, dubbed CES-D (Radloff 1977), and several filler instruments to seventy sixteen- to eighteen-year-old high-school students (thirty-six males and thirty-four females).

The Covariation of Discrepancy Scores

The first matter addressed by Paprota was the relationship between real-/ideal-self and real-/undesired-self discrepancy scores. If the correlation between the two scales approximated −1.00, that would mean that both scales measure the same dimension of self-assessment. On the other hand, if the correlation between the scales was low, support would be given to the proposition that real-/ideal-self and real-/undesired-self discrepancies are separate dimensions.

In Paprota's study, the correlation between the two measures was .06. This means that, for this sample of high-school students, one cannot predict an individual's real-/undesired-self discrepancy score by knowing his or her real-/ideal-self discrepancy score or vice versa. This makes sense in that many of these young people consider that they have a life-time of reaching goals ahead of themselves and, thus, may estimate that there is a considerable amount of distance between where they are now and when their bests will be forthcoming. Being close to, or far from, their worst at the present time is a very different, and quite independent, judgement.[4]

This result supports the view that ideal-selves and undesired-selves do not lie on the opposite poles of a single dimension. Findings to be reported later show that the correlations between real-/ideal-self and real-/undesired-self discrepancies fluctuate from sample to sample. For example, the correlation rose to .37 in a sample of young adult females and returned to .06 in a sample of older adult males and females. Our speculations regarding what these results may indicate appear later in this report.

Depression

The other focus of Paprota's research was on the relationship between the two types of discrepancy scores and depressive affect. It would seem to be self-evident that persons who judge themselves to be close to their worst (that is, those who obtain low real-/undesired-self discrepancy scores) are likely to obtain relatively high scores on depression. Reversing the causal implications of the previous statement, people who are depressed are also likely to view themselves as operating close to their worst. Self-evident as either formulation might be, to actually test the relationship presented an opportunity to, once again, challenge psychology's relentless focus on real-/ideal-self discrepancies. For example, Higgins and his associates have shown in several studies that real-/ideal-self discrepancy scores are predictive of depression mood-states whereas real-/ought-self discrepancies are more indicative of anxiety (Higgins, Klein & Strauman 1985; Higgins, Bond, Klein & Strauman 1986). Attending only to the former pattern of results, it was predicted that both real/ideal-self and real-/undesired-self discrepancy scores would be significantly related to depression scores *and* that the relationship would hold more strongly for real-/undesired-self discrepancies. With one exception, all hypotheses were confirmed. For the entire sample, the correlation between real-/ideal-self discrepancies and CES-D scores was $-.33$ ($p < .005$). Broken down by sex, however, it was shown that the correlation for females was $-.46$, but for males, it fell to $-.05$.

The prediction that real-/undesired-self discrepancies would correlate more strongly with the CES-D measure of depressive affect than would real-/ideal-self discrepancies was confirmed for the entire group and for both sexes with $r = -.56$ ($p < .0001$) for sexes combined, $r = -.67$ ($p < .0001$) for females, and $r = -.40$ ($p < .01$) for males. Also, the prediction that the worst-scale covaries more strongly with depression scores than does the best-scale was statistically confirmed, $z = 1.706$, $F(z) = 0.955$ ($p < .05$). Finally, the results of regressing the depression variable onto the best-scale and worst-scale revealed that the latter variable (real-/undesired-self discrepancy) explained more than 40 percent of the variance. The corresponding figure for the real-/ideal-self measure was less than 5 percent of the variance.

In a follow-up study, Fuzzi demonstrated in 1989 that the same pattern of results occurs using a modified version of a method developed by Higgins. In Higgins's work, subjects are asked to list up to ten traits or attributes associated with three different self-concepts: the actual self, the ideal self, and the ought self.

Discrepancy scores are derived by first determining the numbers of synonyms and antonyms used to describe any two pairs. Then, the number of matches is subtracted from the number of mismatches, and the resulting figure is used as the discrepancy measure. For example, if a subject used five synonymous attributes (matches) to describe her real-self and her ideal-self and two antonyms (mismatches) in making the same comparison, her real/ ideal-self discrepancy score would be -3.00.

As has already been indicated, Higgins has shown consistent relations between real-/ideal-self discrepancies and dejection-related emotions and between real-/ought-self discrepancies and agitation-related emotions. Since Fuzzi's interest was in replicating Paprota's study, she substituted ought self descriptions with undesired-self descriptions. Thus, in this design, participants were asked to create three lists of ten traits and attributes descriptive of their actual-, ideal-, and undesired-selves. Real-/ideal-self and real/ undesired-self discrepancy scores were determined using Higgins's method of calculation.

A sample of ninety undergraduates (thirty-seven males and fifty-three females) was administered Higgins's task—as modified by Fuzzi—along with the CES-D scale and several filler instruments used to separate the primary measures. The results showed the same pattern of results found by Paprota. For the entire sample, the correlation between real-/ideal-self discrepancy scores and depression scores was $.32$ $(p < .002)$. For males, $r = .26$ $(n.s.)$, and for females, $r = .35$ $(p < .008)$. The corresponding figures for real-/ undesired-self discrepancies and depression were stronger. For the entire sample, $r = -.60$ $(p < .0001)$. Here, again, there was a sex difference. For females, $r = -.66$ $(p < .0001)$, and for males, $r = -.48$ $(p < .008)$.

Thus, the best-scale and the worst-scale (Paprota 1988) and Higgins's modified method (Fuzzi 1989) show similar patterns of results regarding the relationships between real-/undesired-self and real-/ideal-self discrepancy scores and depressive affect. That is, the relationship between real-/undesired-self discrepancies and depressive affect is stronger than the relationship between real-/ideal-self discrepancies and depressive affect, and this pattern holds more strongly for females than for males.

YOUNG-ADULT SEX DIFFERENCES

Just and Clark both conducted a replication study of self-discrepancy, depression, and life satisfaction involving 323 young adults (174 females and 149 males) (Just 1988; Clark 1988). Using the best-scale and worst-scale measure of real-/ideal-self and real/ undesired-self discrepancies, predictions that real-/undesired-self discrepancy scores (worst-scale) would covary more strongly with depressive mood states and life satisfaction than would real-/ideal-self (best-scale) discrepancies were confirmed. For both sexes, the worst-scale measure was a better predictor of both life satisfaction and depression than was the best-scale measure. The study also re-affirmed a pattern of results that had been seen in other studies regarding sex differences. That is, for every prediction, the real/undesired-self discrepancy measure was more strongly related to outcome variables for females than for males. In every case, correlation figures were at least twenty-five points higher for females than for males when the worst-scale was correlated with the CES-D and life-satisfaction scales.

One instrument used in this study asked participants to state the age at which they were or expected to be at their worst. Following that, they were asked to write about what being at their worst was, is, or will be like. A content analysis of written descriptions of at-worst states was conducted in order to deepen our understanding of sex differences that were now emerging on a regular basis. A sample of two-hundred statements was randomly selected from the available pool of 323 documents (one-hundred female and one-hundred male responses). Just (1988) developed content analysis categories on an inductive basis using half of the sample that had been selected. After the categories was established and were defined well enough to produce high interrater agreement, all two-hundred documents were scored. The results, we believe, have given us a considerable amount of new information regarding worst-scale sex differences. The following is a summary of the content analysis findings.

1. Thirty percent of the male responses were categorized as defensive. This category includes no response, answers judged to be unrealistic (such as, "I will be at my worst when I am 107 and dead"), and written statements such as "I don't know what you're asking for," and "Listen, I don't even want to talk about it." No female responses were suitable for placement in this category. In addition, 27 percent of the males who described themselves at their worst distanced themselves from their statements by noting that "all that" was in the past and, at the present time, they are in much better shape. Only 15 percent of the females covered over their statements in this fashion.

2. Sixty-four percent of the females stated that their worst took place within the past seven years. Forty-four percent of the males said the same. More than half of all females described their worst to

have been when they were not getting along with their parents or some other member of their immediate families. Only 3 percent of the males referred to similar circumstances.

3. Nearly all females who did not mention past family relations as contexts for worst states wrote about relations with non-family members as context for past, present, or projected future periods of distress. Indeed, 90 percent of the females identified their worst selves as occurring in interpersonal relationships. Only 30 percent of the males made any references to other people. Rather, males showed a greater tendency to be concerned about occupational failures, instrumental ineptitude, and the prospects of physical and mental decline.

Earlier, we stated that two interrelated but separable spheres of mental activity seem to be differentially activated when at-best and at-worst questions are posed. In regards to being at one's best, an abstract list containing roles and general social labels is accessed. At-worst queries tend to activate memories of negative emotional experiences. Results from the content analysis study indicate that females have greater access to the emotional memory system than do males. This idea is consistent with contemporary theory and research findings regarding sex differences and emotion.

For example, several studies have shown that females have an advantage over males in their ability to read emotion cues (Buck 1984). Diener, Sandvik, and Larsen reported in 1985 that females tend to experience emotions at a greater intensity than do males, and they suggested that past affective experiences may be more salient to females. Complementing these results, Malatesta and Kalnok (1984) found that adult females, regardless of age, count emotion as more important to their lives than do men and use the language of affect more frequently.

In a completely different area of psychological investigation, research on cerebral lateralization and hemispheric activation continues to affirm that the left hemisphere of the brain is largely ideational, analytic, and linear. An area of specialization recently added to right-brain functioning is the processing of negative affect (Davidson, Schaffer & Saron 1985; Leventhal & Tomarken 1986; Reuter-Lorenz, Givis & Moscovitch 1983). While we need not rely on brain research to verify gender differences, it seems quite likely that females have greater access to right-brain circuitry than do males. Hints that this may be true comes from the results of the work of Ingram, Cruet, Johnson, and Wisnicki (1988) who reported that females are more responsive than are males to negative affect.

To summarize our own views regarding sex differences, we must backtrack for a moment. First, it was proposed that the undesired-self is a more securely established marker for assessing present-day well-being than is the ideal-self. From this proposition, the prediction was made that real-/undesired-self discrepancies would correlate more strongly with life satisfaction and depressive affect than would real-/ideal-self discrepancies. These predictions were confirmed in several studies and they were especially confirmed for females. Just's (1988) content analysis study showed why that might be so. Young-adult females are far more likely than their male counterparts to identify past incidents of interpersonal disruptions to be times when they were at their worst. This fits well with the emergent view, that females' personal identities are based on connections with others whereas, early-on, males learn that one of their major tasks is to establish their separateness from others (Belenky, Clenchy, Goldberger & Tarule 1986; Gilligan 1982).

It follows from these speculations that persons (primarily females) most invested in maintaining relationships would be more likely to viscerally record instances of disturbances in the flow of their own relationships with others. For these individuals, the discrepancy between "how I feel right now" and "what it is like for me when my relationships are going poorly" (that is, the real/undesired-self discrepancy) would be more tightly calibrated than for individuals (primarily males) who have less specific reference points for making at-worst judgements.

FURTHER STUDIES OF OLDER ADULTS

Periodically, Carlson issues reminders that the world is not peopled entirely by eighteen- to twenty-two-year-old college students (Carlson 1971, 1984). For academic researchers in many areas of psychology, this sobering fact should make us aware that our discoveries in campus labs may be less generalizable than we would like to think. This observation is underscored by the results of replicating our procedures with samples of senior members of the population. As always, when we have done that, our ideas have been expanded. The following study is offered as an example.

In 1988, Clark administered the best- and worst-scales to a sample of fifty-seven noninstitutionalized elderly adults (twenty-four males and thirty-three females) ranging in age from sixty to ninety-seven. Instruments measuring self-perceived health status, life satisfaction, and depressive affect were included in the packet. Here again, sex differences were revealed. Consistent with the findings with young adults, for older females, real-/undesired-self discrepancies correlated more strongly with depression, $r = -.43$ $(p < .01)$ and life satisfaction, $r = .54$ $(p < .001)$ than for older males. For older males, the two correlations were well below statistical significance, $r = -.17$ for depression and .02 for life satisfaction.

However, for the first time in our studies, real-/ideal-self discrepancies were shown to be correlated with life satisfaction, $r = .48$ $(p<.02)$ and depression, $r = -.37$ $(p < .06)$ with real-/ undesired-self discrepancies falling completely out of the picture. These results were obtained from the elderly males. The corresponding figures for elderly females were low and not significant. Although the sample of males was small and the study must be replicated using a larger number of respondents, the trend is a fascinating one. Our interpretation of it follows.

Earlier in table 6.3, it was shown that 63 percent of the elderly males in another sample stated that their best was over. In Clark's sample, 68 percent of the elderly males held the same belief. This suggests that elderly males now have past ideal-self pegs to use in assessing their present sense of well-being, just as females have used the undesired-self as a marker throughout the course of their lives.

In other words, elderly males recall a time when they were at their occupational best or physical peak. For them, it is not a future possible self as the ideal-self is typically portrayed in the literature (Markus & Nurius 1986). Rather, it is a remembered-self of the past. It seems that elderly males rely on cognitive representations of past roles and activities in assessing their current state of well-being which is their analogue to females' life-span reliance on their greater access to affective memory systems.

Further support for this lies in the fact that older males are similar to younger males who were described by Just (1988) as being defensive when asked to write about themselves at their worst. That is, while half of the older males, like older females, stated that the worst was yet to come, the older men cited unrealistic ages (generally, age one-hundred or older) at which they believed they might experience their worst. Thus, older males distanced themselves from the affect-laden undesired self, just as did many of the younger males who experienced difficulties in responding to our worst-selves inquiries.

Clark then attempted to replicate the stepwise regression results that had been obtained with the several samples of young adults. Whenever regression models had been applied to the data sets from young adults (as when depression was regressed onto several independent variables), real-/undesired-self discrepancies were always identified as primary explanatory variables with real-/ideal-self discrepancies arriving at a distant second. The results Clark obtained with her sample of older adults were substantially different.

This time, the stepwise regression model showed that self-perceived health status accounted for 40 percent of the variance in life satisfaction scores, and 24 percent of the variance in depressive affect, with no additional (statistically significant) variance being explained by either real-/ideal- or real-/undesired-self discrepancy scores. When a similar analysis was done by sex, marital status was a significant predictor of depression for older males, and level of education predicted depression for older females. Married males and better educated females were less depressed than were their same-sexed peers.

Thus far, our theorizing about these and related results has gone in the following directions. In later life, the ideal-self and the undesired-self both lose their edge. This is not to say that they have become blurred and forgotten. Indeed, our older respondents are similar to Paprota's high-school students with respect to making independent judgements regarding real-/ideal-self and real/ undesired-self discrepancies. The correlation between these discrepancies in both samples was .06. This statistic, however, probably masks an important difference.

Most high-school students preparing for college admission and/or careers imagine their best to be several years away in the future. At-worst judgements are independent of the former assessment. Older adults make clear distinctions between worst and best states, but the importance of these conditions in relation to well-being is considerably diminished.

Instead, marital status (for older males), educational level (for older females), and health status (for both males and females) are what matter. Surely, income would also stand out if lower economic groups had been included in Clark's sample.

As previously mentioned, middle-aged individuals have been neglected in our research. Were we to study them, our prediction would be that there is a rise in the covariation between real-/ideal-self and real-/undesired-self discrepancy scores throughout the first half of life. We have shown that correlations between these variables increase in young-adult samples. We envision that figure as taking another leap among individuals who are presently raising children and/or who are at or near the heights of their careers. Several times throughout this chapter, it has been suggested that individuals refer to two independent and interacting domains of mental activity when making at-best and at-worst assessments. With middle-aged individuals, we would stress the *interactive* aspect of this formulation of how these assessments are made. That is, we suspect that there is a stronger relationship between progress on immediate goals and affective experiences during this period of life. However, beyond middle-age and into older age, what had become increasingly aligned along a single best/worst dimension once again becomes differentiated and multidimensional. In effect, ideal-selves become less compelling and undesired-selves less threatening in later life.

Our line of thinking is consistent with recent theoretical developments in the area of cognition. In 1985, Labouvie-Vief proposed that adult thinking is more pragmatic and tempered by reality than is the thinking of younger persons. Riegel (1976) views human development as a dialectic process involving an increased ability to accept contradictions leading to higher levels of integration.

Kramer (1983) identified three forms of thinking: (1) mechanistic, a form often characteristic of adolescence that involves a commitment to absolute truths, idealism, and dichotomization; (2) relativistic, a more advanced form of thinking that includes acceptance of change and contradictions and the realization that there is no absolute reality; and (3) dialectic/organismic, a more integrated form of thinking that manages to organize earlier relativistic positions in a manner that unifies seemingly unrelated patterns into a larger vision of the whole. Dialectic thinking—perhaps a key element of wisdom—is a likely component of successful life review that Erikson promoted in 1963 as a vital aspect of the final stage of life.

Our words regarding the blunting of real-/ideal-self and real-/undesired-self discrepancies and concomitant dialectic forms of thinking are not nearly as vivid in conveying our ideas as are the words of an eighty-three-year-old man who participated in one of our surveys. He said, "My best and worst? My best and worst are over. And you know something? The best was never all that great, and the worst was never as awful as I thought it would be. I wish I had known that before. I wouldn't have struggled so much. I could have done what I do now. I get up, experience the day, and then I go back to bed. Had I discovered the joke when I was a young man, I would have gotten more accomplished, had more fun doing it, and would have had a lot more time for others along the way. But I have no regrets. Things pretty much had to be the way they were."

In summary, one never knows in advance where revelations on a dreary day will lead. In this instance, it led to several studies to ferret out how the undesired-self affects self-judgements and ended with a memorable quotation from an elderly gentleman. His thoughts about his life assist us in reminding ourselves and the reader that neither the ideal-self nor the undesired-self are isolated, static entities. They are part of the fabric of the self in motion. Their contents evolve and change, are variously more important and less important, as individuals face ongoing and age-related challenges of making meaning from their life experiences.

NOTES

1. The final version of this chapter makes use of responses to an earlier draft made by Richard D. Ashmore and the two editors of this volume, Richard P. Lipka and Thomas M. Brinthaupt. The observations of these individuals were of particular value in assisting us in being more explicit about the theoretical underpinnings of our research. We are grateful for their comments.

2. We want to stress that emphasis is placed on *self-generated* information in all of the research which we report. While it would make our lives as researchers considerably easier if we surrendered to the sometimes powerful temptation to use experimenter-generated lists of words and categories, we are committed to using our research participants' own vocabularies whenever the option arises. This commitment enables us to avoid the trap of insisting that individuals rate themselves on words, phrases, and dimensions that are outside their own experiences. One of the remarkable capacities of being human is our ability to judge the applicability of almost anything to almost anything else—even when we have no idea what either one or both of those *things* are. This is especially so for research subjects, most of whom are very good at (and many of whom are granted course credit for) following instructions. Admittedly, we are overstating the point but we do so to draw attention to the problem of what meaning researchers make of an array of scores and ratings some of which make sense to respondents and others that have no bearing on their everyday experience. (See also Brinthaupt & Erwin 1992).

3. Here and in other places in this report, *life satisfaction* is used as a primary dependent variable. The more common term applied to what we

refer to as *life satisfaction* is *self-esteem*. The two measures we used for life satisfaction—one for young adults and the other for older adults—contain several items that either duplicate or come close to duplicating items on standard self-esteem inventories (M. Rosenberg 1979). For example, the Life Satisfaction Questionnaire administered to young adults contained the items "On the whole, I am satisfied with my life" and "I generally think of myself as a happy person." Comparable items on Rosenberg's self-esteem instrument are "On the whole, I am satisfied with myself" and "I take a positive attitude toward myself." Older adults completed a modified version of the Life Satisfaction Index A (Neugarten, Havighurst & Tobin 1961). Two items on this instrument are "When I think back on my life, I didn't get most of the important things I wanted" and "As I look back on my life, I am fairly well satisfied." Items written in the same tone from Rosenberg's scale are "All in all, I am inclined to feel that I am a failure" and "I feel that I'm a person of worth, at least on an equal plane with others." We have not collected the data necessary to compute correlations among our instruments and instruments featuring self-esteem, but the overlapping surface appearances of most items in these various measures lead us to suspect that all of them ask respondents to assess how much they value themselves as individuals. In other words, it is probably justifiable to use *life satisfaction* and *self-esteem* interchangeably. We have kept the former label, not from any attachment to it, but because it was the term used in the original study from which the others were derived (Ogilvie 1987a).

4. The finding that "me at my worst" and "me at my best" are not opposite ends of a bipolar dimension parallels the work of investigators who have decomposed other dimensions previously assumed to be bipolar. For example, Constantinople (1973) was among the first to point out that masculinity and femininity should be viewed as independent and multifaceted phenomena rather than personality conceptions resting at opposite ends of a simple-minded dimension. Similarly, in the area of emotion, Diener and Emmons (1985) showed that positive and negative affect are relatively independent in several self-report studies.

REFERENCES

Ansbacher, H. L., and Ansbacher, R. R. 1956. *The individual psychology of Alfred Adler.* New York: Basic Books.

Ashmore, R. D., and Ogilvie, D. M. 1992. He's such a nice boy . . . when he's with grandma: Gender and evaluation in self-with-other representations. In *The self: Definitional and methodological issues,* edited by T. M. Brinthaupt and R. P. Lipka. Albany: State University of New York Press.

Bailey, R. C., and Bailey, K. G. 1971. Perceived ability in relation to actual ability and academic achievement. *Journal of Clinical Psychology* 27:461–463.

Beard, B. H., and Pishkin, V. 1970. Concept changes in training medical and nursing students. *Diseases of the Nervous System* 31:616–623.

Belenky, M. F.; Clenchy, B. M.; Goldberger, N. R.; and Tarule, J. M. 1986. *Women's way of knowing: The development of self, voice, and mind.* New York: Basic Books.

Berg, N. L. 1974. Self-concept of neurotic and sociopathic criminal offenders. *Psychological Reports* 34:622.

Boshier, R. 1972. The effect of academic failure on self-concept and maladjustment indices. *Journal of Educational Research* 65:347–3351.

Brinthaupt, T. M., and Erwin, L. J. 1992. Reporting about the self: Issues and implications. In *The self: Definitional and methodological issues,* edited by T. M. Brinthaupt and R. L. Lipka. Albany: State University of New York Press.

Buck, R. 1984. *The communication of emotion.* New York: The Guilford Press.

Burke, E. L. 1978. Some empirical evidence for Erikson's concept of negative identity in delinquent adolescent drug abusers. *Comprehensive Psychiatry* 19:141–152.

Carlson, R. 1971. Where is the person in personality research? *Psychological Bulletin* 75:203–219.

———. 1984. What's social about social psychology? Where's the person in personality research? *Journal of Personality and Social Psychology* 47:1304–1309.

Carroll, J. L., and Fuller, G. B. 1969. The self and ideal-self concept of the alcoholic as influenced by length of sobriety and/or participation in Alcoholics Anonymous. *Journal of Clinical Psychology* 6:363–364.

Clark, M. D. 1988. Real-/ideal-self and real-/undesired-self discrepancies as predictors of life satisfaction and depression. Unpublished master's thesis. New Brunswick, N.J.: Rutgers University, Department of Psychology.

Clifford, E., and Clifford, M. 1967. Self-concepts before and after survival training. *British Journal of Social and Clinical Psychology,* 6:241–248.

Constantinople, A. 1973. Masculinity-femininity: An exception to a famous dictum. *Psychological Bulletin* 80:389–407.

Czaja, S. J. 1975. Age differences in life satisfaction as a function of discrepancy between real and ideal self concepts. *Experimental Aging Research* 1:81–89.

Davidson, R. J.; Schaffer, C. E.; and Saron, C. 1985. Effects of lateralization presentations of faces on self-reports of emotion and EEG asymmetry in depressed and non-depressed subjects. *Psychophysiology* 22:353–363.

DeBoeck, P. 1983. Prototype analysis. Paper presented at the joint meeting of the Classification and Psychometric Societies. Jouyen Johas, France. July.

DeBoeck, P., and Rosenberg, S. 1988. Hierarchical classes: Model and data analysis. *Psychometrika* 53:361–381.

Diener, E., and Emmons, R. A. 1985. The independence of positive and negative affect. *Journal of Personality and Social Psychology* 47:1105–1117.

Diener, E.; Sandvik, E.; and Larsen, R. J. 1985. Age and sex effects for emotional intensity. *Developmental Psychology* 21:542–546.

Eisenman, R. 1970. Birth order, sex, self-esteem, and prejudice against the physically disabled. *Journal of Psychology* 75:147–155.

Erikson, E. H. 1963. *Childhood and society.* 2d ed. New York: W. W. Norton.

Fordham, F. 1953. *An introduction to Jung's psychology.* London: Penguin Books.

Freud, S. 1959. *Beyond the pleasure principle.* New York: Basic Books.

Fuzzi, P. 1989. Self-discrepancy and depressive affect: A replication study. Undergraduate honors thesis. New Brunswick, N.J.: Rutgers University, Department of Psychology.

Gara, M. A., and Rosenberg, S. 1979. The identification of persons as supersets and subsets in free-response personality descriptions. *Journal of Personality and Social Psychology* 37:2,161–2,170.

Gilligan, C. 1982. *In a different voice: Psychological theory and women's development.* Cambridge, Mass.: Harvard University Press.

Gottlieb, J. 1969. Attitudes toward retarded children: Effects of evaluator's psychological adjustment and age. *Scandinavian Journal of Educational Research* 3:170–182.

Gough, H. G.; Fioranvanti, M.; and Lazzari, R. 1983. Some implications of self versus ideal-self congruence on the revised adjective checklist. *Journal of Personality and Social Psychology* 44:1124–1220.

Higgins, E. T.; Klein, R.; and Strauman, T. 1985. Self-concept discrepancy theory: A psychological model for distinguishing among different aspects of depression and anxiety. *Social Cognition* 3:51–76.

Higgins, E. T.; Bond, R. N.; Klein, R.; and Strauman, T. 1986. Self-discrepancies and emotional vulnerability: How magnitude, accessibility, and type of discrepancy influence affect. *Journal of Personality and Social Psychology* 51:5–15.

Hoge, D. R., and McCarthy, J. D. 1983. Issues of validity and reliability in the use of real-ideal discrepancy scores to measure self-regard. *Journal of Personality and Social Psychology* 79:63–67.

Horney, K. 1950. *Neurosis and human growth.* New York: Norton.

Ingram, R. E.; Cruet, D.; Johnson, B. R.; and Wisnicki, K. S. 1988. Self-focused attention, gender, gender role, and vulnerability to negative affect. *Journal of Personality and Social Psychology* 55:967–978.

Jorgensen, E. C., and Howell, R. J. 1969. Changes in self, ideal-self correlations from ages 8 through 18. *Journal of Social Psychology* 79:63–67.

Just, N. 1988. A replication and extension of research in self-discrepancy: Sex differences and the undesired-self. Undergraduate honors thesis. New Brunswick, N.J.: Rutgers University, Department of Psychology.

Kramer, D. A. 1983. Post-formal operations? A need for further conceptualization. *Human Development* 26: 91–105.

Labouvie-Vief, G. 1985. Intelligence and cognition. In *Handbook of the Psychology of Aging.* Edited by J. E. Birren and K. W. Schaie. 2d ed. New York: Van Nostrand Reinhold Co. 500–520.

Leventhal, H., and Tomarken, A. J. 1986. Emotion: Today's problem. *Annual Review of Psychology,* 37:565–610.

Lindowski, D. C., and Dunn, M. A. 1974. Self-concept and acceptance of disability. *Rehabilitation Counseling Bulletin* 18:28–32.

Malatesta, C. Z., and Kalnok, M. 1984. Emotional experience in younger and older adults. *Journal of Gerontology* 39:301–308.

Markus, H., and Nurius, P. 1986. Possible selves. *American Psychologist* 41:954–969.

Neimeyer, R. A., and Chapman, K. M. 1980–1981. Self-ideal discrepancy and fear of death: The test of an existential hypothesis. *Omega: Journal of Death and Dying* 11:233–24.

Neugarten, B. L.; Havighurst, R. J.; and Tobin, S. 1961. The measurement of life satisfaction. *Journal of Gerontology* 16:134–143.

Ogilvie, D. M. 1987a. The undesired self: A neglected variable in personality research. *Journal of Personality and Social Psychology* 52:379–385.

————. 1987b. Life satisfaction and identity structure in late middle-aged men and women. *Psychology and Aging* 2:217–224.

————. 1987c. Beliefs about satisfaction over the life-span. Invited address at the Max Planck Institute. Berlin, Germany.

Ogilvie, D. M., and Lutz, M. 1984. The representation of multiple identities. Unpublished manuscript. New Brunswick, N.J.: Rutgers University, Department of Psychology.

Paprota, M. 1988. Real/undesired-self discrepancies and depression in male and female high school students. Undergraduate Honors Thesis. New Brunswick, N.J.: Rutgers University, Department of Psychology.

Parsons, O. A.; Yourshaw, S.; and Borstelmann, L. 1968. Self-discrepancies on the MMPI: Consistencies over time and geographic region. *Journal of Counseling Psychology* 15:160–166.

Perlman, G. 1972. Change in self- and ideal self-concept congruence of beginning psychotherapists. *Journal of Clinical Psychology* 28:404–408.

Radloff, L. S. 1977. The CES-D Scale: A self-report depression scale for research in the general population. *Applied Psychological Measurement* 1:385–401.

Rank, O. 1971. *The double.* Chapel Hill: The University of North Carolina Press.

Reuter-Lorenz, P.; Givis, R. P.; and Moscovitch, M. 1983. Hemispheric specialization and the perception of emotion: Evidence from right-handers and from inverted and noninverted left-handers. *Neuropsychologia* 21:687–692.

Riegel, K. F., 1976. The dialectics of human development. *American Psychologist* 31:689–700.

Rogers, C. R. 1954. The case of Mrs. Oak: A research analysis. In *Psychotherapy and personality change,* edited by C. R. Rogers and R. F. Dymond. Chicago: University of Chicago Press.

Rosenberg, M. 1979. *Conceiving the self.* New York: Basic Books.

Rosenberg, S. 1977. New approaches to the analysis of personal constructs in person perception. *Nebraska Symposium on Motivation.* Vol. 24. Lincoln: University of Nebraska Press. 174–242.

Sharma, S. 1970. Self concept and adjustment. *Indian Psychological Review* 6:71–76.

Stephenson, W. 1953. *The study of behavior.* Chicago: University of Chicago Press.

Stern, D. 1985. *The interpersonal world of the infant.* New York: Basic Books.

Sullivan, H. S. 1953. *The interpersonal theory of psychiatry.* New York: Norton.

Van-Dyne, W. T., and Carskadan, T. G. 1978. Relations among three components of self-concept and same and opposite-sex human figure drawings. *Journal of Clinical Psychology* 34:537–538.

JOHN H. MUELLER
W. CALVIN JOHNSON
ALISON DANDOY
TIM KELLER

7

Trait Distinctiveness and Age Specificity in the Self-Concept

INTRODUCTION

This chapter will examine self-concept differences between young and elderly adults. Such differences are significant for what they may tell us about age-related changes in personality, and also how these personality changes may affect cognitive processes.

A critical concern in our research has been how memories are affected by involvement of the self-concept. Past experiences are presumably organized into memory structures, concepts, or schemas, and, when a current event can be integrated into one of these pre-existing units, it seems to be more durably encoded.

Recent developments in personality research have focused on the special value of the self-concept as an organizing structure, with particular attention to its benefits relative to semantic concepts or schemas involving other people (Rogers, Kuiper & Kirker 1977). Thus, research on how self-referencing affects memory tells us about how new events are combined with old information in memory—specifically how the self-concept functions to interpret our experiences—and the form of the memory-effects may tell us indirectly about the structure of the self-concept.

Five primary questions will be addressed in this chapter. First, does the self-concept serve as effectively as a mnemonic aid for elderly adults as appears to be the case with young adults? This is important because elderly adults often show some memory deficit relative to younger subjects, and this may be due to a failure to spontaneously utilize various memory techniques.

Second, are elderly subjects less self-aware than young adults? This is important because of what it may reveal about age-related personality differences, and also because degree of self-awareness often moderates the benefits of self-referential processing.

Third, do we have age-specific vocabularies to describe young and elderly adults, reflecting age-appropriate traits? This is important because of what it may reflect about the content of the self-schema as we grow older, as well as the view of older people as they are constituted in the other-person schemas of younger people.

Fourth, if there are such age-specific traits, do such limits on the content of the self-concept moderate the memorial effects of self-referential processing? It appears that the activity of self-referencing is most effective when the event is a part of the self-concept, so that any age-related differences in content may limit those benefits.

Finally, is age-specificity fairly general in terms of traits, or is it more apparent for self-content that is distinctively true of the individual? These questions will be addressed using procedures developed in social-cognition research (Srull 1984). The main technique will be briefly described before considering these specific questions.

SELF-REFERENCE AS AN ENCODING STRATEGY

Origins and Background

The orienting-task methodology is widely used in memory research to control which attribute of an event is encoded in order to determine how that attribute affects retention. For example, subjects who are required to generate a synonym for each study word will subsequently remember the study words better than subjects who generate a rhyme or otherwise superficially process the study items. Although this technique is readily compatible with the levels of processing theory (Craik & Lockhart 1972), it predates that framework and the procedure itself can be extended to other interpretations.

This methodology was applied in social cognition experiments that introduced encoding decisions involving personality attributes as exemplified in trait adjectives, such as honest and friendly. Some studies employed orienting decisions with photographs of people, and found that this led to better retention of the faces than when physical features were examined by subjects (Bower & Karlin 1974; Courtois & Mueller 1979). Other studies used personality decisions to examine how the traits themselves were processed, and what that might reveal about how personality information is stored in memory. For example, Rogers, Kuiper, and Kirker (1977) included study decisions such as "Does this word describe you?" and compared retention with these self-reference decisions to retention with semantic encoding (such as synonym generation) and nonsemantic encoding (rhyme generation).

Several early experiments with the self-reference procedure demonstrated that trait adjectives involved in self-reference judgments were generally better remembered than those involved in other decisions. Such an outcome suggested that the self-concept is a highly organized structure, which readily accommodates new experiences and assures their retention. Furthermore, in addition to enhancing memory, these experiments often also showed that the speed of making a self-reference decision was faster than for other-descriptiveness decisions, as if the information in the highly developed self-concept was more readily accessible (Kuiper & Rogers 1979).

However, comparing self-reference to semantic decisions essentially compares a personality judgment to a nonpersonality dimension, so it is not clear whether the benefit is a special feature of the self-concept or some benefit that would also occur for an encoding that involves a schema for any other person as well. One way to test this point is to have the self-reference condition compared to another person, such as when the control question asks "Does this word describe your best friend?"

When self-descriptiveness encoding is compared to other descriptiveness encoding, the self-reference benefit also occurs, but it may be smaller when the other person is someone whom we know well, such as a best friend, compared to a target other who is less well-known to us, such as George Bush (Bower & Gilligan 1979; Keenan & Baillet 1980).

Self-reference Benefits and Aging

Effects involved in the self-reference paradigm have been reviewed elsewhere (Greenwald & Pratkanis 1984), and we will limit our attention to the life-span implications here. The demonstration that activating the self-concept during encoding enhances memory is potentially relevant to a general concern in gerontological research. Specifically, there is a tendency for elderly subjects to typically show some deficit on laboratory memory tasks relative to college students (Kausler 1982; Salthouse 1982). This deficit is often small, and it can be reduced sometimes by explicitly requiring the elderly subjects to use some encoding strategy, such as forming images.

Given the benefits of self-referencing, we can ask how this activity may be involved in cognitive processing as we grow older, and three general concerns arise. Is just using the self-concept a problem for the elderly? Or is the use somehow constrained in its effectiveness by age-related changes in the content of the self-concept? Or is it moderated by some related process, such as self-awareness or self-esteem?

One possibility is that elderly subjects are simply less likely than young adults to spontaneously activate the self-concept, just as they seem less likely to generate images or other effective mnemonics. If this is the case, then requiring them to make self-comparisons could activate the self-concept and yield the corresponding memory benefits. Thus, an experiment using a self-reference task could answer two questions: First, do elderly subjects show the young-adult pattern of self-reference benefits relative to other-reference and semantic encoding? Second, do the elderly still show a deficit relative to young adults when self-reference is explicitly induced? The relevant research is limited, but it seems to suggest that both questions can be answered in the affirmative.

Spees, Cates, Nakfoor, and Lapsley (1987) compared young- and elderly adults using self-reference, synonym, and rhyme encoding decisions. They found that the best recall was associated with self-reference encoding, followed by semantic and acoustic, as expected. Elderly subjects recalled less than did young adults in every condition. Thus, even with imposed self-reference, the elderly subjects did not perform as well as did the college students.

Whereas Spees and colleagues used a between-subject design, Mueller, Wonderlich, and Dugan (1986) examined the self-reference strategy in a within-subject design with young and elderly adults in which each subject made some self-descriptiveness decisions and some decisions about other people. In this case, the subject made both decisions about people, as opposed to comparing a person-schema and a nonperson decision as in the procedure used by Spees and colleagues. Thus, the within-subject design should be more sensitive to self-other differences.

As usual, young adults showed better incidental recall, and self-reference led to better retention than did other-reference. However, once again, there was no age-by-encoding task interaction. In other words, elderly subjects did benefit from self-reference as a task relative to other-referencing, but the young-old recall advantage was not overcome even with self-reference.

Thus, the result seemed to be independent of whether each subject made just one encoding decision for every word (between-subject) or made each decision about different words (within-subject), and whether the comparison involved self-reference versus semantic encoding or self-reference versus the schema for another person. Furthermore, Mueller and Ross (1984) found a recall deficit even after elderly subjects made both self- and other-descriptiveness decisions for every word. Therefore, the general outcome seems to be well-established. Elderly subjects can employ and benefit from self-referencing, but this strategy does not completely eliminate the age-related recall deficit.

Of course, there may be some related process that varies with age which moderates the ability of elderly subjects to benefit fully from self-reference encoding. One candidate for such a process is "self consciousness," which has been shown to be a factor in determining the magnitude of self-reference benefits with young adults (Agatstein & Buchanan 1984). In other words, college students differ in the extent to which they are self-examining, and those who are most self-aware seem to benefit most from using the self-reference strategy. The question may then be asked as to whether elderly subjects as a group show less self consciousness, thereby suggesting another mechanism in the recall deficit as well as an age-related difference in personality. In addition, it would be of interest within the elderly group to know whether elderly subjects who are more self-aware benefit more from self-reference encoding in the same way as do young adults. Thus, there are several reasons to examine the personality dimension of self-awareness in elderly subjects.

SELF-AWARENESS IN ELDERLY ADULTS

A number of studies have tried to identify personality dimensions that change or do not change as we grow older. For example,

McCrae and Costa have presented cogent arguments and considerable data to indicate essential stability of the personality over the life span, (McCrae & Costa 1982; Costa & McCrae 1980). On the other hand, Gaber (1984) found some evidence that the self-concept of elderly subjects was structured somewhat differently than for younger people, being composed of perhaps just three factors rather than five. Nehrke, Hulicka, and Morganti (1980) also noted some change in the self-concept, even when the subject pool was restricted to the upper end of the age range. Other investigators have examined changes in views of related dimensions with age, such as well-being (Ryff 1989) and attributional style (Burns & Seligman 1989).

However, few studies have specifically examined self-awareness or self-monitoring in the elderly. This activity seems critical as a component of the personality, as a mechanism for enriching and articulating the content of the self-concept, and as a factor in fully utilizing self-reference as an encoding strategy. If elderly subjects are deficient or merely different in some way in terms of self-awareness, that would have ramifications for the interaction of the self-concept with other cognitive functions.

A number of inventories have been used by personality theorists to assess self-awareness, and the Self-Consciousness Questionnaire (SCQ) (Fenigstein, Scheier & Buss 1975; Buss 1980) has been used in some studies comparing young and elderly adults. The SCQ has also been used in a few studies with elderly subjects alone (Schultz & Moore 1984). But the values obtained in that manner are difficult to compare to the scores for young adults assessed at a different time and place and by possibly noncomparable testing procedures. This instrument provides three subscales: (1) social anxiety or arousal provoked by the presence of others; (2) public self-consciousness or awareness of how we appear to others; and (3) private self consciousness, which is awareness of our moods, motives, and other inner aspects of our selves that are not directly observable by others.

An important initial concern is whether there are age-related changes in any of these components of self-awareness. A number of experiments in which the SCQ was used with both young and elderly subjects are summarized in table 7.1. It would appear that there are consistent differences in that virtually every comparison of the young subjects' mean to the elderly adults' mean shows elderly subjects to have lower scores on all three dimensions of the SCQ, but especially so on the private self-consciousness scale.

Table 7.1

Self-Consciousness Scores (SCQ, Fenigstein et al., 1975)
in Several Studies Comparing Young and Elderly Adults

	College Students				Elderly Adults			
	N	Private	Public	Social Anxiety	N	Private	Public	Social Anxiety
Mueller, Wright, and Kausler (1980)	491	34.1	26.6	19.0	33	26.3	21.5	17.0
Mueller and Ross (1984)	10	36.7	26.4	17.3	10	22.0	19.6	18.4
Mueller, Wonderlich, and Dugan (1986)	20	34.6	19.1	25.6	20	28.1	15.7	22.6
Mueller & Johnson (1990)	20	33.2	26.7	17.3	20	28.0	20.9	14.7
Mueller, Grove, and Vogel (1989)	35	33.8	26.3	17.2	17	27.0	19.8	16.8
Wells and Rankin (1987)	96	24.8	20.5	12.6	89	21.4	18.4	13.7

Thus, while it is necessary to keep in mind possible cohort effects in these comparisons, the pattern is consistent with the presumption of lower levels of consciousness of self in elderly adults.

It is possible to examine these differences more closely, and table 7.2 shows the specific item content that revealed significant dif-

Table 7.2
Items from the SCQ that Show a Significant ($p < .05$) Difference
for Young versus Elderly Adults*

Private Self-Consciousness
   I'm always trying to figure myself out.
   Generally, I'm not very aware of myself.
   I reflect about myself a lot.
   I'm often the subject of my own fantasies.
   I never scrutize myself.
   I'm constantly examining my motives.
   I sometimes have the feeling that I'm off somewhere watching myself.
   I'm alert to changes in my mood.
   I'm aware of the way my mind works when I work through a problem.

Public Self-Consciousness
   I'm concerned about the way I present myself.
   I'm self conscious about the way I look.
   I usually worry about making a good impression.
   One of the last things I do before I leave my house is look in the mirror.
   I'm concerned about what people think of me.
   I'm usually aware of my appearance.

Social Anxiety
   I have trouble working when someone is watching me.

*Source: Based on Mueller, Wright & Kausler 1980

ferences in one comparative study (Mueller, Wright & Kausler 1980). Nine of the ten items on the private self-consciousness subscale show elderly adults scoring lower in self awareness than young adults, and six of the seven public self-consciousness subscale items show the same pattern, whereas the age-related difference is virtually absent for social anxiety. Thus, it would appear that the self-awareness deficit is not specific to an inner versus an outer focus of attention, in that the age difference was apparent for both private and public self-consciousness. In terms of general social anxiety generated by the presence of others, however, the young and elderly subjects showed no overall difference, although elderly subjects profess to be less troubled at working when someone else is watching.

There are a few related studies involving other dimensions related to self awareness. For example, Ross and colleagues examined body consciousness in young and elderly adults (Ross, Tait, Grossberg, Handal, Brandeberry & Nakra 1989). The Body-Consciousness Questionnaire (Miller, Murphy & Buss 1981) yields three components: awareness of inner or private sensations, concern with external or public appearance, and feelings of physical competence.

Healthy elderly subjects showed no difference from young adults for private body consciousness, but older subjects were higher than young adults in public body consciousness and feeling of competence. The higher concern with appearance may reflect anticipated negative evaluation of appearance due to a loss of youthful features, whereas the higher body competence may reflect the selection process which deliberately focused on healthy elderly subjects who likely represent the high end of the elderly distribution of actual physical health, in which case the feelings of greater body competence relative to their peers are presumably veridical.

Some aspects of self-awareness may derive from general intellectual activity, in which case greater self consciousness for young adults could just reflect in part a generalized commitment to or enjoyment of introspection of all forms, and not solely the development or involvement of the self-concept per se. Thus, it would be useful to separately evaluate general introspective tendencies in conjunction with specifically self-focused attention.

The Need for Cognition (NC) scale (Cacioppo, Petty & Kao 1984) assesses the extent to which an individual engages in effortful cognitive activity, as in "I really enjoy a task that involves coming up with new solutions to problems". This dimension has not been thoroughly examined in the elderly, nor has its possible connection to self-consciousness measures been established even in young adults. However, both of these questions seem pertinent to a more complete understanding of how introspective processes change with aging, and how the change affects cognitive processing.

One study (Mueller & Johnson 1990) included both the NC and SCQ measures in a study with young and elderly subjects. Although the elderly subjects showed lower self-consciousness scores for both private and public self-consciousness (table 7.1), they did not differ from the young adults in terms of need for cognition scores (*Ms* = 57.8 and 60.9). Thus, it appeared that the elderly subjects do not have a generalized deficit in terms of introspective processes, and that the deficit is more focused on self-related cognitions.

A second aspect of self-awareness is its apparent role as a moderating factor in enhancing or limiting the benefits of self-referential encoding, and specifically whether the moderating effects of self-awareness are the same over the life span. Self-consciousness does not always yield a significant correlation with self-reference effects with young adults, but when such effects occur it appears that subjects who are high in self-consciousness show greater benefits, as if their self-concept was better articulated and more accessible so they could more readily incorporate new experiences (Agatstein & Buchanan 1984). The data in table 7.1 indicate that elderly subjects as a group generally seem to score lower on self-consciousness, but there is also an individual differences question which requires an examination of the effect of self-consciousness differences within the elderly group, rather than a between-age-groups comparison.

Mueller and Johnson (1990) found that need for cognition was not significantly correlated with either private or public self-consciousness $(rs\ (40) = .16$ and $-.14)$, but it was correlated with social anxiety $(r\ (40) = -.40,\ p < .01)$, especially for the elderly subjects $(r\ (20) = -.62,\ p < .005)$. These data further suggest that the age-related differences in self consciousness noted in tables 7.1 and 7.2 do not derive from some global difference in introspective tendencies in general. However, it could still be true that the pattern relating self-awareness to self-reference benefits is not the same for young and elderly subjects.

Table 7.3 presents some correlations between SCQ scores, NC scores, and decision speed (Mueller & Johnson 1990), for traits that were judged descriptive of self and other people (shown under Both) or just self alone. Unfortunately, in this experiment the young adults did not show a significant correlation between SCQ scores and self-reference benefits (that is, faster access to self or better memory), but neither did the elderly subjects. In this case, higher need for cognition was associated with greater recall, at least for the distinctive self-only trait adjectives, for both young and elderly subjects.

Thus, although the conclusion is tempered by the absence of significant SCQ effects, these data do not show age-related differences in the way these aspects of self awareness interact with self-reference processing. In other words, although elderly adults seem to show lower levels of self awareness—a fact that is of interest in its

Table 7.3
Correlations with Questionnaire Data,
by Subject Age, Pooled over Item Age, and Likability

	Endorsements		Latency		Recall	
	Both	_Self only_	_Both_	_Self only_	_Both_	_Self only_
College students						
Social Anxiety	.04	−.09	.22	−.01	−.08	−.11
Private Self-Consciousness	.31	.15	.21	−.12	−.21	−.15
Public Self-Consciousness	.43*	.22	−.01	−.20	−.01	−.29
Need for Cognition	−.41	.30	.13	.09	.19	.52*
Elderly adults						
Social Anxiety	−.30	.31	−.23	−.25	−.17	.15
Private Self-Consciousness	−.15	.09	.24	.11	.07	.41
Public Self-Consciousness	−.33	.30	−.30	−.26	−.11	.08
Need for Cognition	.04	−.23	−.16	−.07	.45*	.49*

Note: (N = 20 each)
* ($p < .05$)

own right—there is no evidence that self-awareness moderates the benefits of self-reference encoding in any different manner for young and elderly adults. To the extent that some age-related component does qualify the use of the self-concept, we must look elsewhere, and specifically at the content of the self concept as it may differ over the life span.

SELF-CONCEPT CONTENT OVER THE LIFE SPAN

Age-specific Traits

There seems to be little doubt that the content of the self-concept may affect how it is applied to help us understand our experiences. For example, Markus has shown that we define ourselves with respect to certain dimensions but not others, and only the traits on which we are schematic are used to judge other people (Markus 1983; Markus & Smith 1982). A number of other studies have tried to show that a distorted or limited self-concept can place boundary conditions on the benefits of self-referential encoding, and perhaps the work on depressive self-concept distortion is more widely known in this regard (Davis & Unruh 1981; Derry & Kuiper 1981; Ross 1989; Ross, Mueller & de la Torre 1986). This work argues that depressed subjects' self-concepts are disproportionately negative compared to nondepressed people, and this bias precludes integrating positive content into the self-concept to the same extent as normals.

As a consequence, in the self-reference task, depressed subjects might show enhanced recall for negative items (such as bleak or gloomy) but not for positive items (as in amiable or charming), whereas nondepressed subjects would tend to show the reversed pattern with benefits for positive content and not for negative content, even though both groups of subjects are forced to engage in self-referential encoding of both types of material. This characterization of limits on self-reference processing has been labeled the *content specificity hypothesis* by Kuiper and his colleagues (Derry & Kuiper 1981). Only that content which is in the self-image can benefit from activation of the self-concept during encoding.

If a biased self-concept has such a limiting effect, we can ask whether the self-concept becomes distorted in some systematic way over the life span. In particular, is there evidence for an analogous age specificity in self-concept across the life span? The issue of age stereotypes has been examined in a number of studies, both in terms of how the elderly are perceived by others (Brewer, Dull & Lui 1981; Linville 1982), and in terms of the way that may impact on how the elderly view themselves (Rothbaum 1983). These perceptions should interact with actual age-related changes and combine internally with the cumulative effect of actual life experiences, thus creating the necessary conditions for a somewhat different self-image in elderly people.

These changes may be operationalized in various ways, including asking subjects about the age appropriateness of various behaviors and by noting "age specificity" in the vocabulary used to describe the personality of young and elderly subjects. In one large-scale effort, Heckhausen, Dixon, and Baltes (1989) examined belief systems in young, middle-aged, and elderly adults with regard to the appropriate age at which various traits should emerge. Subjects were able to identify behaviors as prototypically youthful or elderly, and young and old raters showed considerable agreement as to the age-appropriateness of the traits.

Heckhausen and colleagues also noted that not all of the characteristics associated with elderly subjects were undesirable, with the expected age of onset for many positive traits being past the middle of the life span, nor were all the desirable traits associated with youth. In addition, the elderly adults displayed more complex views of the process of personality development, presumably due to the continued expansion of their general knowledge base and personal experience with various stages of developmental maturity.

Mueller, Wonderlich, and Dugan (1986) had young and elderly subjects rate, using a five-point scale, nominally positive and negative trait adjectives as to whether the term in general was typically used to describe either young (1) or elderly (5) people. The average rating for each for the one-hundred traits is shown in table 7.4, for raters in each age group.

Those traits for which the average value of young and old raters showed a significance difference are indicated. However, that difference is not as important as whether the mean in each case is at the same end of the scale for the life span. For example, the significant difference for *brash* is not that meaningful, because both young and elderly subjects clearly located that trait at the young end of the scale (midpoint = 3.0).

Cases of greater interest would be those in which the mean rating for young subjects was clearly on the opposite side of the midpoint from the mean rating by elderly subjects, and there are very few where that reversal was notable. Thus, traits that were

Table 7.4
Trait Adjective Ratings for Age Specificity by Young and Elderly Adults

Trait	Average Rating		Trait	Average Rating		Trait	Average Rating	
	Y	E		Y	E		Y	E
Active	1.83	1.90	Experienced	4.35	4.53	Quick	1.55	1.59
Admirable	3.55	3.28	Fearful	3.61	3.53	Realistic	3.59	3.84
Adventurous	1.64	1.46	Feeble	4.65	4.71	Reckless	1.66	1.59
Ambitious	1.57	1.65	Fickle	2.63	2.15	Repetitive	3.96	4.34
Arrogant	2.32	2.09	Forgetful	4.42	4.59	Respected	4.40	4.09
Attractive	1.64	1.90	Forlorn*	3.87	4.09	Rigid	4.07	4.21
Awkward	2.55	1.96	Frail	4.61	4.40	Robust	2.55	1.96
Boastful	2.01	2.09	Gentle	4.14	3.96	Rude	2.18	2.21
Bold	1.66	1.71	Healthy	1.59	1.65	Sensible	3.55	3.28
Bossy	3.59	4.03	Honorable*	4.05	3.40	Serene	4.14	4.28
Brash*	2.23	1.15	Hopeful	2.38	2.03	Sloppy	1.90	2.34
Bright	1.75	1.96	Idealistic*	2.27	1.53	Slow	4.35	4.40
Broadminded*	2.33	3.34	Ill	4.51	4.53	Spoiled*	1.53	2.09
Careless	1.79	2.09	Immature*	1.22	1.65	Strong	1.63	1.65
Changeable	1.72	2.15	Impatient	2.42	1.90	Superficial	2.05	2.03
Cheerful	2.72	2.59	Impetuous	2.22	1.65	Suspicious*	3.51	4.09

Trait	Y	E
Composed	3.83	3.90
Confident	2.35	2.21
Confused*	2.88	3.78
Considerate	3.18	2.84
Courageous*	2.16	2.96
Cranky	4.55	4.40
Curious	1.77	1.78
Deliberate*	3.16	3.96
Dependent	3.07	3.03
Depressed	3.59	3.28
Dignified	4.31	4.34
Distinguished	4.31	4.40
Eager	1.72	1.78
Eccentric	4.14	4.40
Egocentric*	2.18	3.03
Energetic	1.77	1.90
Enterprising	1.96	1.90
Enthusiastic	1.57	1.71
Impulsive	1.48	1.59
Inactive	4.66	4.59
Inconsiderate	2.11	2.03
Inexperienced	1.38	1.40
Inquisitive	1.67	1.53
Kindly	4.25	4.34
Lazy	2.22	1.90
Lonely	4.44	4.34
Mature	3.90	3.96
Moralistic*	4.29	3.53
Naive	1.53	1.53
Needy	4.14	4.21
Noble*	4.07	3.46
Noisy	1.57	1.46
Optimistic	2.31	2.09
Patient	4.05	4.15
Peaceful	4.29	3.90
Persistent	2.48	2.59
Thorough	3.92	3.84
Thoughtful	3.46	3.34
Tired	4.46	4.28
Tolerant	3.70	3.90
Tranquil	4.25	4.15
Unreliable	1.94	2.34
Useless	3.88	3.78
Vigorous	1.98	1.65
Violent	1.88	1.90
Virile	1.76	1.65
Vulnerable	2.98	2.34
Wasteful	1.83	1.78
Weak	3.92	3.96
Wise	4.64	4.40
Withdrawn	3.70	3.78
Worldly*	4.03	3.40

Note: 1 = youthful; 5 = elderly

Y = young; E = elderly

* (p < .05)

age-bound could be identified. There was also good consensus as to whether a given trait was appropriately young or old for both age groups of raters.

These ratings and trait desirability ratings (Anderson 1968) allowed the classification of traits into four categories: those which were young-positive (such as ambitious or robust); young-negative (brash or noisy), old-positive (dignified or wise), and old-negative (cranky or feeble). (See Mueller, Wonderlich & Dugan 1986, table 1).

The content of this four-fold classification was very similar to that obtained by Rothbaum (1983), but with essentially middle-aged subjects in that case. The present outcomes also corroborate the findings of Heckhausen and colleagues in 1989 in showing *both* positive and negative traits at both ends of the life span, and in showing agreement by young and old subjects as to what those traits are.

Thus, it seems that age-specific vocabularies do exist to some extent, although whether these constitute the cause or the effect of underlying age stereotypes or myths is difficult to determine (Schonfield 1982). Having identified the actual usages by both young and elderly people, however, we can take the next step and ask whether the stereotypes of old and young people affect individual self-images and thereby moderate the impact of self-referential encoding.

Self-descriptiveness ratings in table 7.4 were obtained from college students and elderly adults for traits identified as typically young or old (Mueller, Wonderlich & Dugan 1986). An age-specificity endorsement pattern would show elderly subjects saying "yes" to more elderly traits than young adults would, and young adults saying "yes" to more young traits than elderly adults would. This expectation was supported for the young traits, as young subjects endorsed more of those than elderly subjects did ($Ms = 12.0$ versus 10.5), but the elderly traits showed no such differentiation for young and elderly subjects ($Ms = 10.9$ and 10.8). There was some indication in the latency data that elderly subjects had more rapid access to traits associated with older people, but that was the only indication of age specificity for the elderly. The recall data did not reflect any age specificity for either group of subjects.

These results indicated that elderly subjects do not show much age specificity, whereas young adults do. That is, the young adults saw themselves more in terms of the youthful traits, whereas the elderly saw themselves about equally in terms of both young and elderly traits. One interpretation consistent with this outcome is that, having been young once, the elderly remember once possessing the youthful personality characteristic being described, and this residual still constitutes some part of their self-image (Brewer & Lui 1984). This is also consistent with the observation by Heckhausen et al. (1989) that their elderly subjects had more complex self-images. The youthful subjects, however, have not had the opportunity to develop the features characteristically associated with old age, and thus realistically have a more constrained self-image. Thus, the expectation of a restricted self-image at both extremes of the age range may be overly simplified.

One common effect in self-reference research with young adults is the generation of a positive-self image, whereby positive traits are claimed more often than are negative traits by young adults. This was present for both age groups in the work of Mueller, Wonderlich, and Dugan (1986) but the effect was significantly greater for the elderly subjects than for the college students. This outcome is subject to various interpretations, but it is consistent with the body-competence results found by Ross et al. (1989) as already noted. It is plausible that healthy elderly subjects do enjoy a positive self-image in terms of veridical comparisons with age-mates and by virtue of being the survivors among their cohorts.

Trait Distinctiveness

These varied outcomes offer support for the basic notion of age-appropriate trait vocabularies and age-specificity, at least in the self-concepts of young adults. Of course, the identification of age-specificity with the scaling techniques already described is normative, and although some general life-span differences in self-image may be revealed in that way, it seems likely that considerable individual differences exist in both young and elderly subjects. Thus, a more individualized assessment of self-image content may reveal further aspects associated with age-specificity, including further details about how life-span self-concept differences limit information processing.

One way to obtain idiographic information would be to separate common or shared traits from those that are more specific to the individual. At first glance, it might seem that subjects could just be asked to rate how much a given trait characterizes them, but this procedure does not precisely address the distinctiveness dimension in terms of shared versus unshared traits (Mueller, Thompson & Dugan 1986). In other words, just as some physical traits are not very distinctive (such as tall, thin, or brown hair), some psychological traits may be general enough that they describe many people, whereas other traits may be less common. This separation can be achieved in the self-reference format by having each trait adjective judged twice, once in terms of whether it describes other people and then again in terms of whether it is true for one's self.

This produces a classification with four types of traits: (1) descriptive of self and others, or shared traits; (2) descriptive of self but not others, or unique traits (self-only); (3) descriptive of others but not self, other-only; and (4) not descriptive of self or others (Mueller, Ross & Heesacker 1984). This should identify not just whether a trait is a part of the self-concept, but how distinctive the trait is for the individual. Thus, it may provide a more sensitive determination of age-specific content, with even elderly subjects showing some age-specificity in the self-concept when the traits are more central.

This approach to identifying trait distinctiveness was used by Mueller and Ross (1984) in a comparison of college students and elderly adults. They found that (1) elderly adults generated fewer self-only traits than did young adults (Ms = 13.9 versus 20.1); (2) elderly and young adults generated the same number of shared traits (Ms = 45.4 versus 45.0), those judged descriptive of both self and other (best friend); and (3) elderly adults generated more traits considered to be not descriptive of either self or other (Ms = 45.8 versus 40.7). This pattern also seems consistent with the observation by Heckhausen and colleagues in 1989 that elderly subjects show a more complex self-image, although the traits examined here were not specifically screened for age-specific content.

In terms of relative decision speed, elderly subjects were slower than young adults for all four item types, as is commonly observed (Kausler 1982; Salthouse 1982), but the age-span difference was proportionally greater for the self-only items (elderly at 53 percent slower than young adults) than for the common (or both) traits (42 percent slower), and smallest for the mutually nondescriptive items (30 percent slower). As for absolute decision speed, elderly adults took more time for traits ultimately judged as descriptive when compared to nondescriptive traits (Ms = 4,919 versus 4,638 msec), whereas young adults did not show such a pattern (Ms = 3,337 versus 3,331 msec).

Finally, elderly subjects actually recalled more of the shared (or both) traits than did young adults (Ms = 29 percent versus 19 percent), but there was no difference for the unique self-only traits (Ms = 18 percent versus 19 percent). It was only for the nondescriptive traits, other-only and neither combined, that elderly subjects showed a recall deficit compared to young adults (Ms = 17 percent versus 26 percent).

In sum, the separation of unique and common traits revealed some age-span differences, notably fewer unique traits for the elderly and slower access to them. This could occur artifactually if the elderly subjects merely see themselves as more like others, thus possessing fewer distinctive traits as a by-product of that impression of greater commonality. However, that seems not to be the case, because the elderly subjects generated no more of the shared traits than did young adults. Instead, the elderly adults actually generated more mutually nondescriptive (neither) items than did young adults. This could reflect some type of criterion difference in acknowledging the presence of a trait.

These data are of interest, but the traits examined were not systematically selected as age-delimited. Thus the outcomes do not bear directly on the question of age-specific self-image content. However, this general technique was extended to age-bound traits in an experiment by Mueller and Johnson (1990).

Trait Distinctiveness and Normative Trait Age

The double-judgment methodology which idiographically defines trait distinctiveness can be used in conjunction with the trait adjectives that have been normatively rated for age level. This combined approach to identfying trait distinctiveness should be especially sensitive to age-related variation in the content of the self-concept. Specifically, although young adults seemed to display some age specificity even with the normative classification (Mueller, Wonderlich & Dugan 1986), elderly subjects did not seem to differentiate the young and old items to the same extent. However, if elderly subjects are required to identify traits as shared or specific, it might be expected that the self-only traits would tend to be predominantly items rated as appropriate for older people (that is, there would be content specificity), whereas the shared (both) traits might tend to include both young and old items.

Mueller and Johnson (1990) selected young and old traits from the norms described in the discussion of table 7.4—half positive and half negative traits in each case—and had college students and elderly subjects make both self- and other-descriptiveness decisions about each one. After both judgments were obtained for each word, every trait was classified as descriptive of self and other (both) or self-only. The classification data indicated that the self-only items showed little variation with subject age, as elderly subjects produced about the same number of unique young items as the college students did (Ms = 2.93 versus 3.31), and somewhat fewer unique old items (Ms = 4.23 versus 5.21). On the other hand, for the common items (those judged to be descriptive of self and most people) elderly subjects generated significantly fewer shared young traits than did college students (Ms = 5.70 versus 8.07), and about the same number of old traits (Ms = 6.13 versus 5.57).

In other words, trait age did not make much difference to either young or elderly subjects when the traits were seen as characteristic primarily of one's self, nor did trait age matter to elderly subjects when the trait was seen as more commonly true. However, trait age was critical to college students for the shared traits, as college students much more readily saw young traits as characteristic of themselves and most people than was the case for old traits. This may reflect somewhat different perspectives on what is meant by the target-other (here, most people), but it does continue the pattern whereby trait age is more pertinent to young adults than to older adults.

As observed earlier, the only evidence of a trait-age effect for the elderly was in decision speed, as older adults made their decisions about old traits faster than they did for young-traits, and young adults showed no trait-age latency effect. Elderly subjects were slower than college students overall, but this deficit was more pronounced on the distinctive self-only items than on the shared items, corroborating the finding by Mueller and Ross (1984) using more general traits.

Trait Distinctiveness: Real- and Ideal-Self-Concept

The self-reference paradigm has focused primarily on traits that are truly possessed by the subjects. This focus on the real-self is quite clear in the content-specificity hypothesis in which it is even assumed that the absence of self-reference benefits can be used to map distortions of the self-concept (Derry & Kuiper 1981). The results discussed here suggest that—at least in the case of aging—the real- and present-self provides an incomplete picture of the value of self-referential processing. Specifically, the results with elderly subjects seem to imply some residual effect of past-self, whereby young traits still show processing benefits with elderly subjects.

Furthermore, some other recent results suggest that future-self may also play a critical role in the case of young adults. In 1986 Markus and Nurius explored the motivational effect of ideal- or possible-selves, whereby the way in which we want to be accounts for our present action or actions in striving for that goal. In this connection, Grove and Mueller (1988) demonstrated that the concept of an ideal-self exists as a sufficiently well-developed schema for most young adults, and that encoding events relative to our ideal-selves will benefit performance very well, much in the same way that encoding events relative to well-known others (such as best friend) yields performance benefits comparable to those obtained with self-reference (Bower & Gilligan 1979; Keenan & Baillet 1980).

The Grove and Mueller study, with only young adults as subjects, compared a semantic decision (of synonym judgment) and a physical structure decision (on word length) to a decision about whether or not the trait word actually described the subject (that is, the real-self) and a decision about whether or not the trait word described how the subject would like to be (that is, the ideal-self). As usual, the incidental recall results indicated better performance for the semantic decision compared to the structural task, but, more importantly, both types of self-reference decisions led to performance even better than the semantic task, with no significant difference between the actual- and ideal-self decisions. Thus it seems clear that, in general, the knowledge structure associated with how we would like to be is sufficiently well-integrated to yield a self-reference benefit. However, it is somewhat unclear as to what extent this derives from the certain partial overlap of the real- and ideal-self. Answering this part of the question requires a different technique.

In an experiment with college students alone, Mueller, Grove, and Vogel (1989) adapted the unique-shared trait double-decision procedure to provide a closer look at the question of real versus ideal self. Just as traits may differ in the extent to which they are true of self and others (that is, distinctiveness in the real self), the degree of correspondence or overlap between the way we are and the way we would like to be can vary as well. That is, some things we want to be may, in fact, be true of us, whereas other things we want to be are not true of us. It is only the latter description that clearly fits the idea of a possible- or future-self. Fortunately, we can make this separation easily using a variation of the double-judgment procedure previously discussed.

Each of several trait adjectives was judged twice, but, in this case, the decision was real-self ("I am") on one occasion. On the second occasion, the decision was for ideal-self ("I would like to be"). After each trait was judged, the traits could be classified into four groups based on the yes-or-no answers to each question: (1) real, ideal, or actualized traits; (2) real-only traits; (3) ideal-only traits; or (4) neither. Because subject age was not a factor, the traits were not selected for age-specificity, but both likeable and unlikable traits were employed. The traits that were judged true for both real- and ideal-self tended to be predominantly socially desirable features, and these actualized traits led to quicker decisions than did the more distinctive traits that were judged to be real-only or ideal-only.

However, actualized traits were not recalled any better. Instead, unlikable traits that were true of the real-self (actualized and real-only pooled) were recalled significantly better than unlikable traits not true of the real-self ($Ms = 30.7$ percent versus 23.2 percent), whereas likable traits were remembered better when they were not true of the real-self (ideal-only and neither combined, $M = 30.5$ percent) than when true of real-self (real-only and actualized combined, $M = 19.5$ percent). In other words, we tend to remember best our undesired traits and our desired but unachieved traits. (For further discussion of the significance of the undesired self, see Ogilvie 1987, and chapter 6 of this volume).

These data show that this variation of the double-judgment task may provide a useful way to test the role of the future-self in various cognitive processes. In fact, it seems quite useful in that, in this way, it becomes clearer that the ideal- and future-self, although closely related, are not just one and the same. Some aspects of the ideal-self already exist in the present- or actualized-self, and some do not (ideal-only, unactualized, and future-only). It would seem that the future-self would be especially pertinent to young adults still actively engaged in personality and career development, as well as leaving home and making other major commitments for perhaps the first time. Thus, this is the subject population used in the limited number of ideal-self studies conducted so far.

However, it also seems that, as one progresses through the years and presumably reaches a more stable and fully developed self concept, it might be that the role of the future-self would be moderated somewhat—although we hasten to add that it does not seem likely that it disappears altogether. This loss of influence from a future-self may be one way of looking at increased depression in older subjects, for example. This thought raises the prospect that a life-span perspective on the self-concept as it relates to information processing must consider not just the real- or present-self but the past-self and the future-self as well. In other words, with young adults the ideal-self (especially the ideal-only traits) may function as conceived by Markus and Nurius in 1986—that is, be a motivating future-self. However, with elderly subjects, the ideal-self may include some youthful aspects that cannot realistically be conceived as attainable in the future. Thus, they comprise a past-self at best—albeit a still preferred- or ideal-self in some sense. In one experiment just completed, we explored this tripartite view and tried to relate it to trait age as well.

Real- and Ideal-Self: Aging and Trait Age

In this experiment, we followed the procedure of having young and elderly subjects decide for each of several trait adjectives whether it was descriptive of them as they actually are (real-self) and, then, in a second phase, whether it was descriptive of how they would like to be (ideal-self). The real and ideal decisions were counterbalanced as first and second phases. The sixty-four traits judged were selected to be either typically young or old characteristics, using the Heckhausen et al. (1989) norms and the norms in table 7.4.

To simplify analysis and interpretation, extremely positive or negative traits were not used, and the items selected had a predominantly mild positive connotation. For example, the young items included active, adventurous, assertive, curious, helpful, and idealistic, whereas the nominally old items included complicated, deliberate, dignified, moralistic, patient, and peaceful. The rating phases were followed by an unannounced recall test, and three questionnaires: the Self-Conscious Questionnaire (Fenigstein et al. 1975), the Need for Cognition scale (Cacioppo, Petty & Kao 1984), and the Self-Esteem Inventory (Coopersmith 1967).

The subjects in this experiment were college students (mean age = 19.0) at a large public university in a college town in the midwest, recruited from introductory psychology courses, and healthy elderly adults (mean age = 75.2). As in our other studies, not only were the elderly subjects in good health and living at home, but many were retired faculty members and spouses, or otherwise well-educated, accustomed to the demands of questionnaires and related assessment procedures, and continuing to be active in the community or on campus.

Although the income levels of the elderly subjects may be lower than desired in some cases, that was more an artifact of limited retirement packages than socioeconomic status more broadly defined. Their verbal ability scores as a group did not differ significantly from those of the younger subjects, with some elderly individuals easily exceeding the younger subjects in that regard.

The self-descriptive decisions were used to classify each trait into one of the four distinctiveness categories: (1) true of real-self and ideal-self (both); (2) real-self only; (3) ideal-self only; or (4) neither. In addition to these endorsement data, decision speeds for each phase (real-self or ideal-self) were examined, as was the probability of recall on the incidental test.

The young traits revealed no significant differences between young and elderly subjects for any of the four distinctiveness categories. However, as can be seen in figure 7.1, the old traits showed

Figure 7.1
Endorsements by Subject Age for Young and Old Traits Judged to Be
Descriptive of Both Real and Ideal Self, Real-self Only, or Ideal-self Only

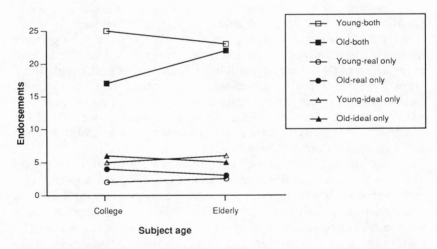

elderly subjects generating significantly more actualized old traits (both) than did young adults, and significantly fewer real-only and ideal-only old traits. For the young traits, elderly and young-adults produced comparable numbers of actualized and real-only traits; elderly subjects did generate slightly more young ideal-only traits than did college students, but not significantly more. Thus, some degree of age specificity was apparent, especially for the actualized old traits, and, as noted throughout our discussion, it is the young subjects who show the age-limited self-concept more clearly.

Other aspects of the data are summarized in table 7.5. As noted by Mueller and colleagues in 1989, actualized traits generally produced quicker decisions overall than did the unique traits. In terms of decisions about the real self, elderly subjects were slower than young adults in general, as is common, but the deficit varied somewhat. For one thing, the elderly were significantly slower for actualized (both) traits and ideal-only traits, but not significantly slower for real-only traits.

However, the most notable effect is the subject-age by trait-age interaction for real-only traits. Young subjects made their fastest decisions for young traits, and elderly subjects made their fastest decisions for old traits. Thus, for the most distinctive features, elderly subjects showed an age-specific accessibility effect. This repeats what appears to be a pattern, namely elderly subjects displaying age-related differences in the self-concept in terms of decision speed rather than ultimate endorsement outcome.

In the case of decisions about the ideal self, the elderly subjects were significantly slower for all four trait distinctiveness subtypes. However, the real-only items showed a significant trait-age by subject-age interaction, as college students showed no difference in decision speed between young and old traits, whereas elderly subjects were much slower on the young traits. Thus, elderly subjects accessed distinctive features more slowly whether the target for the decision was real-self or ideal-self.

Recall showed a general deficit for elderly subjects, but it encompassed all four trait distinctiveness subtypes and both young and old traits. Thus, there was no indication of age-specificity or actualization differences in terms of retention.

DISCUSSION AND CONCLUSIONS

The work considered here examined how the content of the self-concept for elderly adults differs from that of young adults, and how that content and related personality processes may affect encoding and retention. Several approaches were employed, including imposing self-referencing as a learning strategy, the identification of traits that may be age bound, the determination of shared and unshared traits, and the separation of real- and ideal-self concepts.

One critical question at the outset was whether any of the deficit in recall that is commonly observed for elderly subjects could be attributed to differences in the content of the self-concept for

Table 7.5

Endorsements, Decision Speed, and Percent Recall, by Age Group and Trait Age for Each Item Subtype

	Both		Real-only		Ideal-only		Neither	
	Y	E	Y	E	Y	E	Y	E
Endorsements								
Young item	23.9	22.7	0.9	0.9	4.4	5.1	2.8	3.3
Old item	17.5	21.4	3.0	1.5	5.3	3.6	6.2	5.8
All	41.4	44.1	3.9	2.4	9.7	8.7	9.0	9.1
Latency (Real Target)								
Young item	1272	1679	1609	2606	1959	2962	1701	2435
Old item	1418	1710	2085	2207	2013	3209	1742	2404
All	1345	1694	1896	2367	1986	3085	1723	2419
Latency (Ideal Target)								
Young item	1051	1598	1710	4823	1269	2517	1799	2893
Old item	1153	1568	1755	2891	1224	2420	1550	2334
All	1102	1583	1737	3664	1247	2469	1665	2603
Recall								
Young item	25.6	12.1	45.2	25.0	24.6	15.4	26.4	16.6
Old item	24.9	15.1	29.0	8.7	35.2	12.8	36.5	16.9
All	25.3	13.6	35.3	15.9	29.9	14.1	31.8	16.7

Note: Decision times are in msecs.
Y = young. E = elderly.

older subjects, to some failure to involve the self-concept during learning, or to some combination of content and utilitization of the self-image. Overall, there appears to be little question that the self-concept can be used by elderly subjects to encode experiences, with the same benefits relative to other strategies that are obtained by young adults. That is, the pattern of performance for self-reference versus other-reference is generally similar for young and elderly adults. However, there typically remains some recall deficit for the elderly subjects. So it appears that forced involvement of the self-concept during encoding is not sufficient by itself to overcome the entire age-related retention difference.

That a residual deficit remains could be due to relative inexperience with the strategy of self-referencing, with elderly subjects being capable but less adept for some reason. This could occur in several ways, so, for example, as we grow older we may just increasingly use other encoding strategies (such as rote repetition) that do not involve self focusing. Alternatively, if the self-concept eventually stabilizes at some point—possible after the identity-seeking of young adulthood declines—then, at that point, the self may be activated less reliably as a way to understand our experiences. The resulting condition would be reflected in less self-awareness in elderly people. Thus, they would be able to recover some use of the self-reference strategy if obliged to do so, but perhaps with less facility than young adults who are still constantly seeking to define themselves. This could be reflected in age differences in various indices of self-monitoring, and measures of performance other than recall per se, such as decision speed.

In terms of some of the measures of self-consciousness commonly used in social psychology, the pattern reflected in several studies shows elderly subjects to be somewhat less attentive to internal aspects of self-consciousness, as well as some aspects of self-presentation to others. Elderly adults do not seem to differ in terms of an index of need for general intellectual activity, at least in the only life-span comparison of which we are aware.

Therefore it would seem that this deficit in self-awareness is not just one aspect of a generalized decline in thinking about experiences. In addition, in the last study described here, involving real- and ideal-self concepts in the elderly, the elderly subjects actually showed slightly greater self-esteem than did the young adults ($Ms = 44.0$ versus 39.9, $p < .07$), and, as previously noted elderly subjects also showed enhanced views of body competence and certain other features. So it seems unlikely that the reduced self-monitoring simply reflects avoidance of confrontation with an undesirable self concept. Conceivably, reduced self-awareness may follow from the stabilization of the self-concept at some point, and some identity resolution is followed by slower change and, thus, less constant self-concern, as a sense of continuity becomes established. However it is interpreted, the fact that elderly subjects may be less self-conscious could help explain why self-referencing does not totally overcome the age-related differences in recall.

Although there may be some variation in how young and old subjects view a few traits in terms of the appropriate age for the feature, there seemed to be considerable agreement about most traits. Thus, this variation in content does not likely yield a direct accounting of the age-related difference in recall. In addition, however, actual differences in the content of the self-concepts may be involved in more subtle ways.

The evidence reviewed here seems to show that young adults have a self-image that reflects many traits normally seen as appropriate for the young, and few traits that usually characterize elderly people. Thus, young adults may have some elderly traits as part of their ideal or future-self concept, but their present-self tends to be weighted more toward youthful features. This did not seem to be attributable to a simple confounding of youthful traits as the more desirable traits. Overall, although some age-specific aspects are apparent, they seem to have little bearing on life-span differences in recall. Actually, this could imply that young adults would benefit less from self-referencing the elderly traits and thus recall less than elderly adults, which, of course, is the opposite of what happened.

In contrast to the age-bound self-image of young adults, the elderly subjects here often accepted youthful and elderly traits, although there was some sign that perhaps the young traits were less accessible. It can be noted that the relative absence of age-specificity in trait endorsement here is consistent with the results of Gfellner (1986), who used McGuire's (1984) spontaneous self-description procedure with elderly adults to find that, contrary to expectations, they typically did not mention age as a very distinctive trait in their self-descriptions. Of course, elderly subjects might be induced to mention age more when it is made salient, as when they are the only old person in the setting, but, in general, age did not appear to be especially salient for elders, providing some convergent evidence with procedures less structured than those employed here.

Taken at face value, the results suggest some blurring or blending of past and present self for the elderly subjects, perhaps in the interest of yielding a consistent self-image. In addition, it may be the case that elderly subjects subtly alter or raise the criterion for deciding that a trait is present, either for themselves or in general. In any event, it is clear that the analogy between depressive content-specificity and age-specificity is incomplete, with age-specificity more a feature of youth than being present at both ends of the adult life span.

It is possible, of course, to ask the same questions with regard to the lower end of the life span, namely how effectively the self-concept can be used by very young people. The self-concept in children in general is discussed elsewhere in this volume, and there has been extensive work with measures such as self-esteem in children and adolescents. However, there have been very few studies that employ the social cognition strategy discussed here.

With children, Halpin, Puff, Mason, and Marston (1984) found that the self-reference benefit relative to semantic encoding did not emerge until about the fourth grade or about age ten, but Hammen and Zupan (1984) observed a self-reference benefit at an even younger age of seven to eight years. Thus, the data base is limited, but it indicates that the self-concept is sufficiently well-integrated to serve as a useful mnemonic aid at a much younger age than the college students on whom the findings were originally based.

However, there was no direct comparison with a young adult sample in either study. Thus, the results can only be suggestive of the general existence of a basic benefit for the process of self-referencing in younger subjects. This leaves a number of interesting questions open—such as just when does the self-concept become sufficiently well-developed to serve as a memory aid? Does it achieve that status before or after other schemas? To what extent and how early can the real-self and ideal-self distinction be made with young children? What content-specific limits emerge as dimensions are gradually incorporated and refined in the self-image as a part of normal development? The social cognition procedures such as those used here may not completely answer all these questions, but they would seem to be among the useful methods that can be applied.

In sum, several studies, using various methodologies, converge on the conclusion that the self-concept of elderly subjects is perhaps more complicated or richer than that of young adults. One aspect of this complexity may be the residual presence of (1) some traits that were possessed when the subject was younger (past self), or (2) youthful features that are still part of an ideal-self which may or may not realistically be a future self. No single strategy seems capable of fully illuminating personality change or development across the life span, but procedures such as the real-ideal self double-judgment task seem well-suited to further examination of this tripartite self-concept.

REFERENCES

Agatstein, F. C., and Buchanan, D. B. 1984. Public and private self-consciousness and the recall of self-relevant information. *Personality and Social Psychology Bulletin*, 10:314–325.

Anderson, N. H. 1968. Likableness ratings of 555 personality-trait words. *Journal of Personality and Social Psychology* 9:272–279.

Bower, G. H., and Gilligan, S. G. 1979. Remembering information about one's self. *Journal of Research in Personality* 13:420–432.

Bower, G. H. and Karlin, M. B. 1974. Depth of processing pictures of faces. *Journal of Experimental Psychology* 103:751–757.

Brewer, M. B., and Lui, L. 1984. Categorization of the elderly by the elderly: Effects of perceiver's category membership. *Personality and Social Psychology Bulletin*, 10:585–595.

Brewer, M. B.; Dull, V.; and Lui, L. 1981. Perceptions of the elderly: Stereotypes as prototypes. *Journal of Personality and Social Psychology* 41:656–670.

Burns, M. O., and Seligman, M. E. P. 1989. Explanatory style across the life span: Evidence for stability over 52 years. *Journal of Personality and Social Psychology* 56:471–477.

Buss, A. H. 1980. *Self consciousness and social anxiety*. San Francisco, Calif.: W. H. Freeman.

Cacioppo, J. T.; Petty, R. E.; and Kao, C. F. 1984. The efficient assessment of need for cognition. *Journal of Personality Assessment* 48:306–307.

Coopersmith, S. 1967. *The antecedents of self esteem*. San Francisco, Calif.: W. H. Freeman.

Costa, P. T., Jr., and McCrae, R. R. 1980. Still stable after all these years: Personality as a key to some issues in adulthood and old age. In *Life-span development and behavior*. Vol. 3. edited by P. B. Baltes and O. G. Brim. New York: Academic Press.

Courtois, M. R., and Mueller, J. H. 1979. Processing multiple physical features in facial recognition. *Bulletin of the Psychonomic Society* 14:74–76.

Craik, F. I. M., and Lockhart, R. S. 1972. Levels of processing: A framework for memory research. *Journal of Verbal Learning and Verbal Behavior* 11:671–684.

Davis, H., and Unruh, W. 1981. The development of the self-schema in adult depression. *Journal of Abnormal Psychology* 90:125–133.

Derry, P. A., and Kuiper, N. A. 1981. Schematic processing and self-reference in clinical depression. *Journal of Abnormal Psychology* 90:286–297.

Fenigstein, A.; Scheier, M. F.; and Buss, A. H. 1975. Public and private self-consciousness: Assessment and theory. *Journal of Consulting and Clinical Psychology* 43:522–527.

Gaber, L. B. 1984. Structural dimensions in aged self-concept: A Tennessee Self Concept study. *British Journal of Psychology* 75:207–212.

Gfellner, B. M. 1986. Age salience in older adults' spontaneous self-concept. *Perceptual and Motor Skills* 63:1196–1198.

Greenwald, A. G., and Pratkanis, A. R. 1984. The self. In *Handbook of social cognition*. Vol. 3. Edited by R. S. Wyer and T. K. Srull. Hillsdale, N.J.: Lawrence Erlbaum Associates. 129–178.

Grove, T. R., and Mueller, J. H. 1988. The real, ideal, and valuational selves: Some consequences and implications. Paper presented at the annual meetings of the Midwestern Psychological Association. Chicago, Ill.

Halpin, J. A.; Puff, C. R.; Mason, H. F.; and Marston, S. P. 1984. Self-reference encoding and incidental recall by children. *Bulletin of the Psychonomic Society* 22:87–89.

Hammen, C., and Zupan, B. A. 1984. Self-schemas, depression, and the processing of personal information in children. *Journal of Experimental Child Psychology* 37:598–608.

Heckhausen, J.; Dixon, R. A.; and Baltes, P. B. 1989. Gains and losses in development throughout adulthood as perceived by different adult age groups. *Developmental Psychology* 25:109–121.

Kausler, D. H. 1982. *Experimental psychology and human aging.* New York: Wiley.

Keenan, J. M., and Baillet, S. D. 1980. Memory for personally and socially significant events. In *Attention and performance.* Vol. 8. Edited by R. S. Nickerson. Hillsdale, N.J.: Lawrence Erlbaum Associates. 651–669.

Kuiper, N. A., and Rogers, T. B. 1979. Encoding of personal information: Self-other differences. *Journal of Personality and Social Psychology* 37:499–514.

Linville, P. W. 1982. The complexity-extremity effect and age-based stereo-typing. *Journal of Personality and Social Psychology* 42:193–211.

Markus, H. 1983. Self knowledge: An expanded view. *Journal of Personality* 51:543–565.

Markus, H., and Nurius, P. 1986. Possible selves. *American Psychologist* 41:954–969.

Markus, H., and Smith, J. 1982. The influence of self-schemas on the per-ception of others. In *Cognition, social interaction, and personality.* Edited by N. Cantor and J. F. Kihlstrom. Hillsdale, N.J.: Lawrence Erl-baum Associates.

McCrae, R. R., and Costa, P. T. 1982. Self concept and the stability of per-sonality: Cross-sectional comparisons of self reports and ratings. *Journal of Personality and Social Psychology* 43:1282–1292.

McGuire, W. J. 1984. Search for the self: Going beyond self-esteem and the reactive self. In *Personality and the prediction of behavior.* Edited by R. A. Zucker, J. Arnoff, and I. Rabin. New York: Academic Press.

Miller, L. C.; Murphy, R.; and Buss, A. H. 1981. Consciousness of body: Private and public. *Journal of Personality and Social Psychology* 41:397–406.

Mueller, J. H., and Johnson, W. C. 1990. Trait distinctiveness and age spec-ificity in self-referent information processing. *Bulletin of the Psy-chonomic Society* 28:119–122.

Mueller, J. H., and Ross, M. J. 1984. Uniqueness of the self concept across the life span. *Bulletin of the Psychonomic Society* 22:83–86.

Mueller, J. H.; Grove, T. R.; and Vogel, J. M. 1989. Trait distinctiveness in the ideal-self concept. Paper presented at the meetings of the Mid-western Psychological Association. Chicago, Ill.

Mueller, J. H.; Ross, M. R.; and Heesacker, M. 1984. Distinguishing me from thee. *Bulletin of the Psychonomic Society* 22:79–82.

Mueller, J. H.; Thompson, W. B.; and Dugan, K. 1986. Trait distinctiveness and accessibility in the self-schema. *Personality and Social Psychol-ogy Bulleti* 12:81–89.

Mueller, J. H.; Wonderlich, S.; and Dugan, K. 1986. Self-referent processing of age-specific material. *Psychology and Aging* 1:293–299.

Mueller, J. H.; Wright, R.; and Kausler, D. H. 1980. A normative study of self-consciousness in young and elderly adults. Unpublished manu-script. University of Missouri, Columbia, Missouri.

Nehrke, M. F.; Hulicka, I. M.; and Morganti, J. B. 1980. Age differences in life satisfaction, locus or control, and self concept. *International Journal of Aging and Human Development* 11:25–33.

Ogilvie, D. M. 1987. The undesired self: A neglected variable in personality research. *Journal of Personality and Social Psychology* 52:379–385.

Rogers, T. B.; Kuiper, N. A.; and Kirker, W. S. 1977. Self-reference and the encoding of personal information. *Journal of Personality and Social Psychology* 35:677–688.

Ross, M. J. 1989. Self-schematic instability in mild depression. *Journal of Social Behavior and Personality* 4:119–126.

Ross, M. J.; Mueller, J. H., & de la Torre, M. 1986. Depression and trait distinctiveness in the self schema. *Journal of Social and Clinical Psychology* 4:46–59.

Ross, M. J.; Tait, R. C.; Grossberg, G. T.; Handal, P. J.; Brandeberry, L.; and Nakra, R. 1989. Age differences in body consciousness. *Journal of Gerontology* 44:23–24.

Rothbaum, F. 1983. Aging and age stereotypes. *Social Cognition* 2: 169–181.

Ryff, C. D. 1989. In the eye of the beholder: Views of psychological well-being among middle-aged and older adults. *Psychology and Aging* 4:195–210.

Salthouse, T. A. 1982. *Adult cognition: An experimental psychology of human aging.* New York: Springer-Verlag.

Schonfield, D. 1982. Who is stereotyping whom and why? *The Gerontologist* 22:267–272.

Schultz, N. R., and Moore, D. 1984. Loneliness: Correlates, attributions, and coping among older adults. *Personality and Social Psychology Bulletin* 10:67–77.

Spees, M.; Cates, D.; Nakfoor, B.; and Lapsley, D. K. 1987. The self-reference effect in senescence. Paper presented at the annual meetings of the Midwestern Psychological Association. Chicago, Ill.

Srull, T. K. 1984. Methodological techniques for the study of person memory and social cognition. In *Handbook of social cognition.* Vol. 3. Edited by R. S. Wyer and T. K. Srull. Hillsdale, N.J.: Lawrence Erlbaum Associates.

Wells, P. D., and Rankin, J. L. 1987. Age, self-consciousness, and sympathy for stigmatized others. Paper presented at the annual meetings of the Midwestern Psychological Association. Chicago, Ill.

RICHARD P. LIPKA
THOMAS M. BRINTHAUPT

8

Summary and Implications

The purpose of this volume was to arrive at a broad understanding of the study of the self across the life span. In this final
chapter, we return to that initial issue and examine critically each
of the chapters. We consider several of the similarities and differences in how the contributors have addressed the life span as
well as additional issues raised by examining the total array of
contributions.

Anderson's work with third- and sixth-graders represents the
classic case of a study that raises more questions than it answers.
While it is possible that the proposed theoretical relationship between self-esteem and self-complexity is not accurate in childhood,
other issues appear as more probable. For these two age groups,
might different areas of the self (such as physical competence) show
a stronger relationship between complexity and esteem?

Support for considering other competence areas can be derived
from Shirk and Renouf's chapter in which they demonstrate physical appearance and social acceptability as more powerful determinants of self-worth for the age groups being studied by Anderson. Or,
staying within the scholastic competence mode, are report cards an
important feature?

A complete analysis of the responses during the open-ended
self-description task might reveal more salient dimensions of scholastic competence to serve as the independent variable. Or, given
the results found by Lipka, Hurford, and Litten in this volume,

Anderson's present findings may be a case of large but opposite gender effects that are washed out when utilizing intact grade levels for analyses.

In our way of thinking, a report card may be analogous to a total scale score on a standardized instrument which may lack the sensitivity and salience found in subscales. Perhaps weekly quizzes, good works posted on bulletin boards, happy grams, and similar methods may be a more salient indicator of scholastic competence for these age groups.

It may also be that a card-sorting task for these age groups is inappropriate. The examination of self-complexity research with other age groups may yield important developmental data on the esteem-complexity relationship as well as the most suitable methodology. For example, is there a developmental period before which esteem and complexity are *not* related? What is the esteem-complexity relationship in early and late adolescence or middle and late adulthood?

In their chapter, Shirk and Renouf demonstrate that the movement from childhood to early adolescence is characterized by the stage-salient developmental issues of mastery and identity. Further, these pivotal tasks embrace four subtasks: accuracy in self-evaluation, coordination of self-worth with perceived competence, conservation of self, and the maintenance of self-esteem. Shirk and Renouf's codification of literature for each of the four subtasks should lead the reader to a number of interesting questions and concerns for future research.

For example, the conservation of self is a most rich metaphor conjuring up a number of issues and questions. How closely tied is conservation of self to increasing cognitive abilities? Further, is this cognitive complexity the result of quantitative or qualitative changes in competence domains? That is, is it more important to have a variety of domains or to rank-order the domains in such a fashion that would promote high levels of congruence between perceived competence and the importance of the competence domain?

Might conservation of self be a largely social-comparison, social-normative process? It may not be the numerous transitions faced by these age groups that challenge the conservation of self, but rather the timing of the transition in relation to one's peers or cohort. The Simmons work reviewed by Shirk and Renouf clearly suggests this, as does the research discussed by Lipka, Hurford, and Litten within this volume. Clearly, being old or young for one's grade level can be facilitating or debilitating depending upon the grade level in which the comparison takes place. That is, can individuals adequately conserve in an environment in which they see themselves as "off time"? Further, if conservation is largely a social process, then the differential socialization by gender must become an important issue of future investigation.

Shirk and Renouf's notion of self-development gone awry is an intriguing idea with many interesting implications. For example, is the late-childhood and early-adolescence period especially susceptible to things going awry, when compared to other developmental periods? What insights might a focus on maladaptation tell us about the normal development of the self? And finally, are there similar or different tasks that adults and the elderly must resolve? That is, can this type of analysis be utilized by researchers who are studying the self at different age ranges?

The chapter by Lipka and his colleagues reflects research by individuals interested in the impact of contextual and situational factors upon the self. It also raises several interesting questions concering the differential effects of transitions on self-esteem.

Lipka and his colleagues provide evidence for both age and gender differences in terms of the transition to middle school. Why should age matter for these students? Are there any obvious differences with respect to younger or older students within the same grade? Why should age matter differentially for boys and girls? How aware are students of existing age differences within the classes? Lipka and his colleagues suggest some possible answers to these questions. But, as they note, more research needs to be done.

Another interesting issue raised by the notion of being "on" or "off time" concerns other types of transitions. Lipka and his colleagues noted that similar types of questions arise when we consider transitions such as getting married, having children, starting a new career, or retiring from a career. How much weight is age given during such transitions? Does being on or off time really make any difference for the self-esteem of the adult? It may be that age is particularly important to school-age populations but decreases in importance once a certain age is reached (say, eighteen or twenty-one) or a certain transition is made (such as completing one's formal schooling).

Finally, Lipka's and his colleagues' discussion of the issues involved in disentangling age, cohort, and time of measurement effects has a great deal of potential usefulness for researchers interested in studying the self across the life span. As they have shown, there are ways in which to finesse the thorny problems that confront the life-span-oriented researcher. With the type of design sophistication advocated by Lipka and his colleagues, a greater understanding of the effects of contexts and transitions on the self is within our reach.

Demo and Savin-Williams make a case for the idea that change and discontinuity are not synonymous with instability of the self-concept, and that it is the exception rather than the rule that adolescence is a period of storm and stress. Further, they propose that adolescents and parents have a reciprocal and bidirectional impact on the selves of each other, and that relying on one family member's account to understand another family member is risky business. In fact, to understand the nature of the interaction process will require careful investigation of the timing and sequence of family formation, disruption, and reconstitution across the entire life span of a family.

The family formation, disruption, and reconstitution process may also be a fruitful metaphor to understand the effects of attending a new school, passage through grades, and progress within a school. This metaphor may also be helpful in the explanation of gender differences as a function of situational and environmental fluctuations. As Demo and Savin-Williams suggest, numerous interactions impact upon early adolescent and adolescent self-concept, and to sort out these influences will require both nomothetic and idiographic approaches to research into the self.

Demo and Savin-Williams' distinction between experienced and presented self-esteem also raises several interesting implications for researchers into the self. This approach brings together the elements of self—and other—perception, and, in so doing, emphasizes the social nature of the self. Does the relationship between experienced and presented self-esteem change depending on the developmental period under consideration?

For example, is childhood characterized by an experienced-presented self-esteem relationship that is stronger or weaker than the adolescent's? What are the effects of entering adulthood on experienced self-esteem, presented self-esteem, and the relationship between the two? Changes in the impact or importance of social influence and peer relations all across the life span should have discernable effects on this relationship.

In her work, Wells affords us an opportunity to learn about the Experiential Sampling Method (ESM) as an important addition to research on studying the self. Further, we are afforded the study of women in a postcollege and pregeriatric setting—a population which is woefully understudied in the literature on the self. One compelling question generated by this research is tied to the view that, as there are many different aspects of self-concept, so are there many different aspects of self-esteem. How are the different self-esteem aspects affected by different contexts? This seems to be a very fruitful area for future research. Further, how must or should we define context and how can we look at more than one feature of the context at a time?

Especially interesting is Wells' notion of self-esteem as an on-going or moment-by-moment phenomenon. Her consideration of some of the effects of different contexts on the self-esteem of working mothers raises several issues. For example, one implication of Wells' approach is that different criteria are used for evaluating the self at different developmental periods. The ESM methodology can be easily used to investigate this possibility. The emphasis on current on-going self-esteem also suggests that global or generalized self-esteem is something quite different (and perhaps not worth studying) when we are interested in the effects on context and situation on the self.

Finally, Wells's use of a baseline or set-point notion of current self-esteem (also alluded to by Demo and Savin-Williams) offers many implications for future research. As Wells noted, set points may exist both within and across specific contexts. In addition to the possibility that fluctuations can occur within and between contexts (as Wells's data suggest), is it possible that dramatic events or life experiences can change set-point levels either temporarily or permanently? What are the effects of major developmental changes and life transitions on on-going self-esteem? When we look at self-esteem as Wells does, these are some of the questions that arise.

Ogilvie and Clark introduce us to a heretofore new concept in research into the self known as the *undesired-self*. Their research with young and older adults suggests that the ideal-self is more abstract and conceptual while the undesired-self is more concrete. Would this also be true for younger subjects? At what point will cognitive development create a floor effect for this methodology? Given their striking gender findings, disaggregating the data by sex will also be necessary for these younger populations. At present, Ogilvie and Clark have by their own admission utilized samples of convenience that do not reflect the precollege age population or working adults beyond the completion of the college years. Such a powerful research area as the undesired-self clearly requires testing across the life-span.

There are several other interesting implications of the undesired-self for researchers into the self. First of all, the fact that the real-/undesired-self relationship is more predictive of life satisfaction than is the relationship between the real- and the ideal-self suggests that people are more concerned with avoiding a bad self than acquiring a good self. This suggests that a self-protective motive may be operating here as opposed to self-enhancement or self-consistency motives.

Second, it is interesting to consider the implications of Ogilvie's and Clark's proposal that the ideal self is more abstract and conceptual and less concrete than is the undesired-self. If the undesired-self is easier to imagine than the ideal-self, then the former may be more susceptible to the effects of specific events or experiences, be they negative (such as failures or embarrassments) or positive (such as successes or favorable social outcomes). Does the undesired-self play a stronger role in on-going self-esteem than does the ideal-self? With increasing age and development, does the undesired-self grow in its detail and complexity?

Finally, it is interesting to speculate about Ogilvie and Clark's notion of at-best and at-worst self-judgments. What accounts for the differences between young and older adults in their judgments?

For example, it would be interesting to analyze subjects' reasons for why the "best is yet to come" or the "worst is yet to come." Is it because one is young or old? Are different judgmental criteria used by young and older respondents? The same types of questions can be asked of male and female subjects as well in an effort to better explain the gender differences found in Ogilvie and Clark's research.

The work of Mueller and his colleagues illustrates the power of the cognitive approach to studying the self across the life-span. By drawing upon paradigms from this research area, they are able to address several questions relating to the self as a mnemonic device.

Mueller's and colleagues' approach and results give rise to several issues and implications. For example, the major finding based on this experimental approach is that elderly adults do not perform as well as do young adults on laboratory self-referencing tasks. What are the implications of such age differences for other less contrived, and more natural tasks? Does the recall-deficit of the elderly generalize to or manifest itself in common, everyday activities relating to work, leisure, or interpersonal relationships? Thus, a further assumption in need of verification is that the self-referencing effects are important outside the laboratory.

Another interesting issue concerns the finding that explicitly inducing self-referencing among elderly subjects serves to close the deficit relative to young adults. Even though this deficit is not completely closed—and Mueller and colleagues are most interested in trying to account for the remaining difference—the fact that training seems to improve self-referencing is an important observation.

First, it suggests that elderly subjects are not necessarily unable to use self-referencing as a mnemonic aid. If we shift the focus away from why a deficit still exists and toward why explicitly inducing self-referencing narrows the gap, then interesting issues emerge. Are we to assume, for example, that the research supports the argument that elderly subjects are indeed less likely to spontaneously activate the self than are young adults? If so, why might this be? Why do we need to *require* the elderly to make self-comparisons? Are the elderly less selfish or self-centered? It would also be interesting to assess the effect of explicit self-referencing on the self-awareness of the elderly. Does this increase private self-consciousness, or does it have no effect on self-consciousness?

The work of Mueller and his colleagues also suggests that the self-concept of elderly subjects is richer and more complicated than that of young adults with this richness created by a mix of past, present, and future selves. What is not clear, however, is the ratio or weighting within the mix of different selves. Is, as Ogilvie and Clark suggest, the future self more heavily weighted by young adults while the past self is more heavily weighted by elderly subjects?

It appears to us that the strategy of self-referencing is similar to a mental filing cabinet activity. Which aspect of the tripartite (past, present, and future) self-concept serves as the major alphabetizer for the young? For the old? And, might the complexity of the refiling task manifest itself as the reaction time results in elderly subjects for real-self traits? What Mueller and colleagues offer as stabilization of the self-concept with age may be a task-specific manifestation of this complex refiling activity—a process which is detrimental to the discussion of traits, yet perhaps advantageous to the discussion of roles or attributes possessed by the individual—a logical extension of this research endeavor.

A conceptual matrix formed by all the chapters in this volume suggests to us the following themes and implications for future reserach with self across the life span.

Gender, in terms of the potential for male and female differences in the structure, content, and processes of the self, must be given major attention in the research community. Attendant issues will be the methodologies and instruments that are sensitive to differing socialization patterns for males and females, and for individuals of different ages.

In this vein, how is culture different from context or situation? How does acculturation differ from socialization? Exploring these definitions might help us to understand culture, gender, and age similarities and differences. Further, the need to value *no difference* on a par with *significant difference* when examining socially relevant issues of gender, race, and age must be embraced by the research community.

We also advocate the utilization of a common theme across the life span to explore change of the self over time. For example, the utilization of a recurrent developmental task—perhaps in line with the tasks suggested by Shirk and Renouf—might be used to explore the relationship between one's sense of self and, say, "learning to get along with age mates of the opposite sex."

Finally, more attention must be paid to the sequential strategies that are emerging in the designs utilized with life-span developmental psychology. The application of sequential strategies when studying the self allows us to examine the relative significance of ontogenetic (individual) and generational (historical) effects such as those considered by Lipka and colleagues. Within the research on self—and our volume is a modest exception—there is little empirical evidence bearing on the nature of the age-cohort-time of measurement relationship.

As in our volume one, contributors have illustrated many interesting facets about the self across the life span. Their careful research and reviews have added to both our knowledge base and our reservoir of yet-to-be-answered questions.

Contributors

Karen M. Anderson
Department of Psychology
Santa Clara University
Santa Clara, California

Thomas M. Brinthaupt
Department of Psychology
Middle Tennessee State University
Murfreesboro, Tennessee

Margaret D. Clark
Department of Psychology
Rutgers University
New Brunswick, New Jersey

Alison Dandoy
Department of Psychology
University of Missouri
Columbia, Missouri

David H. Demo
Department of Sociology
Virginia Polytechnic Institute and
    State University
Blacksburg, Virginia

David R. Hurford
Department of Psychology and Counseling
Pittsburg State University
Pittsburg, Kansas

W. Calvin Johnson
Department of Psychology
University of Missouri
Columbia, Missouri

Tim Keller
Department of Psychology
University of Missouri
Columbia, Missouri

Richard P. Lipka
Center for Educational Services, Evaluation and
    Research
Pittsburg State University
Pittsburg, Kansas

Mary Jo Litten
Department of Educational Psychology
Kansas State University
Manhattan, Kansas

John H. Mueller
Department of Educational Psychology
University of Calgary
Calgary, Alberta, Canada

Daniel M. Ogilvie
Department of Psychology
Rutgers University
New Brunswick, New Jersey

Andrew G. Renouf
Department of Psychology
University of Denver
Denver, Colorado

Ritch C. Savin-Williams
Department of Human Development
    and Family Studies
Cornell University
Ithaca, New York

Stephen R. Shirk
Child Study Center
Department of Psychology
University of Denver
Denver, Colorado

Anne J. Wells
Center for Family Studies
The Family Institute of Chicago
Chicago, Illinois

Subject Index

A

Academic self-concept: (see also School structure)
academic achievement and, 22–25, 28;
feedback and, 28, 39–41, 44, 257;
versus nonacademic, 18
Adler, Alfred, 187, 189
Adolescence: (see also Early adolescence)
as period of "storm and stress," 4, 54, 70, 72–73, 116–117, 120–121, 132–133, 136–138, 259;
changes during, 70, 117, 119, 135–138;
development of self-esteem in, 131–134, 138–141;
research issues in, 139–140;
self-discrepancies in, 206–207;
teasing and ridiculing in, 122, 125–130
Adulthood: (see also Age differences, Elderly adults, Undesired self)
personality changes in, 223;
role transitions in, 4, 176;
self "at best" and "at worst" in, 202–204, 212–216;
self-concept content in, 234–239;
self-esteem in, 5, 152–179;
undesired self in, 200–204
Affective components of the self: (see also Depression)

accurate self-reports and, 64–65;
and self-consistency, 75–76;
development of, 14;
fluctuations in, 136–137;
in adulthood, 206–207;
in infancy, 166, 176;
self-complexity and, 19–22;
self-esteem and, 79, 131;
sex differences in, 210–212
Age differences: (see also Development of self-concept, Developmental differences)
age stereotypes and, 234–239;
effects of age level within, 102–111;
in self-concept research, 101;
in self-referencing, 223–252;
limitations of research on, 96–98;
school transitions and, 93–112;
social expectations regarding, 111–112
Agency, sense of (see Self-as-subject)
Arena-of-comfort hypothesis, 76–77
Attributions:
across the life span, 228;
in depression, 80

B

Baseline models of self-esteem:
definition of, 75, 171, 177;
in adolescence, 133–134;

Author Index

A

Aboud, F., 65
Abramson, L. Y., 80
Achenbach, T., 61
Acock, A. C., 120, 121, 123, 138
Adam, J., 97
Adler, T., 63, 95
Agatstein, F. C., 227, 232
Agnew, J., 2
Ainsworth, M. D., 13
Ames, C., 22
Anderson, N. H., 238, 256, 257
Ansbacher, H. L., 187, 189
Ansbacher, R. R., 187, 189
Ascher, S. R., 124, 126–128, 140, 141
Ashmore, R. D., 191, 216
Ausubel, D., 59

B

Bachman, J. G., 73, 79, 119, 133
Bailey, K. G., 188
Bailey, R. C., 188
Baillet, S. D., 225, 243
Balla, D. S., 62
Baltes, P. B., 96, 97, 235
Bandura, A., 122
Bannister, D., 2
Barenboim, C., 17, 36, 72, 78
Bargh, J. A., 12
Barnes, J., 17

Basch, M. F., 166, 177, 178
Battle, J., 79, 80
Beane, J. A., 94, 102
Baumeister, R. F., 164
Bayley, H. C., 154
Beard, B. H., 188
Beck, A. T., 79, 80, 166
Belenky, M. F., 212
Bem, D., 63
Bence, P. J., 137
Bengston, V. L., 120
Berg, N. L., 188
Berndt, T. J., 119, 121, 122, 125, 130, 141
Bertenthal, B. I., 12
Bierman, K. L., 121, 125
Bills, R. E., 156
Block, J., 136
Blyth, D. A., 3, 70, 76, 77, 95, 118, 125, 138–140
Boggiano, A. K., 62
Bohan, J. B., 15, 66
Bolus, R., 152, 159
Bond, R. N., 188, 208
Borstelmann, L., 188
Boshier, R., 188
Botwinick, J., 98
Bowen, D., 63
Bradley, G. W., 19
Brand, E., 138
Brandeberry, L., 231
Breckler, S. J., 160
Brewer, M. B., 235, 239
Brewin, C. R., 81